All About
Basic Home Repairs

Created and
designed by the
editorial staff
of ORTHO Books

Written by
T. Jeff Williams

Art direction
and design by
John Williams

Illustrations by
Ron Hildebrand

Photography by
Fred Lyon

Ortho Books

Manager, Ortho Books
Robert L. Iacopi

Editorial Director
Min S. Yee

Editor
Marian E. May

Production Editor
Anne Coolman

Administrative Assistant
Judith C. Pillon

Illustration
Assistance by
Edith Allgood

Copy Editing by
Shirley Manning

Proofreading by
Editcetera
Berkeley, CA

Indexing by
Baxter & Stimson

Typography by
Terry Robinson & Co.
San Francisco, CA

Color Separations by
Color Tech Corp.
Redwood City, CA

Printed by
Webcrafters
Madison, WI

Cover printed by
Graphic Enterprises
of Milwaukee, Inc.
Milwaukee, WI

Acknowledgements
Tool chest on covers
designed and built by
Eric Winter
Winter Woodworking
Sausalito, CA

Address all inquiries to:
Ortho Books
Chevron Chemical Company
Consumer Products Division
575 Market Street
San Francisco, CA 94105

1 2 3 4 5 6 7 8 9 10

ISBN 0-917102-82-7

Library of Congress Catalog
Card Number 79-52989

All About Basic Home Repairs

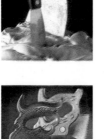

Roofs & Outside Walls

How to repair leaks, chimneys, gutters, downspouts, flashing,
and brick, stucco, masonry and wooden walls.

Safety and Ladders

In making repairs on your home, one of the most important areas to keep well maintained is the roof. And that brings us to the proper use of ladders in getting on and off the roof. Falling off the roof and hurting yourself is not only embarrassing but also foolish.

Take a few minutes to examine your ladder before starting up. Check that there are no cracks along the sides (rails) and there are no loose rungs that could give way under pressure. When you walk the ladder into position, make sure the base is about one-fourth the height of the ladder away from the house. Closer than that and you will tend to sway out from the house when you reach the top; farther out and you will put unnecessary pressure on the middle of the ladder as you climb.

Both feet of the ladder must be set firmly on the ground. If you do a lot of ladder work where the base rests on concrete, it's a good idea to glue some rubber pads on the feet. This will both stabilize the ladder on slightly uneven concrete and help keep it from slipping.

When working on the ladder, keep both hips between the rails while reaching out to work. This practice will keep you from leaning out too far and overbalancing. Once you overbalance and the ladder starts to go, you would be amazed at how fast the ground comes up to meet you.

Another good point to keep in mind on the ladder is always to grip the rails, not the rungs. A loose or cracked rung could pull free with no warning and cause you to topple backwards.

Before you actually start the climb to the roof (get there without stepping on the rain gutter, please), be sure you are wearing shoes with soft rubber soles to minimize your chances of slipping. If the roof is wet and it's covered with slick slate, tile or cedar shakes, you'd better wait until it dries off because these coverings are particularly slippery. If there happens to be an electrical storm going on while you're climbing onto the roof, be sure your last will and testament is in good order.

If you're going to be doing quite a bit of work on the roof, you might as well take the time to make yourself a good roof ladder. It will allow you to work in both comfort and safety.

A ladder with a wooden frame at one end, as illustrated, can be made quickly and bolted to either your wooden ladder or an aluminum ladder. You may also make and use the simpler "chicken ladder" — which refers to hens and not to your level of courage — by nailing cleats every 12 to 15 inches apart on a 1 by 10 board. Make sure the nail points are bent and hammered well back into the board so they won't damage the roof. This ladder, too, should have hooks at one end to keep it on a peaked roof.

If you are going to be on the roof just for a short time — for the annual inspection, say — make your life easier by first securing one end of a rope on the far side of the house and throwing the other end over the roof where you can hang onto it.

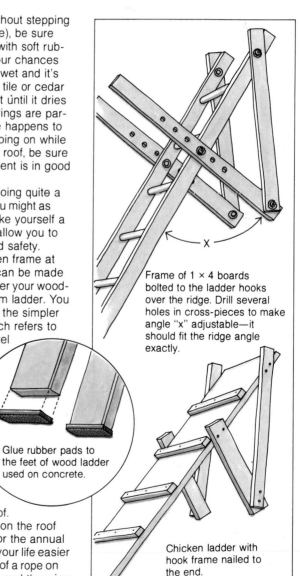

Frame of 1 × 4 boards bolted to the ladder hooks over the ridge. Drill several holes in cross-pieces to make angle "x" adjustable—it should fit the ridge angle exactly.

Glue rubber pads to the feet of wood ladder used on concrete.

Chicken ladder with hook frame nailed to the end.

Finding Leaks

After a general inspection of the roof shingles and flashing, you may not have found anything that appeared to be a potential problem. Then, with the first heavy rain of the year, you discover a leak. Finding the source of that drip takes patience and often the ability of Spiderman to crawl about in cramped spaces.

Almost assuredly, the leak will not be coming through the roof at the same place it is coming through your ceiling, unless you have a flat roof. Water often runs down rafters and ends up far from the leak. If you have an attic or crawl space, take a flashlight and start from the place where the drip is going through the ceiling below. Follow the water line up the rafter and mark its source with a crayon. Handle carefully any insulation batts you have to dislodge, and make sure they're well dried out before you put them back in place. At the source of the leak, try to drive a long thin nail through the roof to help you locate the leak topside when the storm ends. Attempts to plug the leak from the underside are largely ineffective.

If you cannot drive a nail through the leaking spot, find the leak after the storm by using a hose. With one person underneath and the other on the roof, start watering the roof higher and higher over the suspected spot until the leak reappears.

If you cannot get at the underside of the roof because it is covered, measure inside from one end of the house and down from the roof peak to the leak's approximate source. After the storm, use these measurements on top of the roof to give you close positioning. Work your way slowly up the roof, looking for loose roofing or flashing.

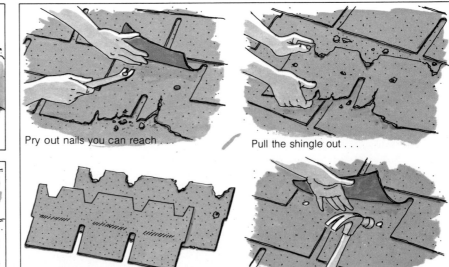

The leak in the roof will probably not be directly above the wet spot in your ceiling. Water often runs several feet down a rafter before dripping.

Roof Repairs

Shingles can work loose or split. Here's how to repair or replace that broken shingle.

■ **Asphalt shingles:** These are generally coated with a coarse sand and are among the most widely used roofing material. When the granular cover wears off, seen as black areas on the roof, the shingles themselves may be worn out. Other problems are split and curled ends, nails pulled loose or the entire shingle loosened.

These shingles are brittle when cold, so try to work on them during warm days. If you must work in cold weather, minimize breakage by heating any shingle with a propane torch before bending it.

A split shingle can be repaired by filling the crack with roofing cement. When the shingle has had a chance to dry out for a couple of days, use a putty knife to push the cement firmly into the crack. Unlike the more rigid roofing tar, roofing cement will expand and contract with temperature changes, and not crack.

Fix curled shingles by applying roofing cement under the curled part and weighting it down firmly. If it won't stay down, nail it in place with a broad

Fill cracks with roofing cement . . .

Put roofing cement under curled edges . . .

Pry out nails you can reach . . .

Cut notches in the new shingle to match any nail tears in the old one . . .

Pull the shingle out . . .

Slide the new shingle into place and nail it. (See text for details.)

headed roofing nail and cover the nail with roofing cement.

■ **Replacement:** To replace an entire shingle, lift the one above it carefully in order not to crack it, and expose the nails. Remove these nails with a prybar and slip the old shingle out. Put the new shingle in place and nail it in the same pattern as the old one. A touch of roofing cement on each nail head will prevent any leaks here.

If you find that the shingle won't slip out because it has been nailed a second time near the top under the upper shingle, split it carefully and tear out the pieces. Then, using them as a pattern, cut out notches at the top of the new shingle to match the old nail holes and slide it into place. Nail it in and give it an additional seal with roofing cement under its flap and under the flap of the shingle above it.

■ **Ridge and hip shingles:** If these shingles on the spine of the house or down sloping hip roofs are just cracked or curled, repair them with roofing cement. If they need to be replaced, leave the old shingles in place but measure them as patterns to cut new ones. Nail the damaged ridge or hip shingle down at the corners, then coat the bottom of the new shingle with roofing cement and put it in place. Finally, nail each corner down and coat the nails with a dab of cement.

■ **Wood shingles:** These are often subject to splitting or, because of their rigidity, being torn out completely by winds. Since you can't lift the upper shingle, remove the damaged one by splitting it apart and then pulling out the pieces. Don't damage the other shingles or the roofing paper underneath. Next, remove the upper nails by sliding a hacksaw blade up there and cutting them. Slide the new shingle into place and secure it with two galvanized nails placed just below the edge of the upper shingle. Seal the nail heads with a dab of roofing cement.

If you have to replace several courses of shingles, break up the damaged shingles and then remove the top row first. This will expose the nails further down. Hacksaw off the upper row of nails and then start from the bottom and work up with the new layer of shingles. Make sure that the joints between the shingles in one row do not coincide with the joints in the row above or below it, which would allow water through your roof.

■ **Flat roofs:** If an air blister forms on the roof, first clean it and the surrounding area of pebbles. Cut the blister down the middle, being careful not to cut the underlayer. Use a putty knife to force some roofing cement inside the blister. Nail down both sides of the opening. Next, cover the entire area and at least 3 inches more all around

it with roofing cement, then lay down a patch that overlaps the cut area by the same amount. Make the patch from heavy roofing felt or an asphalt shingle. Finally, cover this patch with roofing cement and replace the pebbles.

If the roof has been gouged or torn open, it is better to replace that damaged section. Clean the area of any gravel and then cut out a square section around the hole. Be careful not to cut the underlayer. Lift out this piece and use it as a pattern to cut a patch the same size. Coat both the underside of the patch and the hole with roofing cement and then nail the patch in place. Again, cover the patch with roofing cement and lay down another patch with a 3-inch overlay all around. Seal it all with roofing cement, paying close attention to the edges.

■ **Metal roofs:** These are long-lasting roofs with minimum maintenance, but problems can develop.

A small hole in the metal can be repaired by first cleaning the area with steel wool and then filling the hole with epoxy resin. For slightly larger holes, pack them firmly with steel wool and then cover with epoxy. Give them a second coat after the first is dry.

For even larger holes, cut a patch from the same type of metal. Since most metal roofs have distinctive ridge patterns, you probably will have to cut the patch from a matching pattern. Clean the area around the hole by sanding it and then solder the patch in place. On aluminum roofs, that patch can be effectively held in place with epoxy resin, but for galvanized steel or copper, use solder.

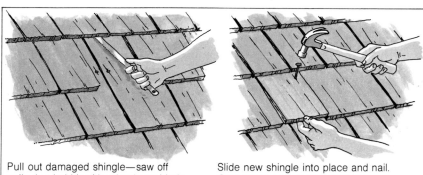

Pull out damaged shingle—saw off nails that held it with a hacksaw blade.

Slide new shingle into place and nail. Cover nails with roofing cement.

Clean off gravel. Slit the blister; do not cut the second layer . . .

Force roofing cement into the slit . . .

Nail down the slit's edges and cover with roofing cement . . .

Nail a patch over the slit; cover with more cement; and replace the gravel.

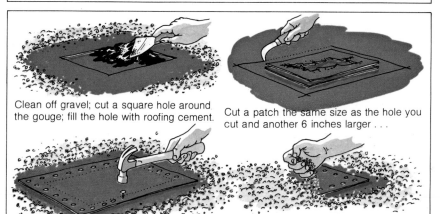

Clean off gravel; cut a square hole around the gouge; fill the hole with roofing cement.

Cut a patch the same size as the hole you cut and another 6 inches larger . . .

Nail the small patch in the hole; cover it with cement; nail the large patch on top . . .

Cover the large patch with roofing cement and replace the gravel.

Chimney Repairs

When it comes to the chimney on your house, it pays to look carefully for problems. Some of these problems could cause your house to burn down.

Consider, first, the soot in the chimney. That overload of soot can ignite, blow up out of the chimney stack and land on the roof. Look also for cracks in the chimney — crumbling mortar or loose bricks. All of these can allow sparks to slip out the side of the chimney onto your roof, or worse, into your attic. Another major item to inspect is the chimney flashing.

Start the inspection by peering down the chimney with a strong flashlight. You will be able to see even better if someone shines a light up from below, or uses a large piece of white cardboard to reflect sunlight up the chimney. If you can't see all the way down a chimney, then there's a real possibility that some creature is living there. Probably a bird in a nest. If that's the case, you can get rid of the nester while cleaning your chimney, and almost assuredly it will need cleaning.

Some people will tell you to close the damper and then begin the cleaning. But later you will have to open the damper and let the soot fall into the fireplace, and some will blow out onto your floor or rugs. Instead, leave the damper open and cover the fireplace opening with a piece of plywood or cardboard draped with rags along the edges to serve as a kind of weather stripping — or soot stripping. Brace it tightly in place. If you have more than one fireplace connecting to the same chimney, don't forget about it.

Now, from the rooftop, lower a burlap bag weighted with rocks and stuffed with balled up newspaper down the chimney. While humming appropriate selections from "Mary Poppins," work the bag up and down the entire chimney to loosen the accumulated soot. Alternatively, you can use a length of heavy chain and jiggle it around inside enough to free the soot, but not the mortar.

Afterwards, vacuum up the soot, including the piles on the damper and the shelf. More things that can go wrong in the fireplace are described on page 41.

The next step in chimney inspection is to check the cap. This is the layer of concrete that slopes away from the flue at the top of the stack. If it is crumbling and coming away from the flue, repair it with some premixed cement mortar, or make your own by mixing 1 part portland cement to 3 parts fine sand. For small cracks in the cap, fill them with exterior-grade caulking or some asphalt cement.

Be sure to maintain the slope away

from the flue to ensure water runoff.

If your chimney has no top on it and is open to the rain and windy downdrafts, consider putting a top on it. At the very least, you should have a wire spark arrester. You can easily make this by cementing some heavy galvanized wire mesh — about 1 inch is a good size — to the top of the flue. Or you can cut it as shown in the sketch and wedge it into the top of the flue. Alternatively, it can be cut to fit around the flue and then wired in place.

To add a top to your chimney, chip away enough room on each corner of the cap for a brick to sit snugly and then build up each corner at least 12 inches. For the top you can probably find a handsome piece of flagstone at a rock shop or pour yourself a 1-inch slab of reinforced concrete.

If you find that the mortar in the chimney has started to disintegrate in several places, clean it out thoroughly. First chip out the crumbled material with a hammer and a ⅜-inch cape chisel, then get rid of the crumbs with

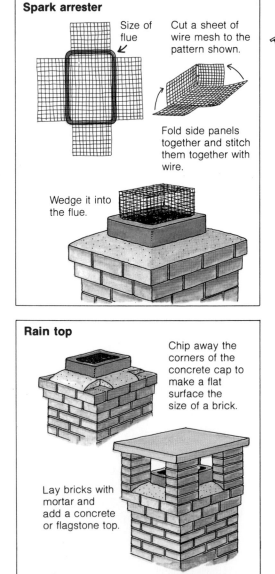

Spark arrester

Size of flue

Cut a sheet of wire mesh to the pattern shown.

Fold side panels together and stitch them together with wire.

Wedge it into the flue.

Rain top

Chip away the corners of the concrete cap to make a flat surface the size of a brick.

Lay bricks with mortar and add a concrete or flagstone top.

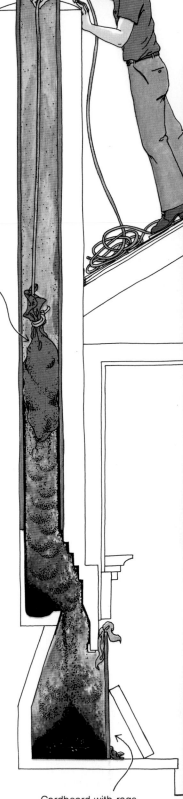

One way to clean a chimney is with a burlap bag weighted with rocks and stuffed with balls of newspaper

Cardboard with rags draped around the edges propped against the fireplace opening.

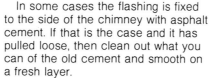

In some cases the flashing is fixed to the side of the chimney with asphalt cement. If that is the case and it has pulled loose, then clean out what you can of the old cement and smooth on a fresh layer.

If the flashing was mortared into the chimney and has pulled loose, then chip out the loose and crumbled mortar to a depth of ½ inch. Use a wire brush to clean it completely, then wet the area, fit the flashing into the groove and cement in place. Use a premixed mortar or make your own of 1 part mortar cement and 3 parts of fine sand. When dry, give some added protection by caulking the seam with some polysulfide rubber.

If the joints where the flashing bends and meets around the chimney have worked apart, use heavy pliers to press them back together. Crimp the edges together and then solder them shut if copper. If aluminum, cover the joints with epoxy resin.

If the flashing is too badly corroded to be repaired, start removing it by chipping out the seams where it's embedded in the chimney. Pull free as carefully as possible. Next, remove shingles that overlap the base flashing (see page 6 on shingle removal). Remove the base flashing, straighten it carefully and use it as a pattern to cut your new flashing.

Remember when reinstalling it that flashing overlaps just as shingles do. Start at the bottom face of the chimney, work around the sides and finish with the upper face for each layer of the flashing. Use roofing nails and asphalt cement to fasten it to the roof. Don't forget that dab of cement over the nail heads.

a wire brush. For details on replacing the mortar, a process called repointing, see page 15.

If you find a loose brick, chip away the mortar, then split the brick with hammer and chisel, and pry it out. Clean the hole, wet it, and then smooth in a layer of mortar (1 part masonry cement to 3 parts fine sand) on the bottom. Fit the new brick in carefully and then pack the sides and top with mortar.

A note of caution here: If you find several loose bricks or cracks, you should test the chimney for smoke leaks. Those openings could allow smoke or sparks into your attic. To test, build a small fire and cover it with green grass or damp leaves to create lots of smoke. Cover the top of the chimney with a wet sack for a minute or less to see if the smoke is escaping from the cracks. If you find extensive leaks, call in an expert for further advice.

The last big chimney problem to hope you don't have is corroded, bent or loose flashing. This is commonly a sheet metal used to keep water out of the joints and angles of a roof, and the joints around vent pipes and chimneys. Normally copper or aluminum, it can also be asphalt roll, galvanized steel or rubber. (There is more about flashing on page 11.)

If the top of the flashing is pulled loose from the mortar in the chimney, or if there are only small cracks where it is bent, it can be repaired. But if there is widespread corrosion, you're better off to replace it all.

There are two layers of chimney flashing. The under layer goes clear around the chimney base and extends out on the sides beneath the roofing material. The top layer fits over this base and stair-steps up the side of the chimney. This part is cemented into the chimney to prevent leaks.

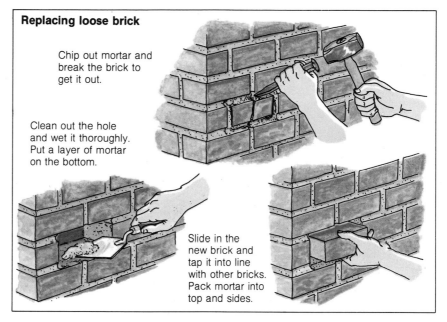

Replacing loose brick

Chip out mortar and break the brick to get it out.

Clean out the hole and wet it thoroughly. Put a layer of mortar on the bottom.

Slide in the new brick and tap it into line with other bricks. Pack mortar into top and sides.

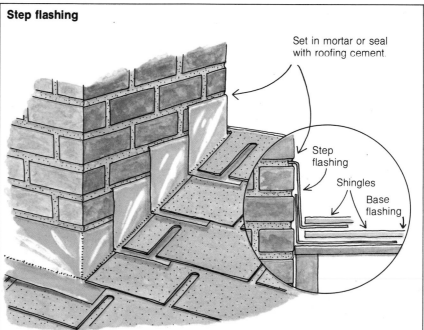

Step flashing

Set in mortar or seal with roofing cement.

Step flashing

Shingles

Base flashing

Gutters, Downspouts and Flashing

No matter what type or shape, all rain gutters have a bothersome habit of getting clogged, and that can give you more problems than you anticipated. Among other things, backed-up water in a gutter can freeze in the winter and break the gutter down. Water can back up under the shingles and run down your interior walls or start the process of rot.

On these cheery notes, let's look at some ways to keep the gutters cleaned and well maintained.

■ **Cleaning:** Gutters should be cleared of debris every fall after the leaves drop and every spring after the winds have died down. Leaf traps covering the downspouts must also be removed and cleaned. Finally, if you haven't already, crimp strips of vinyl coated wire mesh over the gutter to keep out the leaves.

■ **Maintenance and repair:** While cleaning the gutters, look for some of these potential problems: sags, loose joints, loose or broken hangers, small or large holes in the gutter, and splits in the downspout seams.

If you find a sagging gutter, look first for a broken support. There are three major styles, as illustrated.

To correct a sagging gutter, brace it back into position with a long 2 by 4 and then fix the support.

If the rivet holding the hanger at that point has broken but the hanger itself is sound, drill out the rivet and replace it with a small, rustproof nut and bolt. If the strap extending up under the roof is broken, first remove the old piece and join them with an overlay strap of matching galvanized tin.

If the strap has separated from the gutter, resolder it.

Loose joints are another common malady. Leaks generally result here. If you have aluminum gutters, you can usually solve the problem by squeezing a silicone caulking compound into the joints; it acts as a glue as well as a waterproof caulking. For copper gutters, it is more effective to resolder the joint. Should you have the uncommon wooden gutters, the joints can be sealed — when the wood is perfectly dry — with either the silicone caulking compound or a polysulfide rubber caulking.

Holes in the gutter can generally be repaired without a great deal of trouble. Should it be a large tear, however, it is preferable to replace that section of gutter.

For small holes in aluminum gutters, clean the metal thoroughly with steel wool and then smooth in an epoxy resin. If the hole is quite small, two light coats of fibered asphalt cement will fill it.

For larger holes, clean the area, then coat it with fibered asphalt cement and overlap the break with a smooth, double layer of heavy aluminum foil. Top this with another layer of cement.

Wooden gutters can also develop leaks, often stemming from wood rot. When the gutters are dry, inspect closely for any large cracks and poke gently with a dull knife tip to discover any softness that signals dry rot. Fill the cracks with plastic wood. In rotted areas, chisel out all the bad wood, let dry thoroughly and soak the hole with a pentachlorophenol wood preservative. After it is dry, fill the hole with plastic wood and smooth it out. Finally, give the inside of the gutter two light coats of asphalt roofing cement. Do not let it drip on the outside where it will bleed through the protective paint. Treat wooden gutters with preservative every two years.

Gutter hangers

Nailed to roof

STRAP-TYPE: Strap is nailed to roof beneath shingles. Gutter is inserted from below and the hanger hooks to itself under the gutter at the facia.

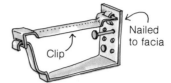

Clip

Nailed to facia

CLIP-TYPE: Hanger is nailed to the facia. Gutter is inserted from above and the clip snaps across the top.

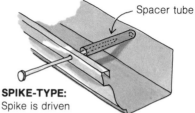

Spacer tube

SPIKE-TYPE: Spike is driven through gutter and spacer tube into facia.

■ **Downspouts:** If these are clogged, clear them with a stout piece of wire or a plumber's snake. The plugged area will probably be in the elbow. You may be able to blow it clear with water pressure from a garden hose.

Leaks sometimes develop around the downspout because it is incorrectly fitted. Some are made to fit smoothly inside the gutter while others are screwed to the outside, then a healthy bead of sealant is put around the join. Double-check your style of downspout.

While you're at it, make sure the gutter and downspout are firmly attached to the side of the house. This will prevent any movement that can cause leaks.

If a downspout or drainpipe splits because of a combination of clogging and ice, clean the seam edges and pull back together with pliers. For aluminum downspouts, fill the crack with an epoxy resin or fiberglass from a mending kit (available in most hardware stores). Reinforce the repair with a binding of several aluminum wires. On copper or galvanized steel downspouts, clean the seam edges, pull into place and then solder shut.

■ **Replacing gutters:** This may be necessary because your gutters are worn out or were set incorrectly and don't drain properly.

Gutters usually come in 10-foot lengths and should be pitched to

Gutter covers

Vinyl coated wire deflects leaves and other debris over the gutter. Install it by sliding it under the first course of shingles so it is flush with the front edge of the gutter.

Mending gutter strap

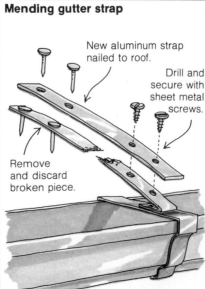

New aluminum strap nailed to roof.

Drill and secure with sheet metal screws.

Remove and discard broken piece.

Installing a gutter

Line level

Mark off a slope of ½-inch drop for each 10 feet of gutter. Snap a chalk line for a continuous guide.

Nail holds string at top of facia.

For a gutter run of over 30 feet, slope it both ways from the middle.

drop ½ inch every 10 feet. To find this proper pitch, don't assume that the fascia board is level. It probably isn't. Find the true level by driving a thin nail into the board just where the upper end of the gutter will be, right under the roof overhang. Stretch a string from this nail to the other end of the fascia board and check with a line level. Drive a small nail to mark the level at this end. Allowing a ½ inch drop for every 10 feet, come down the necessary distance at the end of the fascia board and snap a chalk line. You can now see where the gutters will have to run. If you have more than 30 feet to replace at one time, it is better to split the difference — put the high point at the middle of the fascia board and slope the gutters from there to the two downspouts at the ends.

■ **Flashing:** The roof flashing should be inspected once a year to ensure that it has not worked loose, allowing water to seep under the roof. Small holes in the roofing cement or caulking along the edge of the flashing are difficult to see. If you have any doubts, wire-brush these areas clean and recoat with a fibered asphalt cement. Actual holes in metal flashing can be repaired with epoxy resin quite effectively. For larger holes in aluminum flashing, clean the metal with steel wool until bright and then fix an aluminum patch over the hole with epoxy resin. For added protection, coat the patch and the edges with roofing cement.

For holes in copper or galvanized steel, make the repairs by soldering in a patch.

In closed valley flashing (see illustration) it is possible to repair leaks without removing all the shingles. Cut small diamonds from the same metal as your flashing and, starting from the bottom, work them into position. The few nails you run into can be cut with a hacksaw blade. Allow an overlap of at least 2 inches on each piece of flashing. When in place, nail down through the shingle and coat each nail head with a dab of roofing cement.

Vent flashing replacement

1. Remove old flashing and one or two shingles above the vent. Slide new flashing under one row of shingles.

2. Nail the flashing in place — keep all the nails where they will be covered by shingles.

3. Replace the shingles and seal the joint between the flashing and vent with roofing cement or caulking.

Closed valley

Roofing paper
Metal
Shingles butted

To repair leaks, slide diamond shaped pieces of aluminum under shingles — overlap 2 inches or more.

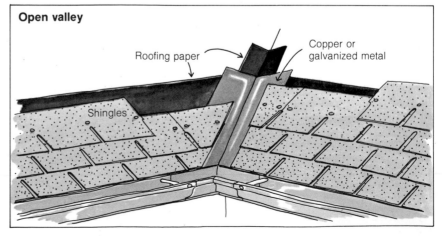

Open valley

Roofing paper

Copper or galvanized metal

Shingles

Caulking

Caulking is a flexible sealant that expands or contracts with temperature fluctuations. It's essential to house-maintenance and a caulking gun plus several varieties of caulking should be kept on hand at all times. It's easy to use and once you start looking around your house, you might be surprised at how much caulking it needs.

The sealant is applied with a caulking gun. There are two types, one that can be bulk loaded and another — which is normally used by homeowners — loaded with cartridges. You can also buy caulking in rope form for pressing into larger holes or in flexible tubes for small jobs.

There is a confusing variety of caulking materials on the market, but each has its own characteristics that are right for certain jobs. They all come in black, white and gray.

Here's a basic list of the varieties and their characteristics:

—oil-base caulking: the most common variety and the least expensive. It cannot be painted over with any success.

—latex-base caulking: drys fast, remains quite flexible and can be painted readily.

—butyl rubber caulking: more expensive but longer lasting. Excellent for sealing joints between masonry and metal.

—polysulfide caulking: good quality, long lasting, sticks readily to painted surfaces and can be painted.

—silicone caulking: the most expensive but also the longest lasting. One drawback — unless the label promises otherwise — it does not adhere well to any painted surface and new paint does not take to it.

Because there are so many brands of caulking, you have to read the label carefully to know you're getting the type you need.

A reminder here: before you race about to fill every crack in sight, remember that you cannot put new caulking over old. You must scrape and chisel out the old first, blow the crumbs away and let the exposed surface dry thoroughly.

■ **Places to caulk:** One of the first areas to inspect for caulking needs are the joints between your outside window frames and the house siding. Settling of the house and shrinkage of wood can cause large gaps here that can cost you money in heating and cooling losses.

With the nozzle on the cartridge cut at a 45-degree angle and the gun held at a similar angle, push a smooth bead from bottom to top of the window frame sides. Make sure the caulking adheres to both the siding and the

45°

Cut the nozzle of the caulking cartridge at a 45° angle.

1.
2.

Load the gun by pulling the handle all the way back; fit the back end of the cartridge over the plunger (**1**) and drop it into the half-barrel (**2**).

Hold the gun at a 45° angle as you push or pull it along.

Caulking the window frame with a caulking gun (see text).

Large cracks require packing with oakum before caulking.

window frame — cut the nozzle at a wider place if the bead is too small.

If the opening is large and deep, pack it first with oakum, a ropelike material that can be bought at most hardware stores. After tamping this firmly into the crack, smooth on the caulking.

Next, have a close look under the window sill. If there is a very large separation here, fill it first with oakum, then cover it with a length of quarter-round molding. Finally, caulk around the molding.

Other places not to miss on your outside inspection tour include:
—joints between door frames and siding;
—around your storm windows;
—along the drip caps over windows and over outside door frames;
—all the roof and dormer flashing and, of course, chimney flashing (page 11);
—around all skylights in the roof.

All these can be treated just as you handled the window frame problem.

■ **Inside caulking:** The area most commonly in need of caulking in the house is around the tub. Each time it is filled, it settles a little and that causes a minor separation from the wall. Splashed water can then work between the tub — or basin — and wall, and start the process of rot.

For bathroom jobs, a small handheld tube of tub and tile caulking is normally sufficient. Clean out the old caulking with a screwdriver, being careful not to scratch the tub or surrounding wall tile. Cut the tip of the nozzle for a moderate-size bead and — when the area is completely dry — push the sealant around the edge in one continuous line.

While you're there, check that the grouting material between the wall tiles is not loose. If you find such a problem, scrape out the loose and flaky material with a screwdriver and lay in a narrow bead of new caulking. Wipe away any excess with a clean damp rag. For replacing tiles, see page 37.

Outside Wood Repairs

These problems largely center around the siding on wood houses and windowsills that are broken or cracked.

Siding on a house, whether it is clapboard, shingles, or board and batten, is subject to cracking, loosening, splintering and rotting. Don't cringe. These replacement and repair tasks are usually pretty easy.

■ **Clapboard:** This common house siding is made from overlapping boards fitted together in any of the four basic styles illustrated. Usually, on the beveled (simple overlap) style, the top edge is thinner than the bottom for a smoother fit, which is why it's called beveled siding. If your siding is drop, tongue and groove or shiplap,

Clapboard siding types

Shiplap   Beveled (simple overlap)   Drop   Tongue & groove

the repair problem is only slightly more difficult.

To repair a split in clapboard siding, pry the crack apart with a stout putty knife and then work in a layer of plastic wood or waterproof adhesive. Press the boards back tightly together and then nail firmly in place with galvanized finishing nails. Countersink the nails, fill the holes with putty and wipe off all excess.

If the board is badly broken or rotted — which is hazardous to the health of your house because it lets in water that can rot the studs — you must replace that section of the board.

Start by driving some narrow wooden wedges up under the section of the board to be removed. Put the wedges just outside the planned saw cut lines. This gives you space to get a keyhole saw beneath the upper board. Finish cutting out the bad section with a backsaw and be careful not to cut the good boards or the building paper underneath.

Once the board is cut, use a chisel to split it lengthwise. Remove that piece and then use a hacksaw to cut the nails in the upper board. Use the wooden wedges again so you can slip the blade in. After the nails are cut, chisel out the remaining piece from beneath the upper board. Tack any cuts in the building paper down with roofing nails and coat with roofing cement.

Cut the new piece of clapboard for an exact fit and tap it into place. Protect the edge from hammer dents with a scrap board. Use galvanized finishing nails, then fill the gap at each

end of the new board with wood putty. Apply a coat of wood sealer before repainting the board.

If you have tongue and groove or shiplap siding, proceed in the same manner but cut the tongue or lap off the replacement board to make it easier to fit in place.

Any breaks in boards or battens are best repaired by simply prying off the entire damaged board and replacing it.

■ **Shingle siding:** Replace in the same manner as described for roofing shingles (page 7). If the building paper is torn in the removal process, tack it back in place and coat with roofing cement before installing new shingles.

If the shingles are merely cracked, fill the crack with plastic wood and tack the sides of the split in place with galvanized finishing nails. If the crack is too large for this, slip a piece of roofing felt up under the crack and hold it in place with some finishing nails.

■ **Windowsill:** For cracks, pry them slightly farther apart, fill with plastic wood and then cinch back together by driving several galvanized 16-penny finishing nails into the crack from the lip of the sill. Countersink the nails and fill the holes with wood putty before repainting.

If the sill contains small pockets of rotted wood, chisel these out and when the area is dry, coat it thoroughly with pentachlorophenol wood preservative. Soak and let dry for at least 24 hours. Afterwards, fill the holes with plastic wood and smooth it in to conform to the sill. Finish the job by repainting the sill.

Repairing split board

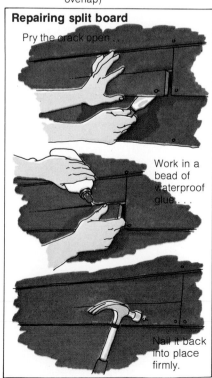

Pry the crack open . . .

Work in a bead of waterproof glue . . .

Nail it back into place firmly.

Repairing damaged siding section (see text).

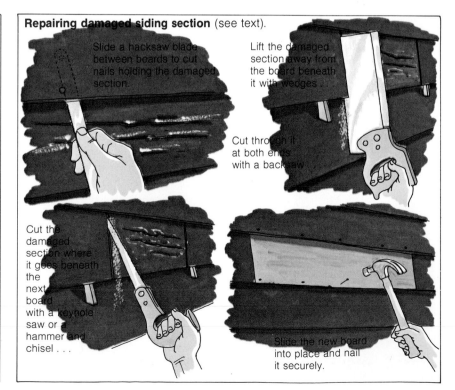

Slide a hacksaw blade between boards to cut nails holding the damaged section.

Cut the damaged section where it goes beneath the next board with a keyhole saw or hammer and chisel . . .

Lift the damaged section away from the board beneath it with wedges . . .

Cut through it at both ends with a backsaw

Slide the new board into place and nail it securely.

Repairing Masonry, Stucco and Brick Surfaces

While strong and long lasting, walls of concrete, brick or stucco can develop problems. Hairline cracks, severe breaks, efflorescence and spalling on bricks, plus stucco cracks are some common headaches. The secret of making good repairs here with the least amount of effort is to get started as soon as you spot the problem. This keeps it from getting out of hand. Here are details on some of the problems and solutions.

■ **Concrete:** Often the most common problems with concrete, whether in walks, steps or walls, are hairline cracks. Generally they do not grow rapidly after appearing unless settling of the wall or walk is continuing to break the concrete, or freezing weather is opening them wider.

Start the repair by cleaning the crack with a wire brush. Remove all dust and small fragments. If there are still some loose elements in there, use a cold chisel and hammer to break them out. The crack must be clean and free of particles that can break loose and reopen the crack.

If a crack completely divides a piece of concrete, as in a walkway, and one side is lower, pry it up and pack sand beneath that section to level it before repairing the pieces.

Wet the crack completely before patching to prevent the old concrete from drawing moisture from the new. Bonds between old and new concrete can be improved by first coating the area to be filled with a commercial bonding agent or common white glue.

The crack can now be filled with premixed concrete or with a masonry patch — latex, epoxy, vinyl or acrylic cement — that comes in a cartridge. Read the label and choose the best kind for your particular job. These patches are fine for small repairs.

For larger breaks, make your own patch from 1 part portland cement and 3 parts sand. Work the repair material deeply into the crack, probing it with the point of the trowel to remove all air bubbles.

Let the patch cure about one week, hosing lightly with water to keep it damp the first 48 hours. Too rapid drying will only crack the concrete again. If you are in an area subject to freezing, the patch must be covered and insulated with sacks or a bit of old carpet.

■ **Broken steps:** If the front edge of a concrete step is broken, you can repair it by making a small wooden form to hold the concrete patch. First use a cold chisel to chip away all the weakened concrete. Try to chisel out a flat "landing" on the edge to hold the patching material. Clean it with a wire brush, blow away the crumbs and dampen.

Make a form to hold the patch in place by cutting a board the same height as the step riser. Block this tightly against the stair and grease the board so the concrete will not stick to it when removed.

Now, trowel in a patch of concrete made from 1 part portland cement to 3 parts sand. Smooth and let cure for a week, keeping the new edge damp for 48 hours.

■ **Brick:** One of the most common problems with bricks is the crumbling away of the binding mortar. In turn, this allows water to begin working deeper and deeper into the bonds and the process of decay is underway. Efforts to repel the water are made when the brick mason finishes each layer of the brick and shapes the bond between in a certain fashion. This is the process called pointing, and some of the more common styles are illustrated on the next page.

If you find mortar crumbling away between joints, it must be repaired promptly. You can use a masonry cutting disc on a power drill to quickly clean out much of the joint. Finish the job with a small cold chisel (a cape chisel is ideal for this) and then scrub clean with a wire brush.

The joint must be cleaned out to ½-inch depth.

Wet the area to be repointed so it won't dry out the new mix. Unless you are experienced with a trowel, you may find it difficult to place your mix cleanly into the joint. Instead, fill the joint by holding a small amount of mix on the trowel just below the joint and then forcing it in with a jointer, stick or small scraper.

The new mix should be 1 part masonry cement to 3 parts fine sand. Wait approximately 5 minutes for the concrete to firm up and then repoint the bond in a style matching the existing work. Pointing tools are handy and inexpensive for this work. For weathered, raked or struck joints, use the trowel to repoint.

■ **Cracked brick wall:** You've got a problem here but you probably really aren't interested in tearing down the wall and putting a better foundation under it. Filling the crack sounds like a much better idea. But before you do, it's a good idea to check if the crack is still widening. If so, there's not much sense in filling it yet. To check, use some epoxy resin to glue a thin piece of glass across the crack. Leave it there several weeks, even three months. If it breaks, the wall is still settling.

When you're ready to fill the crack, wet the inside, then cover the lower portion of the crack to keep the patch from running out. A piece of plywood

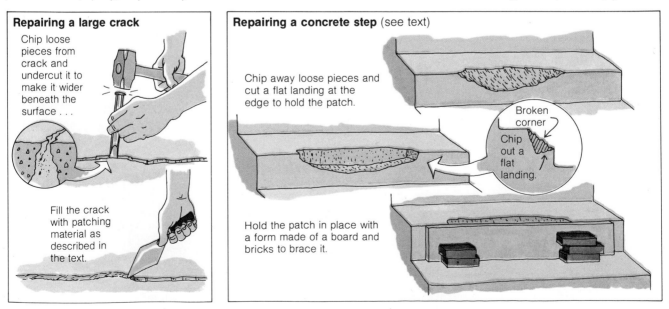

Repairing a large crack

Chip loose pieces from crack and undercut it to make it wider beneath the surface . . .

Fill the crack with patching material as described in the text.

Repairing a concrete step (see text)

Chip away loose pieces and cut a flat landing at the edge to hold the patch.

Broken corner

Chip out a flat landing.

Hold the patch in place with a form made of a board and bricks to brace it.

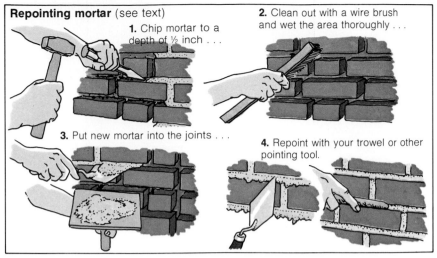

Repointing mortar (see text)

1. Chip mortar to a depth of ½ inch . . .

2. Clean out with a wire brush and wet the area thoroughly . . .

3. Put new mortar into the joints . . .

4. Repoint with your trowel or other pointing tool.

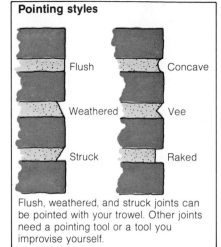

Pointing styles

Flush

Concave

Weathered

Vee

Struck

Raked

Flush, weathered, and struck joints can be pointed with your trowel. Other joints need a pointing tool or a tool you improvise yourself.

---

blocked in place works fine.

It's difficult to get the patching material far back in the crack. Many hardware stores have special grout bags that allow you to more easily squeeze the patch back in there, much like a pastry tube squeezes decoration onto a cake.

Let the lower section set up about 8 hours, then remove the brace and repoint the joints. The next day, brace the upper portion of the crack and repeat the process.

■ **Efflorescence:** This is a fairly common problem that blights new bricks. It is just mineral salts pushed to the surface by moisture in the bricks. Clean the bricks with a wire brush and then apply a coat of 1 part muriatic acid and 4 parts water. Or give it a couple of coats of neutralizer bought at your hardware store. If the problem persists, it's possible that a leak or other source of moisture behind the bricks keeps forcing out those salts. Then you may need an expert's opinion.

■ **Spalling:** This is the result of bricks soaking up water, then chipping apart

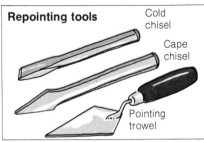

Repointing tools

Cold chisel

Cape chisel

Pointing trowel

in freezing weather. To repair, replace severely damaged bricks, repair any loose mortar, then coat the entire wall with a clear brick sealer.

■ **Stucco:** To repair cracked stucco, first clean the crack with a wire brush. Then, without widening the crack, use a stiff putty knife to chip out an inverted V to better hold the patching material. Dampen the crack and then work in a patch made of 1 part masonry cement and 3 parts fine sand. Add mortar pigment until you think the patch and wall match. But don't count on good results. You might as well plan on giving the whole wall another finish coat.

Keep the repair dampened for two

days so it will cure properly.

Where whole areas of stucco are coming loose, chip the stucco down to a firm layer. Remember that stucco goes on in three coats and normally the first coat is applied over a layer of chicken wire. If the wire is broken, repair it so the stucco will be properly supported. Wet the area, then apply the base or "scratch" coat through the wire and up to within ½ inch of the surface. When the mortar begins to set, scratch the surface with nails in a board so that the next layer gets a good grip.

Keep the first layer damp for 48 hours and then apply the second layer, which should come within ⅛ inch of the surface. Keep this layer damp for 2 days and then let it cure properly for 4 or 5 more days. Now put on your finish coat complete with the matching pigment. Like the other coats, it is made up of 1 part masonry cement and 3 parts fine sand. Be careful not to make the mix too wet or it will tend to run. Apply it over a damp wall and keep it just lightly damp for 2 days, then let it cure.

Crack in stucco (see text)

Clean out loose material . . .

Undercut the crack—widen beneath . . .

Dampen and work in patching material.

Hole in stucco (see text for specifics of mixing & application)

1st LAYER: Dampen the area of the hole and apply the base coat through the wire and to within ½ inch of the surface. When it begins to set, scarify the surface . . .

2nd LAYER: Dampen the area and apply the second layer to within ⅛ inch of the finished surface . . .

3rd LAYER: Dampen the area and apply the finish coat. When it sets, texture it to match the surrounding stucco.

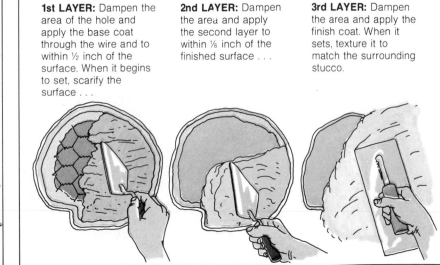

Doors & Windows

How to fix stuck, warped or sagging doors; replace hinges, locks, latches and knobs. How to solve problems with thresholds, sliding doors and screen doors. How to repair stuck windows, sliding and casement windows, shades, blinds and drapery rods. How to replace broken glass.

Doors and Hinges

In this unstable world, it's nice to know there are a few things you can still count on: doors will stick, windows won't open (or close when it's raining) and hinges will come loose.

It's also nice to know that you really don't have to hand over a week's salary to have them fixed. Spend that money instead on some more tools for yourself, and do your own work. The sooner you build up a proper array of tools to do the job right, the more you will enjoy doing it. (See page 97 for basic tools.)

Before starting to correct some problems you might have with doors, take a look at how yours are made. Exterior doors are usually solid, for protection, while inside doors are usually hollow core — just two pieces of plywood sandwiched over a frame. The outside doors, which are more exposed to temperature fluctuations, may stick during damp weather as the wood swells. Before you remove the door and start repairs, decide whether you consider the sticking to be a serious problem or just something to be endured for a couple of months each year.

Because doors are constantly being opened and closed they take more battering than windows and other moving elements of your house. Look at the detailed illustration of a door on page 22 and then look your own doors over to spot the problems: loose hinges, warped or bowed door, loose jamb, or cracked threshold.

Not trying to alarm you, of course, but there are even more things that can go wrong with a door: loose handles, inoperative locks, misaligned strike plates. The list is formidable but fortunately the repairs are not. In fact, once you get into it, you may want to replace an entire door. All the details on how to do that are coming up.

■ **Hinges:** In many cases you are going to have to remove the door before you can work on it. There are two basic types of hinges, the loose-pin and half-pin. The loose-pin is more common. Remove these hinges by holding a screwdriver or large nail under the lip of the top pin and drive it up. For half-pin hinges, open the door about halfway and then lift the entire door to remove it.

When removing the hinges, support the door with a wedge of some type under the latch edge. Then, always remove the bottom hinge first to prevent the door from toppling over and cracking the jamb.

With these basics in mind, you are ready to start repairing those stuck, sagging or warped doors.

Stuck and Sagging Doors

It's almost inevitable that a door will stick in your house. This is particularly likely if you have moved into a new house, because it is going to settle a little and that puts a door out of "true" or "square."

Doors also tend to expand during damp weather and then shrink back when they are dry. Prying these stuck doors open is not only frustrating to you but can be damaging to your house: the door handle may come loose, the edge of the door may split, and you may break the door jamb.

The first things to check on a door that sticks are the hinges. Open the door wide and see if all the screws are tight in both the door and jamb. You may be able to solve your problem right there.

If the screw turns without tightening, it probably means that the wood it grips has stripped away. For an immediate repair, remove the offending screw, fill the hole with plastic wood and let dry. Then predrill for the screw and replace the screw.

If the door is still binding, the next step is to mark exactly these spots. If you can't readily see where the door rubs, move a thin sheet of paper between door and jamb. Outline the sticking areas with light pencil marks.

Now check your hinges again. If you find one that is bent, the only solution

Loose-pin removal

Tap gently at the pin bottom to loosen . . .

then drive the pin up and out.

Sticking doors

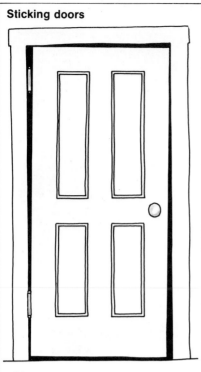

Slide paper between the door and jam — it will bind where the door is sticking. If a door sticks at the top of the latch side, tighten the top hinge screws, chisel the top hinge mortise deeper or shim out the bottom hinge.

To correct sticking at the bottom of the latch side, tighten screws or deepen the mortise of the bottom hinge or shim out the top hinge. If it binds on the hinge side, shim one or both hinges as needed. If this fails, plane off part of the door and repaint.

Shimming a hinge

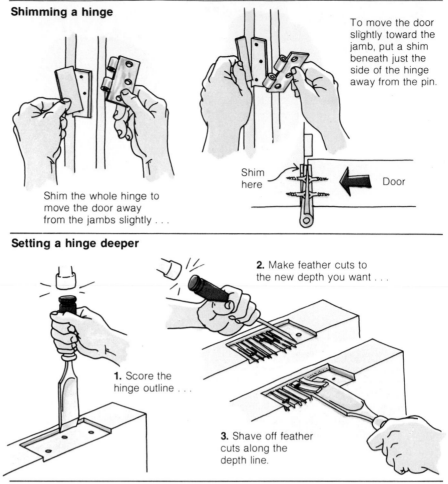

Shim the whole hinge to move the door away from the jambs slightly . . .

To move the door slightly toward the jamb, put a shim beneath just the side of the hinge away from the pin.

Shim here

Door

Setting a hinge deeper

1. Score the hinge outline . . .

2. Make feather cuts to the new depth you want . . .

3. Shave off feather cuts along the depth line.

is to remove it and hammer it straight or buy a new one of the same size and kind.

More often the problem lies with one of the hinges being set deeper or shallower than the other. They worked together in the beginning but as the house settled and the door frame shifted slightly, the door now binds.

■ **Shims:** As illustrated, a door with a top hinge set too shallowly — or the bottom hinge set too deeply — will lean out and bind at the top along the jamb. If your door is binding at the top and the top hinge seems to be set shallower than the lower one, try correcting with a shim on the lower hinge to bring it in line with the upper.

Remove the screws from the lower hinge on the jamb side only. Now slip one or more pieces of cardboard cut to fit the mortise (the cut-out area in the jamb) until you bring the hinge out to match the upper one. Tarpaper makes weather-worthy shims for outside doors that you often leave open, or hardworking doors in steamy places.

If the door binds even worse now, you're going to have to reverse the process: that is, deepen the mortise for the upper hinge. To do this, you must remove the door. First, steady the opened door by inserting a support under the latch side. Lift out the door

if it has half-pin hinges. With loose-pin hinges, use a screwdriver and hammer to knock out the lower pin first so the door won't fall.

With the door out of the way, remove the hinge leaf that is set too shallowly in the jamb. Then, working carefully with a wide wood chisel, scrape out the mortise to the correct depth. Keep the beveled edge of the chisel down and take it easy: you can cut too deeply without any trouble at all. Check your progress often. If you do go too deep, adjust with a shim.

While on the subject of shimming doors: note that sometimes a door resists closing and tends to spring open unless carefully latched. If you look carefully at the hinges just as the door is about to close, you may see them move. In this case, the door is binding against the jamb on the hinge side. This is because the hinges are set too deeply in the mortises.

However, before you remove the door and insert shims at top and bottom, check to see if either hinge was incorrectly set — at a slight angle, either out or in. If this is the problem, you can correct it by loosening the screws on the jamb or door and inserting a shim under only half the hinge in order to bring it back into a true position that will keep the door away from the jamb.

The easiest way to hold a door in a vertical position while you plane or otherwise work on the edge is to nose one end into a corner of the room.

then clamp it. Use scrap wood on both sides of the door to prevent damage from the clamps.

If the crack is more severe, chisel the mortise out another ¼ inch and then repair the crack as above. After the glue has set, cut a shim from a piece of ¼-inch hardwood and fit it into the mortise. Glue and clamp in place and the following day drill new holes and rehang the door. The hardwood shim should give you that extra bit of support to keep the door in place.

■ **Planing the Door:** If your prayers haven't been answered entirely by adjusting the hinges, you can correct the sticking problem by sanding or planing.

First, locate the areas that bind and mark the boundaries with light pencil marks on the door. If you can't see the area that sticks, locate it by running a piece of paper between the closed door and the jamb.

If the bind is slight, try sanding it down. It's slower than planing but more accurate.

If it is a large area or a severe bind, you will have to use a plane. It should be a jack plane or smooth plane to give you the most even cut possible.

Doors that bind on the latch side or top can be worked on while the door is still hung, but the results can be less than satisfactory. It's best to remove the door and brace it securely before planing. Furthermore, the proper way to plane a door is only along the hinge side, even if the bind is on the latch side. This way, any careless work is well hidden. If much wood is removed, the mortises may have to be deepened again for a proper hinge fit.

A warning here: It's easy to remove too much wood and the resulting scallop in your door will be a veritable magnet for inquisitive eyes. So go slow and make long, smooth, shallow cuts. In addition, always plane with the wood grain. Going against it can result in deep gouges.

When planing the top and bottom rails of a door, always work from the outer edge toward the middle. Planing from the middle out to the end can split off large pieces of wood.

■ **Loose door:** If you have an old door that appears to have shrunk and left a gap between it and the jamb — perhaps so much that it will not latch properly — you can bring the door over with a long wooden shim.

First, carefully measure how much of a gap exists, then remove the door and hinges. Cut a strip of wood to the depth of the gap that is also the same length and width of the door edge. Affix it to the hinge edge of the door with glue and screws, countersinking the screws. Cut the hinge mortises again and you're back in business.

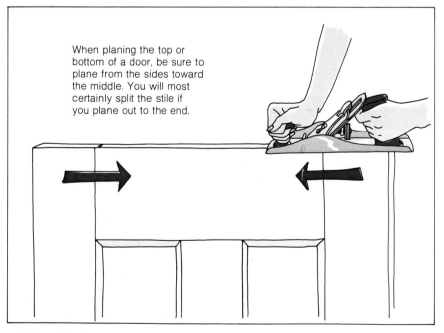

When planing the top or bottom of a door, be sure to plane from the sides toward the middle. You will most certainly split the stile if you plane out to the end.

■ **Broken Mortise:** Sometimes when a screw will not tighten in a door, it is because the wood in the mortise has split.

If the crack does not appear too severe and the door is not too heavy, the repair can be made with white wood glue and clamps. First pry the crack apart slightly and work in a good bead of glue (epoxy resin if it is an outside door that might get wet). Work this thoroughly into the split and

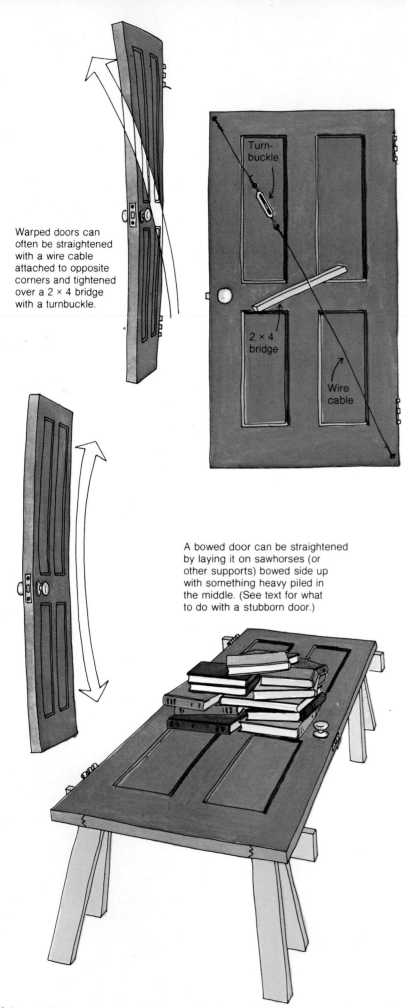

Warped doors can often be straightened with a wire cable attached to opposite corners and tightened over a 2 × 4 bridge with a turnbuckle.

Turn-buckle

2 × 4 bridge

Wire cable

A bowed door can be straightened by laying it on sawhorses (or other supports) bowed side up with something heavy piled in the middle. (See text for what to do with a stubborn door.)

Warped Doors, Thresholds and Other Problems

A warped or bowed door is a fairly common problem. The door will close all right in many cases but there may be a noticeable gap where it twists away from the door stop.

If after the door is removed, you see that it is warped or twisted rather than bowed, drill two holes at the diagonal corners of the twisted part and screw in two eye hooks there. Then, over a 2 by 4 laid on edge in the middle of the door, run a length of wire or light cable. Use a turnbuckle near the middle to begin pulling the door straight. Tighten firmly the first day and then daily thereafter for up to a week, until the door is straight and appears likely to remain that way. Don't try to straighten it completely the first day or you may pull the screw eyes loose.

A bowed door is a little easier to treat. Place the ends over sawhorses or two chairs, bowed side up, and weight it down. This may require 30 to 50 pounds of bricks, books or whatever you have. Put enough weight on to make the door level and leave there about 24 hours. If, when you begin to remove the weights, the door bows up again, add more weights and leave them on 2 or 3 days.

After all this, if the door still bows but you are bound and determined to save it, you're going to have to take drastic measures. Remove the paint or varnish from the middle part of the door, where it is bowed, and then soak that thoroughly by keeping wet rags over the area for 24 hours. After the wood is completely soaked, resume the weight treatment. When straightened, let the door dry slowly and then apply a coat of sealant before you refinish it.

If all of that work sounds a bit formidable and you're saying to yourself that the door is only a little warped, here's a quick solution to hide that gap.

■ **Adjusting doorstops:** Remove the door stop and then with the door closed and held firmly by someone else, renail or rescrew the stop so it fits snugly against the door. The stop is quite flexible and will easily bend to accommodate all but the most severely twisted door. Repaint the jamb and you have a door that appears to close as self-respecting doors should.

■ **Lubricating doors:** Doors, like anything else that moves, need lubricating now and then, unless you are partial to squeaks. After all, what would the great days of radio and Inner Sanctum have been if someone then had a can of graphite? That's right, graphite and not oil for those hinges. Oil attracts dirt. If you have squeaky hinges, check first to see if they are rusty. If so, remove and clean them with steel wool or a wire brush, give them an antirust coating, and when that's dry, shoot some powdered graphite between the hinge parts and along pin.

You can also use a silicone spray for this. For that matter, you can use a light oil, but the graphite is cleaner.

If the door rubs just slightly against the jamb, enough to irritate you on occasion but not enough to warrant removing the door, rub both sticking edges with some paraffin or candle-wax. The same holds true if the door is catching a little along the threshold or the head jamb.

You can give the latch a slight coat of oil but for the door cylinder (knob) and key mechanism, use only graphite to avoid attracting dirt.

■ **Replacing the Threshold:** The threshold in your doorway receives considerable abuse. When it becomes cracked or severely worn, replace it.

The first step is to see if the threshold is merely flush with the jamb or extends under it.

In the first case, removal is quite simple. Take off the door stop and then use a crowbar to pry the threshold up and out.

More commonly, the threshold is designed to fit under the jamb and against the door casing. In this case, remove the door stop and the door too, if it is in the way.

Then cut through the threshold along each side of the jamb and lift this piece out. Now pry or chisel out the two pieces under the jamb.

Do as little damage as possible to the threshold so you can use it as a pattern to mark the new one. If the old one was destroyed, take careful measurements and then make a cardboard pattern before cutting the new threshold.

The new one should be made of a hardwood such as oak or maple for maximum life. When it is cut, tap it gently into place; do not force it. Trim until you have a smooth fit. If it must be raised a little, shim it up with a few layers of roofing paper.

Once in place, drill pilot holes for nails driven in at an angle under the jamb. Attempting to nail without predrilling may split the hardwood. Better yet, screw it down, countersink the holes and fill with wood putty.

■ **Garage doors:** If the garage door binds and sticks while moving, check first to see if the overhead tracks have become loose and misaligned. Tighten any loose screws. Both tracks must be plumb, so check them with a level. If they are out of line, loosen the brackets holding the tracks to make the adjustments.

Also make sure that the wheels or ball bearings are in good working order. Give them and the tracks a light coat of grease.

If you find that the hinges on an out-swinging door are loose and cannot be effectively tightened, then drill through the hinge holes to the other side of the door and tighten them down with nuts and bolts.

Another common problem with the older style garage doors is sagging in the middle when the door is open. If the door already has horizontal reinforcing rods, tighten or replace them. If there are no rods, buy two from a garage door dealer and install them on the inside top and bottom of the door.

To bow the door back into shape, put a 2 by 4 block of wood under the rod in the middle of the door and then tighten the ends of the rods.

Moving a door stop

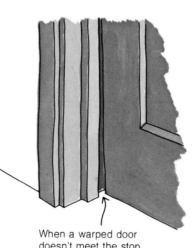

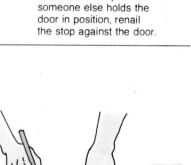

When a warped door doesn't meet the stop at the bottom (or at the top) . . .

Remove the stop. While someone else holds the door in position, renail the stop against the door.

Replacing a threshold (see text)

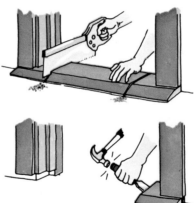

Chisel the ends from under jambs . . .

Use the old threshold as a pattern to mark and cut the new one to fit (or make a cardboard pattern) . . .

After waterproofing the area beneath the threshold with roofing cement, slide the new threshold under the jambs and tap it into place . . .

Drill pilot holes and nail or screw the threshold into place. Set the nails or countersink the screws and finish with wood putty and stain.

Hanging a New Door

While a lot of home repairs are actually fairly easy to do, hanging a new door is not one of them. It takes patience and careful work. Your problems are compounded if the door frame is severely out of square. You can't straighten the frame; you must cut the door to fit. If you have an untrue door frame and serious doubts about your ability here, it will probably be cheaper in the long run for you to hire a carpenter to do the job. Then if the door *still* doesn't hang right, your spouse can yell at him instead of you. However, if you have your nerve up, here's how.

First check the level of the jamb on the side and top. Then measure from the top of the jamb to the bottom at both sides and the middle. Finally, measure the width of the opening at the top, middle and bottom. With these measurements you will be able to see precisely the problems you might have in hanging the new door. Buy a door that comes closest to these dimensions. If you can't get an exact fit, buy one slightly larger and then cut and plane it to fit.

When you get the door home, remove the protective ends on the stiles. Then trim the door according to your measurements with these important considerations: the door should

Parts of a door

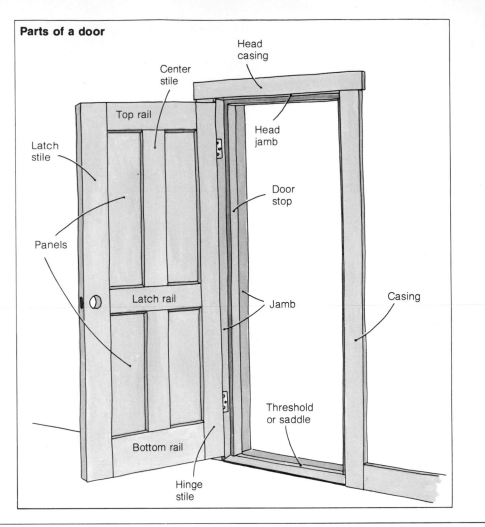

Head casing
Center stile
Top rail
Latch stile
Head jamb
Panels
Door stop
Latch rail
Jamb
Casing
Bottom rail
Threshold or saddle
Hinge stile

Hanging a new door (see text for details)

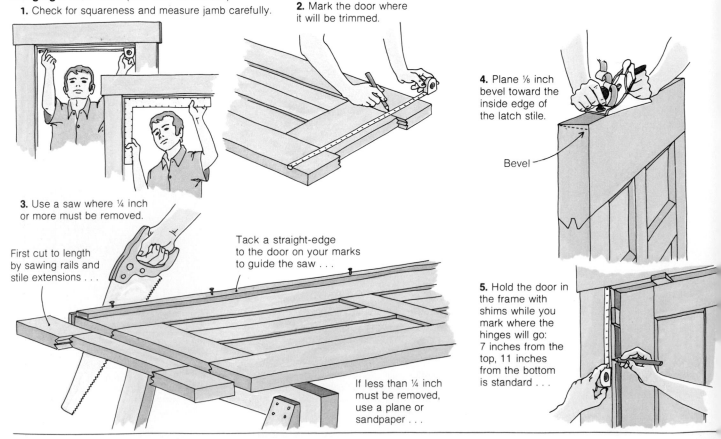

1. Check for squareness and measure jamb carefully.

2. Mark the door where it will be trimmed.

3. Use a saw where ¼ inch or more must be removed.

First cut to length by sawing rails and stile extensions . . .

Tack a straight-edge to the door on your marks to guide the saw . . .

If less than ¼ inch must be removed, use a plane or sandpaper . . .

4. Plane ⅛ inch bevel toward the inside edge of the latch stile.

Bevel

5. Hold the door in the frame with shims while you mark where the hinges will go: 7 inches from the top, 11 inches from the bottom is standard . . .

have a ⅛-inch clearance if it opens over a bare floor and at least ⅞-inch over carpeting.

The trimming of the door can be done with sandpaper if by incredible luck you have little removal to do. For heavier trimming, use a jack plane or saw. If you have more than ¼ inch of wood to remove from the top or sides, keep your sawing straight by tacking a long straight board beside the cut lines as a guide for the power saw. If less than ¼-inch use the plane or sandpaper.

Remember to do all your trimming from the hinge side, particularly if the holes for the latch assembly have already been cut.

Once you think you are close, test the fit of the door and mark any additional areas that need more trimming. It usually takes several fittings to get it just right. After it does fit, take the door down again and use the plane to make a ⅛-inch bevel on the inside edge of the latch stile. This will give it the fraction of space needed to clear the jamb.

Once the door fits, use about 10 small wedges (make them from shingles or use inexpensive regular shims) to hold the door firmly and exactly in the frame. You're now ready to mark and install the hinges.

■ **Hinge installation:** With the door still in place, pencil in the locations of the hinges on the jamb only. The standard mounting has the upper hinge 7 inches from the top and the lower one 11 inches from the bottom. For very heavy doors, add another hinge in the middle.

Remove the door and use a square to carry your pencil marks across the jamb. Then use a leaf of the hinge to draw the exact outline. Be sure to allow for a clearance of at least 3/16 inch between the edge of the hinge and the stop board on the jamb. Closer than that and the door may bind against the board when it closes.

To cut the mortise, start by tracing the outline on the jamb with a sharp knife or outlining it with moderate taps of the chisel. Keep the beveled edge of the chisel toward the opening. If you have a router, use it to cut the mortise; otherwise, with a chisel, make a series of ruffle cuts down the opening, going no deeper than the thickness of the hinge. Remove these pieces with precision by holding the beveled edge of the chisel downward. Check often with the hinge to make sure you don't go too deep. Finally, drill pilot holes and mount the hinges on the jamb.

Now for the mortises on the door. Put the door back up and wedge it exactly in place again. Mark where the hinges will go on the door. (If you try to cut the jamb and the door mortises at the same time, you may find the jamb side didn't go just where you thought it would and now the door won't close right.) After marking, remove the door and, with a square and hinge, mark the outlines on the stile edge. Chisel out the mortises just as you did on the jamb, drill the pilot holes and screw on the hinge leaf. Now put the door up, put in the pins, and the door is hung.

■ **Final adjustments:** If you have a door that swings with no problem, count your blessings. Lesser mortals, however, will have to do a little more work.

If, by dreadful chance, the hinges on the door and jamb don't match up, remove the leafs from the door and remeasure. Extend the mortises up or down until you have a proper match and then mount the hinges again. If the new screw holes are too close to the old ones, pack with plastic wood and allow it to dry before drilling the new screw holes.

Fill any gaps between the new hinges and old mortise lines with wood putty.

More likely your door will bind because of inaccurate cutting or improper hinge mounting. Fix what you can with sandpaper because it is more precise. If you must use a plane, remove the door first for accurate work. If the hinges are set too deep or shallow, see if you can shim them into place as described on page 17.

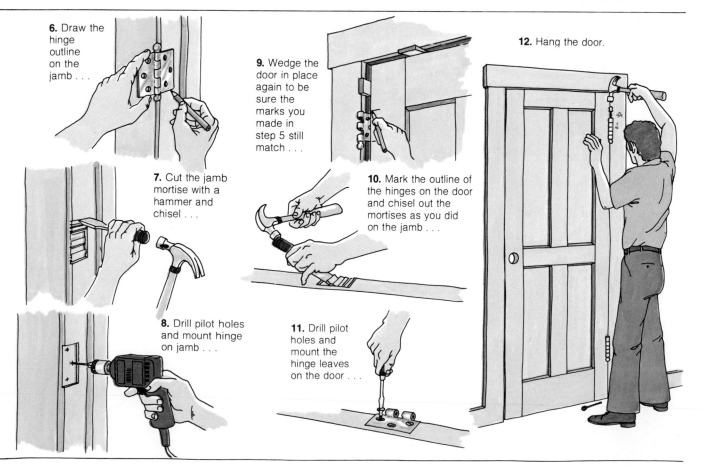

6. Draw the hinge outline on the jamb . . .

7. Cut the jamb mortise with a hammer and chisel . . .

8. Drill pilot holes and mount hinge on jamb . . .

9. Wedge the door in place again to be sure the marks you made in step 5 still match . . .

10. Mark the outline of the hinges on the door and chisel out the mortises as you did on the jamb . . .

11. Drill pilot holes and mount the hinge leaves on the door . . .

12. Hang the door.

Sliding Doors

The light wooden sliding doors widely used for closets or inside doors operate on overhead rails, while heavy glass sliding doors move on floor tracks.

Closet doors sometimes have a bad habit of catching on the rails or jumping off them. Normally you don't have to remove the door to inspect the rails. See that the screws holding the rails are firmly set. Now look at the roller guides to make sure they haven't become misaligned.

If you find either the rollers or the track broken, remove the whole assembly and replace.

At this time it's a good idea to buy larger tracks and rollers than were previously installed, particularly if the others were small and you have trouble with the door jumping loose. The larger tracks and wheels will make a smoother operation.

If the door isn't sliding because it is bowed or warped, you can remove it and attempt to straighten it as outlined on page 20. Alternatively, you can screw door guides to the floor to keep the door from swinging and catching against the frame or the other door.

If the door is hanging at a slant, it's probably because the hangers on the back of the door have come loose. Loosen them more, wedge the door up until it is in line with the door jamb or closet frame, and then tighten.

■ **Sliding glass doors:** The problem here is usually that they just don't slide as they should. The first thing to look for is dirt in the rails. Vacuum the rails thoroughly and then scrape out any hardened dirt, wax or paint that may be catching the rollers. For a first-class job, shine the rails up with steel wool and then shoot a little graphite powder in there. This is better than a light oil, which tends to trap dust and dirt.

If the door still doesn't roll right, inspect the track for a bent rail. To straighten it, use a block of wood and a hammer. Using just the hammer alone will probably put irreparable dents in the rail.

The door may not be sliding properly because it has derailed. On your hands and knees you can spot this problem. The door will be slightly out of line and lower at the leading edge, which is usually the roller that jumps. To correct it, lift the door up and back onto the track.

Many sliding glass doors can be adjusted upward to keep the door base from dragging on the rails. At the bottom of the door on each edge are recessed screws. If the door appears to be dragging and you can't find anything else wrong, turn these screws until you feel the door rise slightly. Adjust both ends equally.

■ **Burglar proofing:** Sliding glass doors have relatively lightweight hooks. Your friendly neighborhood burglar can wedge a small crowbar between the jamb and door, and snap it without too much trouble. Or, depending on how the door was hung, he might be able to lift up one end and remove the whole door.

A simple way to keep the door from being pried open is to put a length of 2 by 2 between the sliding door's edge and the jamb.

In addition, you can prevent the door from being lifted off its rails with a large screw in the middle of the overhead recess. Predrill the hole and then put the screw in deep enough to just clear the door when closed. The door cannot now be lifted out while in that position.

Finally, most hardware stores carry small locking assemblies that screw to the base of the door. These prevent the door from being either pried open or lifted out.

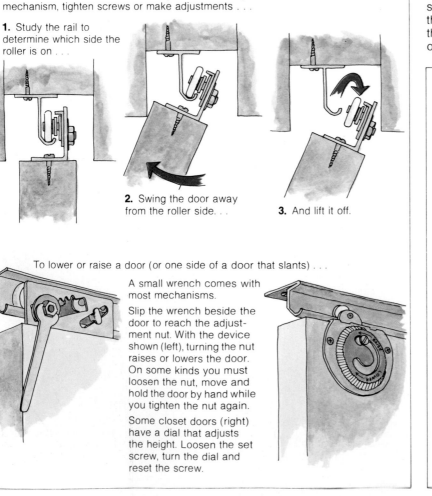

Adjusting sliding doors

To remove a door . . . in order to replace the sliding mechanism, tighten screws or make adjustments . . .

1. Study the rail to determine which side the roller is on . . .

2. Swing the door away from the roller side. . .

3. And lift it off.

To lower or raise a door (or one side of a door that slants) . . .

A small wrench comes with most mechanisms.

Slip the wrench beside the door to reach the adjustment nut. With the device shown (left), turning the nut raises or lowers the door. On some kinds you must loosen the nut, move and hold the door by hand while you tighten the nut again.

Some closet doors (right) have a dial that adjusts the height. Loosen the set screw, turn the dial and reset the screw.

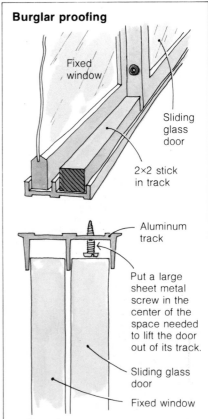

Burglar proofing

Fixed window

Sliding glass door

2×2 stick in track

Aluminum track

Put a large sheet metal screw in the center of the space needed to lift the door out of its track.

Sliding glass door

Fixed window

Screen Doors and Screening

The everyday situation here is that the screen tears, breaks, sags or simply comes out. The problem is getting the replacement screen taut when you put it back in the door. There are two good ways to do it. (If you just want to repair a hole in a screen, see page 31.)

Aluminum screen doors are somewhat easier to work on than wooden ones because they have flexible plastic or metal splines to hold the screen. To remove the old screening, use a screwdriver to pry up one corner of the spline from its channel and work your way around, being careful not to bend the spline. Cut the replacement screen so that it fits to the outer edge of the door all the way around.

Now, using a special roller tool designed for this, put the screen in the bottom channel and replace the spline. Keeping the aluminum door perfectly square, work your way up one side with the spline and all the way around the screen. The combination of the tool and the spline that compresses into the channel will pull the screen tight. Trim the excess screen with wire cutters or a linoleum knife.

For wooden screen doors, start by prying up the molding all around the screen. Carefully, please. Remove all the staples holding the old screen and cut the new piece so it overlaps the opening all around by 1 inch. Staple the screen across the bottom edge of the door only.

To stretch the screen, use either of the two methods illustrated. After the top is stapled, release the tension and staple down the sides. Don't staple the center rail until the very last.

Finally, trim off the excess screen with a sharp knife and replace the molding.

■ **Loose, sagging doors:** For these problems, pry open the joints a little, fill with a waterproof glue and clamp together again.

A more effective cure is to drill through the stile into the end rails and tighten with screws.

Sagging screen doors can also be helped by connecting two wires or light cables across the diagonal and tightening with a turnbuckle.

Replacing the screen on a wood door frame

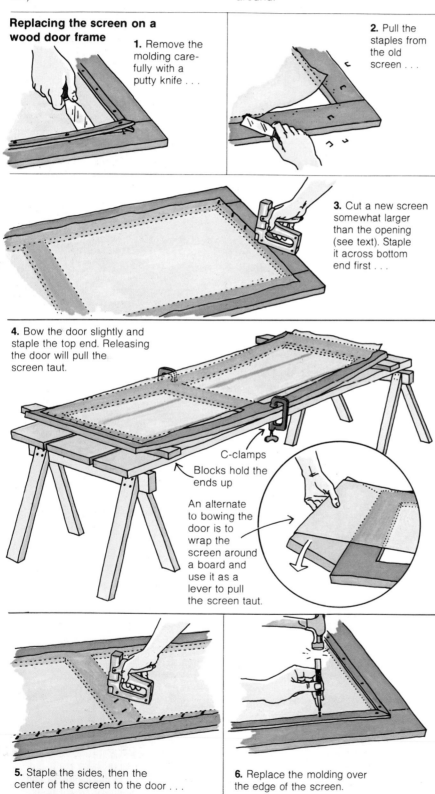

1. Remove the molding carefully with a putty knife . . .

2. Pull the staples from the old screen . . .

3. Cut a new screen somewhat larger than the opening (see text). Staple it across bottom end first . . .

4. Bow the door slightly and staple the top end. Releasing the door will pull the screen taut.

C-clamps
Blocks hold the ends up

An alternate to bowing the door is to wrap the screen around a board and use it as a lever to pull the screen taut.

5. Staple the sides, then the center of the screen to the door . . .

6. Replace the molding over the edge of the screen.

Screen door strengthening

To strengthen corners, countersink long wood screws through the stiles into the ends of the rails.

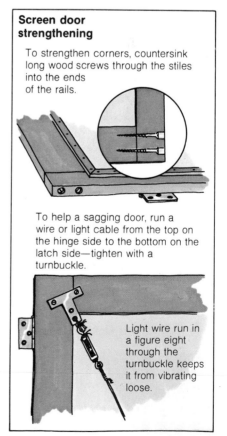

To help a sagging door, run a wire or light cable from the top on the hinge side to the bottom on the latch side—tighten with a turnbuckle.

Light wire run in a figure eight through the turnbuckle keeps it from vibrating loose.

Locks, Latches and Knobs

There are three basic types of locks, each with different characteristics and uses. The most common is the cylindrical lock, which is used on both exterior and interior doors and operates either with a key and inside push button or the button alone.

The second basic lock is the mortise lock, which is recessed into the edge of the door. This is widely used on entrance doors because of its strength and the dead bolt that can be thrown with an extra turn of the key.

Finally, there is the rim lock commonly used for additional security. The simplest varieties are merely screwed to the door and operate only from inside, while others are mounted with a single hole drilled through the door.

■ **Cylinder lock installation:** Like most locks, this comes with a template that outlines the location and size of holes to be drilled. First, select the height you want the doorknob from the ground, which is normally 36 inches. With the template then fitted near the edge of the door, mark the pilot holes for drilling.

The cylinder hole through the door is normally set back 2⅜ inches from the edge of the door. The hole itself is 2⅛ inches in diameter. The smoothest way to drill this is with a hole saw attachment for your power drill. Otherwise use an expansion bit adjusted to the proper size.

With the cylinder hole done, drill the latch hole in the door's edge according to the template marking. This hole is usually ¹⁵⁄₁₆ inches in diameter.

When bored (the hole, not you), insert the latch and mark the outline of the latch plate on the stile edge. With a chisel, carefully trim out this mortise so the plate fits flush with the door.

With the latch bolt installed, insert the exterior knob through the latch holes. Usually, you have to push in the latch bolt for this. Now, slip the interior knob and rose into place and align the screws through the rose with the screw guides on the other side. The knob is now in place.

The final step is to install the strike plate. Put the template up and close the door to make sure it and the latch line up. Mark the drilling point through the template with a nail or awl and bore a ¹⁵⁄₁₆-inch hole about ½ inch deep into the jamb. It must be deep enough to fully accept the latch bolt — but with no spare space that will let a burglar slip in a credit card and flip the bolt.

Center the strike plate over the hole and mark its outline. Then cut that

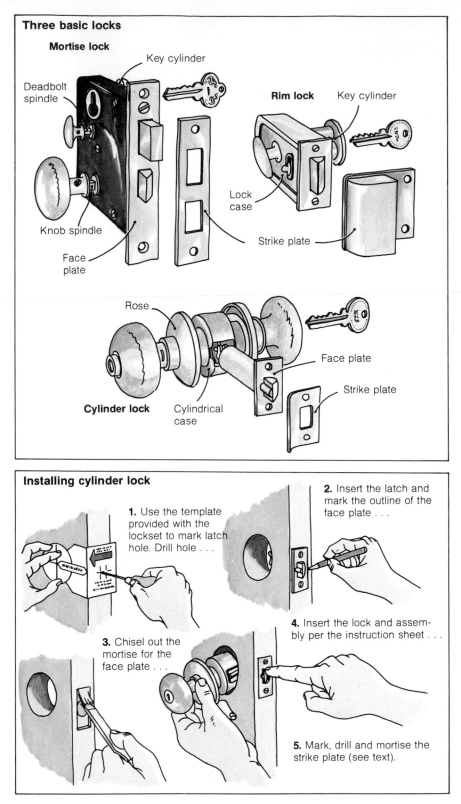

Three basic locks

Mortise lock
Deadbolt spindle
Key cylinder
Knob spindle
Face plate

Rim lock
Key cylinder
Lock case
Strike plate

Rose
Face plate
Strike plate
Cylinder lock
Cylindrical case

Installing cylinder lock

1. Use the template provided with the lockset to mark latch hole. Drill hole . . .

2. Insert the latch and mark the outline of the face plate . . .

3. Chisel out the mortise for the face plate . . .

4. Insert the lock and assembly per the instruction sheet . . .

5. Mark, drill and mortise the strike plate (see text).

mortise with a chisel and screw the strike plate in place.

At this point take note that most hardware stores carry kits that allow you to replace old mortise locks with cylinder locks. It consists basically of a latch that fits into the deep mortise and a doorknob that fits through a long metal escutcheon used to hide the two holes of the mortise lock handle. The strike plate for the new cylinder lock also has a long face

plate to cover the old strike plate mortise.

■ **Cylinder lock problems:**

Key won't turn: Cylinder not properly aligned with bolt; remove rose and realign. Check that key is not a poorly ground duplicate.

Bolt not completely thrown: Strike plate improperly set and out of line with bolt. Hole behind strike plate not deep enough. Door has warped causing misalignment of bolt and strike plate.

Installing a mortise lock

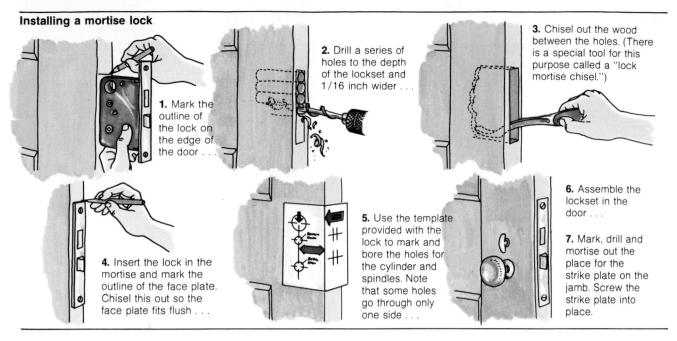

1. Mark the outline of the lock on the edge of the door . . .

2. Drill a series of holes to the depth of the lockset and 1/16 inch wider . . .

3. Chisel out the wood between the holes. (There is a special tool for this purpose called a "lock mortise chisel.")

4. Insert the lock in the mortise and mark the outline of the face plate. Chisel this out so the face plate fits flush . . .

5. Use the template provided with the lock to mark and bore the holes for the cylinder and spindles. Note that some holes go through only one side . . .

6. Assemble the lockset in the door . . .

7. Mark, drill and mortise out the place for the strike plate on the jamb. Screw the strike plate into place.

Readjust strike plates.

Key turns but not the bolt: Latch assembly clogged with dirt, possibly paint. Remove assembly and lubricate with graphite.

Bolt won't turn: Cylinder broken. Remove and replace, or call locksmith.

■ **Mortise lock installation:** These locks probably offer the greatest security. They are mounted in a thin steel case that must be set deeply into the edge of the door. The door must be at least 1⅜ inches thick to receive a mortise lock. In addition to the spring-loaded latch, there is the deadbolt for increased security.

To install a mortise lock, mark the outline on the edge of the door, centering it at 36 inches from the bottom. Drill a series of holes the depth of the mortise lock and 1/16 inch wider. Chisel out, insert the lock and mark the outlines of the upper and lower flanges. These must be mortised into the door for a flush fit.

Using the template that comes with the new lock, mark and bore the holes for the cylinder and spindle. Mount the knob on the interior of the door and the handle on the exterior.

Mark the location of the strike plate on the jamb very carefully and then chisel the mortise for it. Finally, drill out the holes for both the latch and the deadbolt.

■ **Rim locks:** These locks are for additional security. Their installation is quite straightforward. One common type involves drilling a hole through the door for the key cylinder and then connecting the cylinder to a mounting plate and latch assembly on the inside of the door. The only detailed work is cutting a mortise in the door jamb for the strike plate. Simpler varieties are operated from the inside only and merely screwed to the door. They can, however, be locked with keys to prevent someone reaching through a broken window to open them.

■ **Loose doorknob:** Start this repair by having a close look at the knob to see if there is a small setscrew. If there is, loosen it by turning it to the left. Now turn the knob to the right until it feels tight and then reset the screw. It must fit snugly against the flat side of the spindle to be effective.

If this doesn't work, loosen the setscrew and turn the knob to the left to remove it from the spindle. The problem is a worn spindle; take the old one with you when you go shopping for a new one.

If you have an old glass or porcelain knob that remains loose, try squeezing a super glue or epoxy resin between the knob and spindle. If this is unsat-

To tighten loose knob

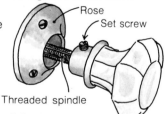

Rose
Set screw
Threaded spindle

1. Loosen setscrew.
2. Hold knob on other side and turn this knob clockwise to fit snugly against the rose.
3. Tighten setscrew against a flat side of the threaded spindle.

To open bath and bedroom doors

These locks are made to open from the outside in case of an emergency.

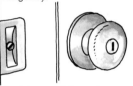

If the lock has a slot as above, turn the slot with a nail file, knife, screwdriver, etc.

If it has a small hole as below, push a nail, knitting needle, etc. into the hole firmly.

isfactory you will probably have to replace the knob and metal shank with a new one.

■ **Locked doors:** Sometimes doors lock when they shouldn't and it often results in a small child crying at you through the door. The bent piece of wire that probably came with the knob for emergency openings generally cannot be found while the kid is screaming to get out. Don't panic. Happiness is a thin strip of metal, such as a narrow screwdriver or a nail file. Just insert in the slot that looks like a keyhole and twist to the right.

If instead of a slot there is just a small hole in the end of the knob, insert a long nail, knitting needle or whatever fits, and push hard. That springs open the twist-lock style of doorknobs.

Now hug your child.

■ **Broken key removal:** There are two approaches to extracting that key if you don't happen to be carrying a pair of needlenose pliers. First, if you must work from the outside, use a piece of wire such as a paper clip with a very tiny hook on the end. Slip that wire into the key slot above the irregular edge of the key. Work it to the end of the key if possible before trying to hook the broken segment. Another tactic is to use a coping saw blade in the same manner if there is room to insert it in the slot.

If you can remove the cylinder from the inside, the key can be readily pushed out the opposite end with a stiff piece of wire or a nail file.

Eliminating Window Sticking

Of the many varieties of windows available, the centuries-old double hung style is most prone to trouble, particularly sticking. There are two basic reasons for this: dirt or paint has worked into the sash molding or the window and frame have swollen in damp weather.

If the window simply won't open, start the repair by working a stiff putty knife around the window between the sash and stops. Do it both inside and outside and break away any paint that may have sealed the window shut. Do not use a screwdriver, for it will just gouge the sash. Use a putty knife. Tap the putty knife in firmly with a hammer and work it back and forth to loosen the window.

If the window will still not move, tap a hatchet blade or metal wedge between the bottom of the sash and the window sill from the outside. Work slowly across the base of the window so it moves upward evenly and doesn't bind.

Once you have opened the window, scrape away any loose paint and clean the pulley stiles, or window channels, thoroughly. This area can be effectively lubricated by spraying it with a silicone lubricant or rubbing the channel with paraffin. Candlewax works well also.

If the window still doesn't move freely, it may be that the wood in the window and the stops has swollen, causing a bind. One way to correct this is to cut a 6-inch length of wood that fits quite snugly in the channel. Hammer it up and down the channel to widen it slightly. This should spread the inside and outside stops enough to let the sash move freely.

If all of this still doesn't result in a smoothly-operating window, the stops and both sashes will have to be removed. For details on that process, see page 30. Once removed, sand or plane down both sides evenly until the window moves freely.

■ **Rattling windows:** Sometimes double hung windows have the annoying habit of rattling in the wind rather than being stuck. A quick solution to the extra space between the window and the stops is to insert a strip of spring-type metal weather stripping in the space. Felt weather stripping could also be used. However, for a more permanent repair, the stop molding should be removed and refitted closer to the sash.

If only the lower sash rattles, this is a relatively simple process. For the upper window, both the stops and the parting strip that divides the two windows will have to be removed.

■ **Sliding windows:** When one of these sticks, first see if it hasn't been painted shut. Clear it by running a putty knife around the edge of the sash to break the bond.

More likely, the sticking is caused by debris in the tracks at the bottom. Vacuum the area clean and then lubricate with paraffin or a silicone lubricant.

Don't try to pry the window loose with a screwdriver or other such tool. You're more likely to bend the tracks permanently out of line than to stop the sticking.

■ **Casement windows:** These windows, which are hinged on the sides and swing out, come in both wood and steel varieties. As with other window types, check first to see that they haven't been painted shut. If so, clear them with a putty knife worked between the sash and frame.

The most common problem with casement windows is a stiff adjusting arm. We deal with this problem on page 31.

Loosening stuck windows

Work a wide putty knife between the sash and stops—inside as well as outside . . .

Drive a wedge or hatchet blade between the sash and sill on the outside. Work slowly across the window so it doesn't tilt and bind . . .

Scrape any paint or hardened dirt from the window channels . . .

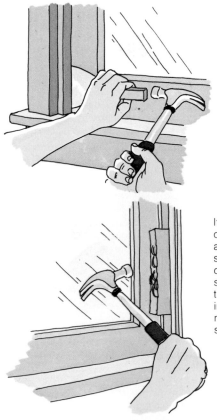

If the channels are clean and smooth and the sash still sticks, cut a block of wood that is slightly too wide for the channel. Tap it into the channel to move the stops slightly outward . . .

When you are able to move the sash but it doesn't slide easily, lubricate the channels with candle wax, paraffin, or silicone lubricant.

Replacing broken glass

1. Remove glass shards . . .

2. Chip out old putty and points . . .

3. Coat bare wood with sealer . . .

4. Apply cushion layer of putty . . .

5. Put in glass with glazier's points . . .

6. Press putty onto edge of glass . . .

7. Smooth putty with a putty knife . . .

8. Paint, after a week or so, when the putty is dry to the touch.

Replacing Broken Glass

After the window is broken, collect both your nerves and the fragments. Then set about removing the shards from the sash. Wear gloves to protect yourself. If the pieces don't come easily, wiggle them and pry with a putty knife.

After the glass is out, remove the putty by scraping with a putty knife. If the putty is too hard, soften it with a soldering iron. Pull out all the glazier's points and then scrape and sand the old wood. Now coat the bare wood with a sealer or linseed oil. This keeps the wood from drawing the oil from the new putty or the glazing compound, which is more elastic than traditional putty.

Once the wood has been prepared, spread on a thin layer — about ⅛ inch — of glazing compound and then insert the glass pane which has been cut ⅛ inch smaller all around than the window opening. Do not press too hard and cause that cushion layer to squeeze out around the glass.

Next, tap the glazier's points in place around the window. Space them about 6 inches apart. Drive them in halfway with a hammer and screwdriver.

To apply the final layer of glazing compound, roll it into a rope about a ½-inch or less thick and press it into place with your fingers. Now, with your putty knife, press the rope in further and leave a smooth, angled bead. Do this by starting at one corner and moving to the next in one continuous stroke.

This final bead should extend to the outer edge of the sash and be as high as the sash edge on the inside of the glass.

When the putty or compound is dry enough to touch without leaving a fingerprint, repaint it. Having cleaned the perimeter of the glass well, let the paint lap onto the glass about 1/16 inch as an added seal.

A safety note: If the window is in a high risk area and has been broken before, use clear acrylic instead of glass. Or, if you feel that will scratch too easily, use tempered glass.

■ **Metal casement windows:** In casement windows, panes are replaced in much the same manner as in wooden frames. However, in removing the putty you will find that instead of glazier's points, the panes are held with small spring clips. These are inserted in holes in the frame.

After the putty has been completely removed, sand the edges and repaint to prevent corrosion. Replace the windowpane as outlined above, using the spring clips instead of glazier's points.

Some varieties of casement windows use metal strips instead of glazing to hold the panes in place. Before screwing these back in place to hold the glass, check that the rubber gasket has not been damaged. If it has, leaks may come through when it rains.

■ **Aluminum windows:** To remove broken glass from sliding windows, the sash must be taken apart. Many types have screws at the corner for this purpose. The glass is held in place by a rubber gasket. After this has been pulled out and all glass particles removed, reinstall the glass and gasket.

■ **Cutting glass:** Mark the point where the cut begins by lightly nicking the glass with the cutter. Wipe the line to be cut with kerosene or turpentine, which helps reduce the chances of chipping the glass. Then slide a steel framing square along the line to guide your glass cutter. Make your cut in a smooth, single sweep. Just score the glass; pressing too hard will chip it. Don't try to go over the line a second time.

The glass is snapped along the scored line by holding it over a dowel or along the edge of a straight board.

Glass cutting

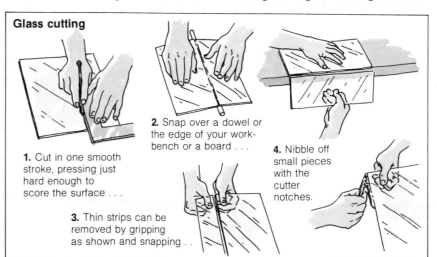

1. Cut in one smooth stroke, pressing just hard enough to score the surface . . .

2. Snap over a dowel or the edge of your workbench or a board . . .

3. Thin strips can be removed by gripping as shown and snapping . .

4. Nibble off small pieces with the cutter notches.

Repairing Windows [and Screens]

■ **Replacing sash cords:** If you have a large house just full of double hung windows that all need repairs, take heart. The more you do the easier it gets.

Start by removing the stop molding along the side that has the broken or tangled sash cord. If this stop is not screwed in place, pry it loose with a chisel from inside the channel if possible to minimize scars.

At this point, note that if it is the upper sash cord that needs repair, you still must first remove the lower sash. To remove the upper window you must next remove the parting strip that separates the two windows. This parting strip is usually set in a groove and can be pulled free with a pair of pliers. Before pulling, however, check that it has not been screwed or nailed in place. And use protective pieces of wood on each side of the parting strip so it is not chewed by the pliers. Slide the upper window down as far as it will go and then, from the top, begin working the parting strip out of the groove. The upper sash cord and weight are removed in the same manner as the lower one.

Once the stop molding on the lower sash has been removed, ease it out of the frame just enough to free the knotted end of the rope from the sash groove. Lower the weight gently and let the knot rest against the pulley.

Now to get at the weight, there may be a small trap door at the bottom of the frame. If it has never been removed, you may not be able to see it under the paint. Search out the grooves with a nail or awl, then find the one or two nails or screws holding it in place. In very old homes this panel may never have been cut completely through and you will have to finish the job with drill and keyhole saw. If there is no access panel, you will have to remove the side of the window frame to reach the weight.

If you have sash cords, replace them with chains to minimize future maintenance. Drop the chain down the channel, run it through the hole at the top of the weight, and wire it securely.

Now, put the window back in its approximate place, as if it were closed, and raise the weight until it is just below the pulley. Fix the chain in the sash groove with two screws through the sash links.

In the upper window, the sash should be all the way up and the weights about 2 inches from the bottom.

Before reinstalling the panel cover and stops, make sure the windows work smoothly.

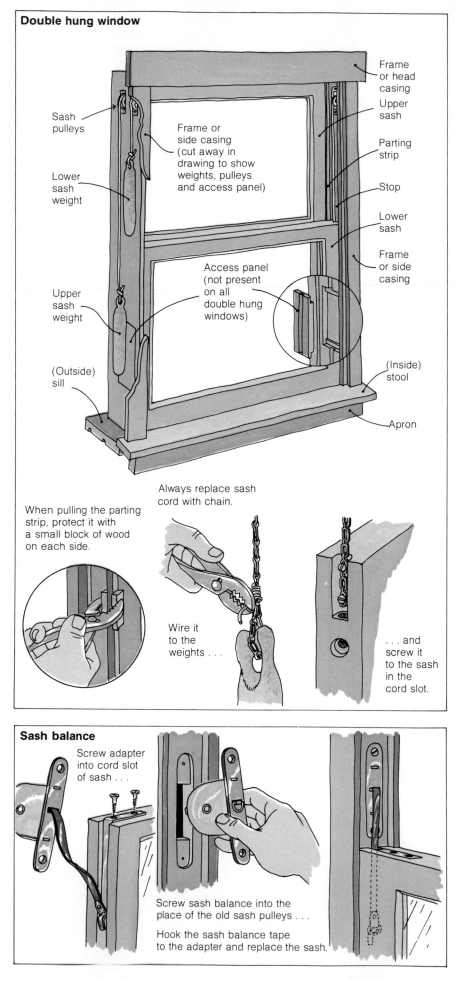

Double hung window

Sash pulleys

Lower sash weight

Upper sash weight

(Outside) sill

Frame or side casing (cut away in drawing to show weights, pulleys and access panel)

Frame or head casing

Upper sash

Parting strip

Stop

Lower sash

Frame or side casing

Access panel (not present on all double hung windows)

(Inside) stool

Apron

Always replace sash cord with chain.

When pulling the parting strip, protect it with a small block of wood on each side.

Wire it to the weights . . .

. . . and screw it to the sash in the cord slot.

Sash balance

Screw adapter into cord slot of sash . . .

Screw sash balance into the place of the old sash pulleys . . .

Hook the sash balance tape to the adapter and replace the sash.

Sash spring lift

Loosen . . .

. . . tighten tension spring.

Spiral rod exits the spring loaded tube out of sight behind the sash . . .

. . . and attaches to the bottom of the sash with screws.

Casement crank

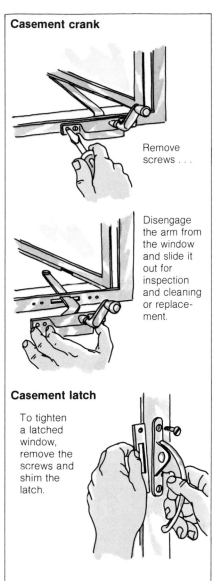

Remove screws . . .

Disengage the arm from the window and slide it out for inspection and cleaning or replacement.

Casement latch

To tighten a latched window, remove the screws and shim the latch.

■ **Spring lift sashes:** You can spot this relatively new device by the metal tube that runs up the window casing channel. It eliminates the need for sash cords and weights, and it can be adjusted to tighten or loosen the window movement.

If the window tends to creep up after opening, the spring is too tight. To loosen it, remove the tube at the top of the window and let the screw unwind two or three turns to the left. Keep firm control of the screw. If the window does not move easily, turn the screw a couple turns to the right to tighten the tension.

■ **Sash balance:** This is one of the easiest of all devices for replacing the sash cords and weights. Built something like a self-retracting steel measuring tape, it is designed to fit into the opening for the pulleys on double hung window frames. An adapter hooks the tape to the sash. These come in different sizes for different size windows. A chart that accompanies the kit will tell you what size you need.

■ **Casement windows:** Wooden windows are usually operated by a simple sliding rod for opening or closing. Clean and lubricate these occasionally with powdered graphite.

Steel windows normally open and shut with a cranking mechanism. When repairs are necesary, check the gears first. To do this, loosen the set-screw on the handle and remove it. Then remove the two screws holding the gear box to the side of the window frame. Finally, remove the arm by sliding it along the slot until it lifts free. In some cases, you have to unscrew the hinged fitting that holds it.

Inspect the gears carefully. If they are dirty, clean them in gasoline or other solvent that won't damage metal, then apply fresh grease. If the gears are worn and are not meshing smoothly, the whole mechanism will have to be replaced. Large hardware stores or lumberyards that sell casement windows can order one for you if they don't have it in stock. Take the old one with you so that exact measurements can be made.

In the event your casement windows do not lock together tightly enough, you can improve on this with a shim behind the locking handle. Just remove the locking handle from the window by removing the two screws and then slip a shim under it. The handle, when reinstalled, will now draw the window sash up snug against the frame.

■ **Sliding windows:** These are largely maintenance free as long as the channel in which they slide is kept clean. If one of the rails is bent, correct it as you would for a sliding door (page 24).

■ **Screen repairs:** What sometimes appears to be a small hole is actually just the screen wires spread apart, as if by a pencil point. Use a nail or awl — or pencil point — to realign them.

For small tears in wire screens, either buy a ready-made patch or make your own from matching screening. For your own patch, cut a square of screen about twice the size of the hole, then unravel all four sides a little. Bend these individual wires at a right angle, push the patch over the hole and bend the wires over.

For plastic screens, this method won't work. On very small holes, align the broken ends and bond them with epoxy resin. On a larger tear, overlay slightly with a matching piece of screen and glue it in place with epoxy resin, which is waterproof. Line up each strand for a smooth job.

Patching a screen

Cut a patch . . .

Pull wires from all 4 sides . . .

Bend remaining wires at right angles and push them through the screen . . .

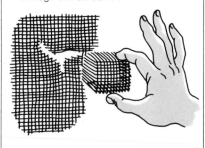

then bend them flat again to secure the patch.

Repairing Window Shades, Blinds and Drapery Rods

■ **Adjusting window shades:** It seems preordained that sooner or later something is going to go wrong with your window shades. They either snap up with a bang or won't go up at all, or fall off the mounts. Fortunately, repairs and adjustments are quite simple, especially once you see how the contraptions work.

The shade goes up and down according to the tension on a spring hidden inside the roller. That spring action is controlled by a simple locking device at one end of the roller. This device, called a pawl, engages a ratchet tooth to hold the shade in position. When the shade is pulled down, the pawl falls away from the ratchet tooth. When the shade goes up, centrifugal pressure keeps the

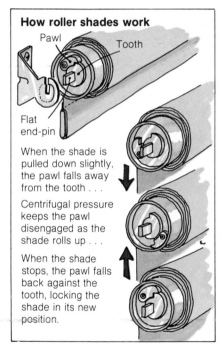

How roller shades work

Pawl
Tooth
Flat end-pin

When the shade is pulled down slightly, the pawl falls away from the tooth . . .

Centrifugal pressure keeps the pawl disengaged as the shade rolls up . . .

When the shade stops, the pawl falls back against the tooth, locking the shade in its new position.

pawl from engaging the ratchet tooth until the shade stops. The pawl then falls into position.

With that operation in mind, here are some of the most common problems and their solutions.

Shade snaps up: There is too much tension on the spring. To correct this, raise the shade to the top and then remove it from the brackets. Unwind it about 24 inches, replace in the brackets and test. If still too tight, unwind some more and test again.

Shade moves sluggishly: In this case the spring is not wound tightly enough. Pull the shade down about two feet, remove it from the brackets and wind the shade back up by hand. Replace it and test. If still too loose, try it again.

Wobbles when moving: This is normally caused by a bent roller pin. Straighten with pliers and clean.

Falls from brackets: If the shade is mounted inside the window frame, remove it and use pliers to pull the pin out a little more. If this is still insufficient, remove both brackets and shim them out more with a piece of cardboard, tarpaper or wood.

If the brackets are on the outside of the window frame, move one of the brackets in slightly.

Shade won't catch: Remove the shade and clean the end with the pawl and ratchet with steel wool. Lubricate with graphite, not oil. Pawl must move easily.

■ **Worn shade:** If the shade is worn only at the bottom, it can be repaired by reversing it. Remove the shade, unroll it and remove the staples holding it to the roller. Trim off the worn section and staple this end to the roller. Make sure it is perfectly straight or the shade will roll up crookedly. Finally, sew a new hem for the slat at the bottom.

■ **Roll up blinds:** These increasingly popular blinds are commonly narrow slats made from bamboo or plastic. They are raised or lowered by ropes that run through two pulleys and are held in place by a tension buckle. They are generally maintenance free but occasionally a rope will break. Replace it with a rope of the same size. To restring the rope, first lower the shade completely. Start at one side by tying off the rope and then go down behind the shade, up the front through the pulley and across to the other pulley. Here, make a long loop for the equalizing buckle, as illustrated, before going down the front of the blind and up the back where that end is secured.

Roll-up blind

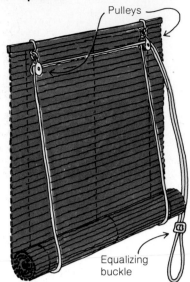

Pulleys

Equalizing buckle

■ **Drapery rods:** There are two basic styles of drapery rods, stationary and traverse. It is only the traverse rod that tends to have problems, and these normally involve the slides and pulleys.

One common problem with traverse rods is the cord either breaking or coming loose from one of the master slides. To see how they must be restrung, study the illustrations for both the two-way and one-way rods. The one-way draw is rather straightforward but the two-way draw involves an important loop in the control slide B.

If you open your drapes but only one side moves, it's quite possible that the cord has slipped off the hook on control slide B.

To readjust these slides, open the curtains by pulling on the cord and bringing control slide A to the edge of the rod. Now, holding the cord so it

Traverse rod draperies

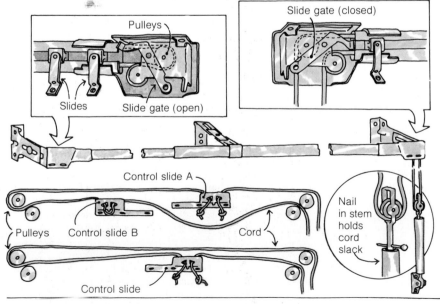

Pulleys
Slides
Slide gate (open)
Slide gate (closed)
Control slide A
Pulleys
Control slide B
Cord
Nail in stem holds cord slack
Control slide

won't move, push control slide B to the other end of the rod. Once there, loop the cord through the opening and over the hook. Both sides should now move simultaneously.

Adjusting cord tension: If after long use the cord running through the pulley stem on the floor or wall becomes loose, it can be quickly tightened.

Pull the stem up 2 inches or more and hold it there with either a built-in latch or a nail through a hole in the stem. Now pull the rope out more on the righthand side of the control slide A and tie a new knot to take up the slack.

Removing unneeded slides: At each end of the rod is a movable gate normally closed to keep the

slides in place. To remove some, snap the gate open and slip out the extra slides.

■ **Restringing venetian blinds:** Even with the best of efforts to keep these blinds clean and neat, ropes and tapes sometimes become severely worn. Replacing them is largely a matter of careful attention to details. Follow these illustrated steps.

Steps in replacing venetian blind cords and tapes

1. Buy new ladder tapes and cord at hardware, variety or drapery store. Be sure new tapes are made for the same width slats.

2. Release the tapes and cords from the bottom bar—be sure to note how they were attached. (Some of the ways are shown in the drawing.)

3. Untie or cut the knots from the ends of the lift cords and pull them just up to the head box.

4. Slide the slats from the tapes and wash or repaint them. While they're drying you can continue with the replacement of cords and tapes.

5. Release the tapes from the tilt tube. There are several methods of attachment. Remember how yours work and save any clips or other gadgets that held them.

6. Cut the new tapes to the same length and number of rungs as the old. Also sew or staple loops or hems on the ends as in the old ones.

7. Attach the new tapes to the tilt tube.

8. Slide the slats into position on the new tape rungs:

9. Replace the lift cord by removing the equalizing buckle and cutting the closed end. Butt-tape the ends of the new cord to the cut ends of the old. Thread the old cords down through the slats and continue pulling them so the new cord follows over all the pulleys and down through the slats. Keep pulling until the loop end of the new cord is at the height you want it to be.

10. Attach the new tapes to the bottom bar. Replace the equalizer bar.

11. Replace the tilt cord by removing the old one (just lift it from its pulley) and remove the decorative pulls. Cut a new cord the same length; attach the pulls; make a loop in the middle of the cord, pass it through the slot in the bottom of the head box and over the pulley.

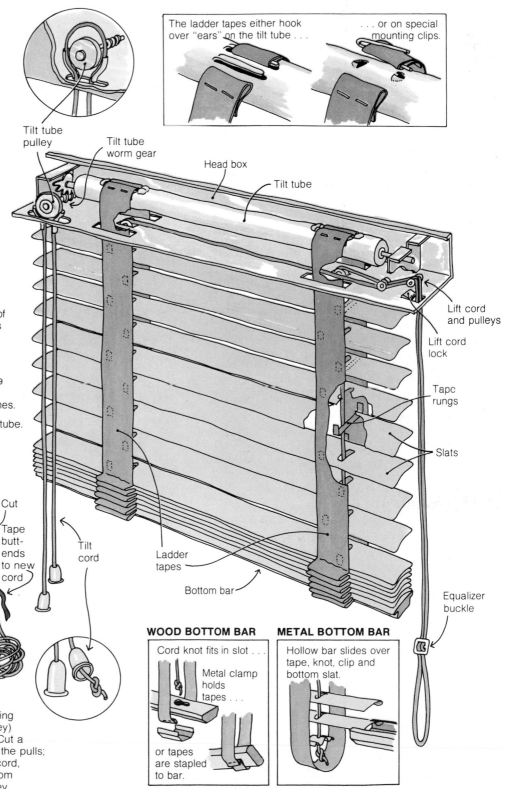

The ladder tapes either hook over "ears" on the tilt tube . . . . . . or on special mounting clips.

Tilt tube pulley

Tilt tube worm gear

Head box

Tilt tube

Lift cord and pulleys

Lift cord lock

Tape rungs

Slats

Cut

Tape butt-ends to new cord

Tilt cord

Ladder tapes

Bottom bar

Equalizer buckle

WOOD BOTTOM BAR

Cord knot fits in slot . . .

Metal clamp holds tapes . . .

or tapes are stapled to bar.

METAL BOTTOM BAR

Hollow bar slides over tape, knot, clip and bottom slat.

Ceilings & Inside Walls

How to repair or replace wood paneling, plaster, wallpaper, ceiling tile, and gypsum board. How to fix fireplace problems.

Repairing Wood Paneling

Wood paneling is commonly put up directly over studs, over furring strips or — for the strongest backing — over gypsum boards. In all instances the panels can be scratched and gouged easily; and in the first two instances, holes can be accidentally punched through them because there is no firm backing.

■ **Scratches:** If the scratches are minor, rubbing with floor wax may hide them. Shoe polish approximating the same color will work. Or pick up a putty stick of the same color at the hardware store.

■ **Gouges:** These are more difficult to hide but if they aren't too severe, you can fill them with a putty stick of the appropriate color. For deeper gouges, fill with wood putty, let dry and sand smooth; then color with a putty stick.

■ **Loose, buckling panels:** Shoot a layer of adhesive onto both the backside of the panel and the stud or gypsum if you can get at it, then nail in

To repair gouges, fill them with spackling compound; sand it smooth; then color it with a putty stick. Scratches can be repaired with just the putty stick.

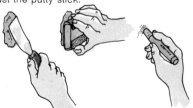

place. Use annular ring nails, countersink the heads and cover with a putty stick.

■ **Replacing panels:** Do this if panels are badly ripped or buckled. Start by removing the baseboard and then use a nail set to drive all the old nails through the paneling. If the panel is glued too tightly for easy removal, split along one edge near a stud so you can get a firm grip for removal.

Once the panels are removed, clear the studs of any nails or adhesive. Start the replacement panels in one corner and take special care to see that the leading edge is vertical. If necessary, cut the trailing edge to conform to a corner that is not square. Glue and nail each panel with ring nails to prevent buckling.

Loose panel

1. Shoot a layer of adhesive beneath the loose edge . . .

Annular ring nail

2. Nail back into place with annular ring nails.

Replacing panel

After removing the baseboard, drive panel nails through panel with nail set . . .

Pull any nails and scrape old adhesive from studs or furring strips . . .

Apply new adhesive . . .

Pull off panel. You may have to break it to get a grip . . .

Nail on the replacement panel.

Repairing Plaster

Once a plaster wall starts to crack, there's not much you can do until it decides to stop. Cracking is usually caused by the house settling or severe vibration. For smaller repairs, use a ready-mix spackling compound but for the larger jobs, you must use a patching plaster. In all repairs, remember to dampen the area first to prevent too rapid a moisture loss from the patch.

■ **Small cracks, nail holes:** Use your fingers or a flexible putty knife to work spackling into the crack after it has been dampened. If your plaster walls are white, gypsum board compound, which is white, may match.

■ **Larger cracks:** These should be widened in the manner of an inverted V which forms a key to hold the patch. Do this with a drink can opener held at right angles to the crack. Blow out loose material, dampen and then fill with spackling compound. Use a flexible putty knife at right angles to the crack to force the compound in deeply. Then let dry, sand and paint.

■ **Deep, wide cracks:** Use a prepared plaster mix available at hardware or masonry supply stores. This dries quickly — in 10 to 15 minutes — but you can slow the process by mixing the plaster with ⅔ water and ⅓ vinegar instead of straight water. Also, it is best to make the repair in 2 or 3 layers to minimize shrinkage which will result in new cracks.

Clean the hole, undercut it, dampen it and fill halfway with plaster. Let dry and then fill to the surface. To get a glassy finish on the last coat, use a square steel finishing trowel and then a wet paint brush. Alternatively, dampen the plaster with the paint brush and smooth with the trowel.

■ **Holes:** In cases where lath is missing, slip a piece of strong wire mesh or perforated cardboard behind the hole and hold in place with a loop of string. Work in a layer of plaster that fills no more than half the depth of the hole. Let dry while holding the backing material firmly in place. Still holding the backing, fill to within ⅛-inch of the surface and let dry. Remove the string, fill the hole and apply the final layer. To get a final layer flush with the wall, scrape the patch while it's still damp with the edge of a steel square. Then use the wet paint brush technique if you want a very smooth finish to match the rest of the wall, or texture to match a rougher surface.

Repairing Large holes

Remove loose pieces from hole and cut some wire mesh a little larger than the hole . . .

Hold the wire in place while you force the first layers of plaster through the mesh. Hold it tight until they set . . .

The next day, apply the final layer of plaster.

Repairing Torn or Blistered Wallpaper

Few things can so quickly transform a room as new wallpaper. But as in any other repair job, problems can and do develop. Before you begin, it's good to have a few specialized tools on hand. These include a seam roller for pressing torn or loose wallpaper firmly and smoothly back in place; a very sharp knife or razor blade for making smooth, precise cuts in the paper; a steel straightedge for guiding the knife while cutting; and white glue or, for extensive repairs, wallpaper glue and brush.

Thus armed, prepare to do battle.

■ **Loose edges:** If the paper is quite stiff, dampen it to soften it. Curl it back and put a thin layer of glue under it and roll flat. A clean, damp rag will also smooth it down. If it is a raised pattern wallpaper, use only the damp rag since the roller may damage the pattern.

■ **Irregular tear:** As with a loose edge, dampen the paper before moving it to prevent cracking. Apply the glue lightly to both the paper and the wall, and then smooth it out carefully.

■ **Blisters and bubbles:** Dampen the blister but be careful not to wet the surrounding area. With the sharp knife or razor blade, make a specialized cut in the bubble: either an L, T or X. Whenever possible, cut along the pattern to help conceal the opening. When pulling back the edges, be careful not to fold them sharply, which may result in a permanent crease. Apply the adhesive to both the paper and wall and smooth out with the roller or clean damp rag.

■ **Large tears:** Here, where it is impossible to glue the tears back, you will have to make a patch that matches the old pattern. Start by cutting a square of matching wall-paper some-

Blister repair

1. Dampen the blister . . .

2. Make 2 or 3 cuts into the bubble appropriate to its shape . . .

3. Apply adhesive . . .

4. Smooth flat.

Cut along part of the pattern when possible . . .

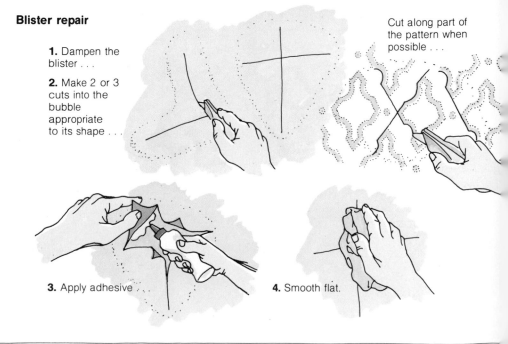

Repairing Ceiling Tiles

You never really notice your ceiling until something goes wrong with it. And then it seems you can't take your eyes off it. It may just be a loose tile or a miniscule bulge but it won't go away.

Ceiling tiles are common in houses because they are easy to install, relatively inexpensive, and effective at deadening sound. Most of them are made from compressed wood fibers but some are made from fiberglass for greater fire resistance.

Tiles are usually installed only with adhesive but sometimes with staples, or both. They can be applied directly to an existing ceiling or on furring strips over exposed joists, as in an unfinished basement.

In addition, tiles can be hung on a metal grid for a suspended ceiling. Problems rarely develop here and replacing a tile involves nothing more than lifting it out and glueing another one in.

■ **Loose or bulging tiles:** If the tile is attached to a plaster ceiling, remove the tile and let the plaster dry thoroughly. Then apply a layer of white glue

Replacing ceiling tile

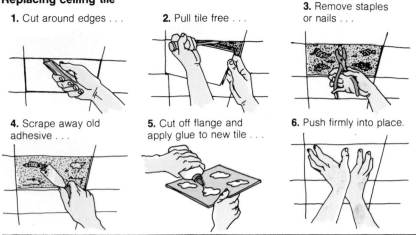

1. Cut around edges . . .

2. Pull tile free . . .

3. Remove staples or nails . . .

4. Scrape away old adhesive . . .

5. Cut off flange and apply glue to new tile . . .

6. Push firmly into place.

to both the ceiling and the tile, and push firmly back in place. Brace it with a long board. Alternatively, drill a hole in the tile and use a cement-coated finishing nail to hold it in place. Cover the nail head with a dab of paint that matches the ceiling tile.

■ **Stained tiles:** First find the cause of the stain, which is likely to be a leak somewhere. After correcting that, brush a coat of paint over the stain that matches the tile. Most ceiling tiles can be effectively painted, with either oil-base or latex paint.

■ **Replacing tiles:** If the tile must be replaced, first cut around the edges with a sharp knife. Pull the tile free and then with a pair of pliers remove any staples or nails. Use a stiff putty knife to scrape away any adhesive on the ceiling.

If the replacement tiles have tongued edges, trim these off evenly with a sharp knife. Apply white glue to the tile, especially along the edges, and push firmly into place. If possible, brace it in position with a board between the floor and ceiling.

---

what larger than the hole to be covered. With masking tape, fasten it on the wall over the tear. Make sure the hole is well covered and that the patterns line up exactly. Using the steel straightedge to guide you, cut out a square around the hole by going through both the patch and old wallpaper.

Now dampen the area inside the square and scrape it clean with a putty knife. Be careful not to damage the surrounding wallpaper as you work.

After the wall is clean, let it dry thoroughly. Inspect the wall and if you find any holes or deep nicks, fill in carefully and evenly with a spackling compound.

When ready, apply a thin, even layer of glue to the back of the patch and another thin layer to the wall and then smooth the patch into position. Roll it smooth if the wallpaper doesn't have a raised pattern. Otherwise, use a clean damp cloth to smooth, and another to wipe up any excess glue.

Patching

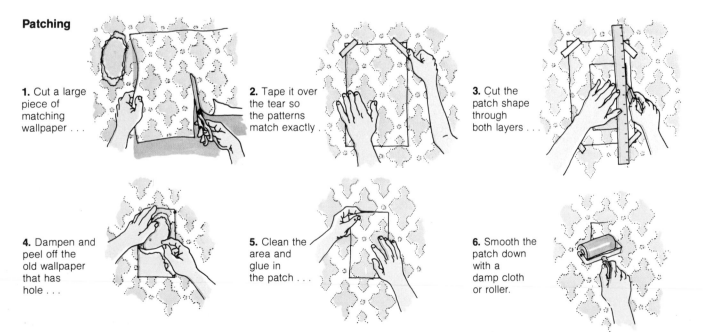

1. Cut a large piece of matching wallpaper . . .

2. Tape it over the tear so the patterns match exactly .

3. Cut the patch shape through both layers . . .

4. Dampen and peel off the old wallpaper that has hole . . .

5. Clean the area and glue in the patch . . .

6. Smooth the patch down with a damp cloth or roller.

Installing Gypsum Board

Gypsum board — which is known as sheetrock or drywall in the trade — is among the best of wall materials. It goes up quickly, is easy to work with and takes any kind of covering. Whether you have only one piece to put up or a whole room, here's how to carry it through.

Standard-size panels are ½-inch thick and come in 4 by 8-foot sections. They also come in lengths of 10, 12, 14 and 16 feet.

Panels are generally put up vertically, particularly if you are working alone. In some cases, however, it may be more practical to place them horizontally. The choice is determined by the least amount of cutting required.

■ **How to cut drywall:** The gypsum boards can be brought into the room where you are working and cut while they are leaning against the wall. For long cuts, make the line with a straightedge or a chalk line on the gypsum side. With a utility knife, deeply score the drywall and then bend it away from you. Now finish the cut by slicing through the paper backing.

Sometimes — when making L-shaped cuts, for instance — you will have to use a drywall saw. Cut the shorter line first with the saw, score the other with the utility knife, snap it over and cut the paper. This method gives you the smoothest, fastest cuts.

■ **Cutting outlet holes:** Nothing ruins more panels or looses more expletives than wrongly measured holes for switches and outlets. The solution is to measure everything twice so you only have to cut once.

One important thing to remember here: Always measure from the *top* of the panel *down* to the opening. This is because drywalls are always attached flush with the ceiling. Any gap below will be covered by the baseboard.

A standard wall switch needs a hole 2¼ inches by 3⅞ inches. Thus, in cutting the hole, measure down from the ceiling to the top of the switch, mark it, add 3⅞ inches and mark that. Now, from either the adjoining panel or from a corner that is already paneled, measure over to the switch's edge, mark it, add 2¼ inches and mark that.

To make the opening, score the lines with a utility knife and then hit the middle of the square with a hammer.

Some home repair books advise you to drill holes at the corners and then saw the piece out. That makes a clean cut but no professional would waste time doing that. Trim the edges with your knife.

■ **Ceiling panels:** If you're covering your ceiling with gypsum, put up those panels before the wall panels. It's awkward, neck-craning work and if you can cajole or coerce one or two people to help, the work will go much faster. Whether with help or alone, make two T-braces as illustrated. They should measure from the floor to the ceiling joists, less ¾ inch. That allows ½ inch for the drywall and ¼ inch clearance for maneuvering the braces.

■ **Wall panels:** Once the ceiling is up, start the walls from one corner. The leading edge of the first panel must be vertical and must cover just half of the stud, leaving the other half as a nailing base for the next panel.

If the corner is not square, you can allow a gap up to ½ inch wide between it and the trailing edge. This will be covered by tape.

If the corner is too much out of square and you must cut, mark the irregularity by holding the panel in a vertical position next to the corner. From the adjoining wall, use a pencil compass to trace the line down the drywall.

When the wall panels are put up, they should be raised until flush with

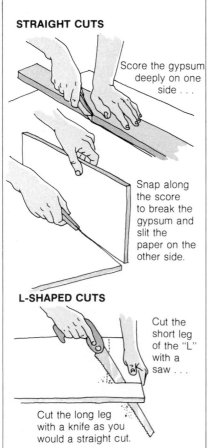

Cutting drywall

STRAIGHT CUTS

Score the gypsum deeply on one side . . .

Snap along the score to break the gypsum and slit the paper on the other side.

L-SHAPED CUTS

Cut the short leg of the "L" with a saw . . .

Cut the long leg with a knife as you would a straight cut.

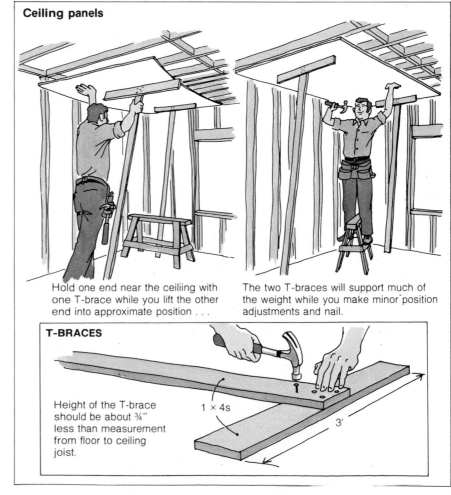

Ceiling panels

Hold one end near the ceiling with one T-brace while you lift the other end into approximate position . . .

The two T-braces will support much of the weight while you make minor position adjustments and nail.

T-BRACES

Height of the T-brace should be about ¾" less than measurement from floor to ceiling joist.

1 × 4s

3'

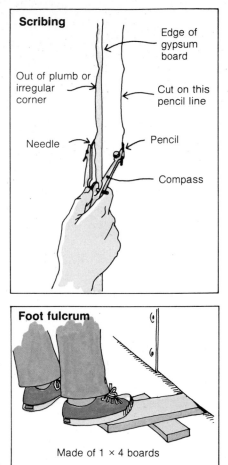

Scribing

Edge of gypsum board

Out of plumb or irregular corner

Cut on this pencil line

Needle

Pencil

Compass

Foot fulcrum

Made of 1 × 4 boards

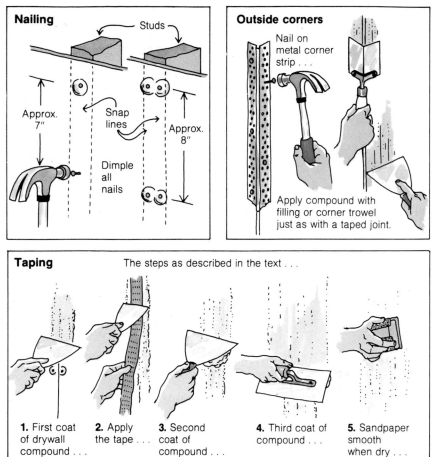

Nailing

Studs

Approx. 7"

Snap lines

Approx. 8"

Dimple all nails

Outside corners

Nail on metal corner strip . . .

Apply compound with filling or corner trowel just as with a taped joint.

Taping The steps as described in the text . . .

1. First coat of drywall compound . . .

2. Apply the tape . . .

3. Second coat of compound . . .

4. Third coat of compound . . .

5. Sandpaper smooth when dry . . .

---

the ceiling. To do this with the least amount of effort, use a foot-powered fulcrum, called a kicker or jack. The end of the kicker should be cut at a 45 degree angle so it will readily slip under the gypsum board. Any space at the bottom is covered by the baseboard.

■ **Removing damaged panel:** If only one panel is damaged and must be replaced, start by slitting the tape on both sides with a utility knife. Next, drive in all the nails with a nail set. Trying to pull them usually results in damage to the adjoining panel. Before putting up the new panel, carefully tear off any loose pieces of tape on the adjoining panel.

■ **Nailing procedure:** Drywall is normally put up with cement-coated drywall nails. For problem areas or for better gripping power, screw-nails with rings on the shank are also available.

Standard nailing calls for driving a single nail about every 8 inches in a wall panel, every 7 inches in a ceiling panel. The first one should be about ½ inch in from the edge.

For greater assurance that the nails will not later pop out, drive two nails about 1 inch apart on each side. Space the pairs of nails about 8 inches apart. It takes more nails and more time, but it probably means you won't have to repair the damage from a popped nail in a year's time or less.

Nails should be driven until flush with the drywall and then with one final blow they must be "dimpled." This blow sets them ⅛ inch or so below the surface so they can be coated and hidden with joint compound. Don't hit so hard that you break the gypsum.

■ **Taping techniques:** There is considerable art to taping panels. Comparing a pro's with your own first efforts may make you cry. When you start, keep in mind that all the bumps and rough edges you leave are going to have to be sanded down, so the smoother you tape, the less sanding you will have to do.

Drywall compound or "mud" goes on in three layers: the first one to hold the tape, the second one to cover the tape, and the final one to hide it and cover shrinkage in the previous layers.

Using a flexible putty knife about 8 inches wide, start by laying a moderately thick bead of compound over the join between the two panels. Work from top to bottom. Into this mud, press the tape and make sure it is centered over the join. The tape is perforated so the mud can grip it. Holding the putty knife at a 45 degree angle, run the blade over the tape to smooth it into the compound. After applying the tape, give the nail heads their first layer of mud. They will require two or three coats also.

Let dry overnight. When the first

coat is dry, sand it smooth and apply the second. Here begins the tricky part. This layer should be feathered out to each side about 8 to 10 inches and applied as smoothly and evenly as possible.

The feathering-out process on each coat is designed to fill evenly the barely perceptible tapering on each side of the gypsum board. When taped properly, a painted drywall will be perfectly smooth and give no indication of where the joins are.

The final coat of compound is feathered out 10 to 12 inches. For the best results here, use a 12-inch putty knife.

When the final coat is thoroughly dry, wrap a piece of medium-grade sandpaper around a smooth block of wood and sand all joins and nail coverings smooth prior to painting or wallpapering.

■ **Inside and outside corners:** Inside corners are done as you would a join between panels, only the tape is folded down the middle to fit equally on both sides. A special trowel is available to smooth inside corners but unless you're doing a lot of drywalling, it is an unnecessary expense.

Outside corners can be protected with a thin metal strip that is nailed up and then covered with mud just as if it were tape. These metal corners are normally available where you buy the gypsum board.

Repairing Holes in Gypsum Board

Drywalls go up fast and are easy to work with but are quite vulnerable. Holes, gouges and dents are common problems. In making these repairs you can use either spackling compound — which is more expensive but dries faster — or drywall compound, which you may have left over from your last drywalling project.

■ **Dents and gouges:** Remove any frayed paper around the blemish and with a putty knife, force the spackling or compound into the dent. Don't try to fill the gouge completely with this first layer. It will shrink slightly as it dries. If the gouge is not too deep, a second layer may be enough. Otherwise, let it dry and apply a third coat. Sand it all smooth after it dries.

■ **Small holes:** If these are only the size of nail or screw holes, simply fill them with compound and finish as you would a dent. If the hole is the diameter of a door knob or more, different treatments are called for.

■ **Large holes:** There are two basic solutions here: covering the hole with tape, or cutting a patch and taping all the edges. If the hole is the size of a fist or smaller, the first method works well; for larger holes, use the second method.

In the first instance, put a moderate layer of mud around the hole, extending it about 3 inches above and below and 6 inches on each side. Smooth the tape over the hole and overlap half the tape's width with each new piece of tape. Allowing the compound to dry overnight each time, apply four or five coats and feather the mud out farther and farther each time. When the last coat is dry, sand it smooth and refinish to match the wall.

For larger holes, some home repair advisors give elaborate details on backing the hole with screen, filling it with several layers of compound and then taping the edges. A professional wouldn't waste time with that.

Instead, find the studs on each side of the hole. The center of one stud to the center of the next is normally 16 inches; in some cases it may be 24 inches. Find the studs just by cutting from the hole over to the stud.

Now cut a patching piece of gypsum board that is at least 2 inches wider than the hole and runs from the center of one stud to the center of the next. Place it over the hole and mark the outline with a pencil. Cut along these lines with a utility knife and then knock that entire damaged piece of sheetrock out with a hammer. Trim off any loose paper.

Now nail the patch in place on each

stud and finish the job by taping all the joints and plugging the nail holes, as previously described.

■ **Popped or bent nails:** Nails can work loose when the studs are crooked and the drywall panel resists bending their way. Pull these nails out. Nails are considered popped also when driven so deeply into the panel they no longer have any holding

power. In both cases, drive another nail about 2 inches above or below the popped one, dimple it and cover with mud as previously described.

If you drive a nail about halfway in then miss and bend it over, pound it in flat and then use the head on a second nail to catch and hold the first nail. Otherwise, the bent nail will straighten itself slightly and pop out.

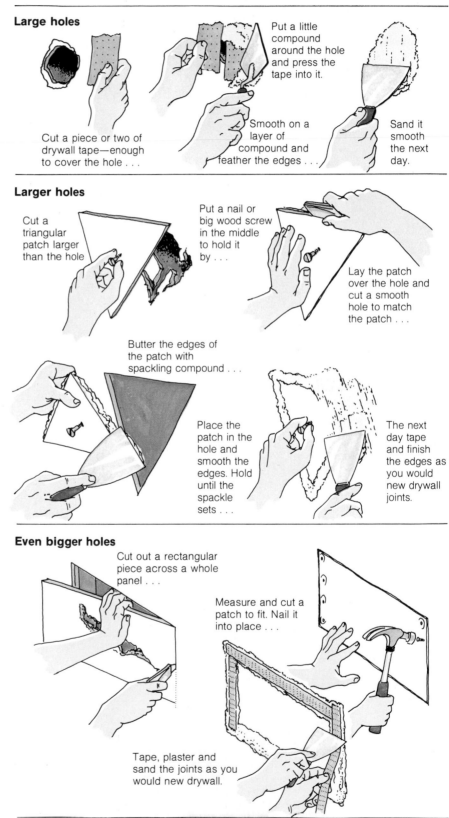

Large holes

Cut a piece or two of drywall tape—enough to cover the hole . . .

Smooth on a layer of compound and feather the edges . . .

Put a little compound around the hole and press the tape into it.

Sand it smooth the next day.

Larger holes

Cut a triangular patch larger than the hole

Put a nail or big wood screw in the middle to hold it by . . .

Lay the patch over the hole and cut a smooth hole to match the patch . . .

Butter the edges of the patch with spackling compound . . .

Place the patch in the hole and smooth the edges. Hold until the spackle sets . . .

The next day tape and finish the edges as you would new drywall joints.

Even bigger holes

Cut out a rectangular piece across a whole panel . . .

Measure and cut a patch to fit. Nail it into place . . .

Tape, plaster and sand the joints as you would new drywall.

Fireplace Problems

Before you light up the fireplace in the fall, it will pay you to give it a quick check over.

Clean the interior of all ashes and use a stiff brush to remove the soot so you can see the bricks clearly. With the aid of a flashlight, check the fire-chamber for loose bricks or crumbling mortar. These should be repaired immediately to prevent flames from working through the cracks to the wood framing behind.

If just occasional bits of mortar are crumbling, use a cold chisel to clean them out at least ½ inch deep and then repoint as detailed on page 15.

For a loose brick, split it with a cold chisel and heavy hammer, and remove. Clean the opening of old mortar and then dampen it before mortaring in a new brick. Because of heat from the fire, the brick must be a firebrick and the mortar must contain fireclay. Mix 1 part of this kind of mortar to 3 parts fine sand. Butter the base and sides of the opening with mortar, insert the brick, squeeze in the top layer of mortar and repoint the joints.

If you have no problems with loose mortar or bricks within the fireplace, look up the chimney. Even if the chimney is offset, as most are, you should be able to see daylight at the top. If you can't, assume something is blocking it. If it is a stork nest inconveniently located halfway down the chimney instead of on top of it, use a chain or sack of balled up paper weighted with rocks on a rope to break the blockage up (page 8).

While getting dirty in the fireplace, do a little work on the damper. Clean it with a wire brush and oil the rod at each end. Remember to keep the damper closed when you're not using the fireplace, or that chimney will suck warm air from the house just as an open window does.

If your chimney doesn't draw properly but instead tends to smoke, especially on windy days, there are a couple of things to look for. For one, the top of the chimney must be at least 2 feet above the peak of the roof. If you have a flat roof, it must be 3 to 4 feet above it.

Another problem may be too large a fire chamber for the size of fire you build. Check this by raising the grate the height of one or two bricks. If this makes a decided difference, cement in a new layer or two of firebrick.

Finally, make doubly sure that the damper opens and shuts completely and that the smoke shelf just above and behind the damper is not packed with soot and ashes. A clean shelf is important to proper air movement in the chimney.

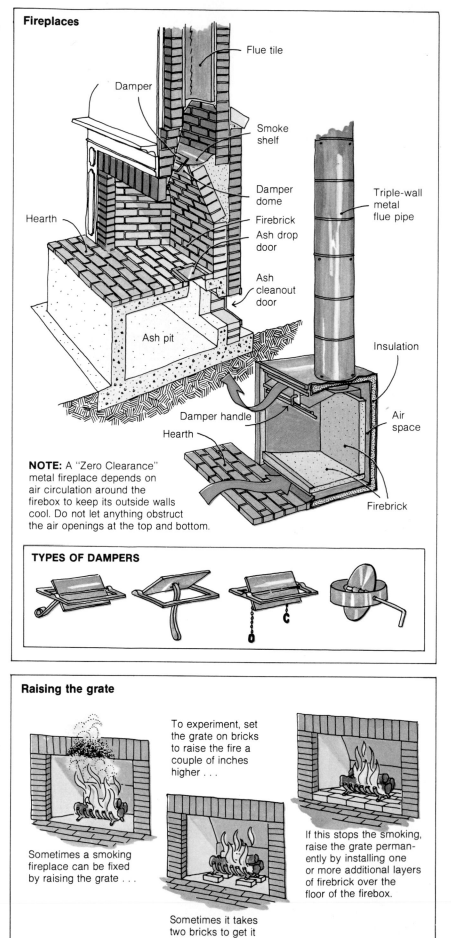

Fireplaces

Flue tile

Damper

Smoke shelf

Damper dome

Firebrick

Ash drop door

Ash cleanout door

Hearth

Ash pit

Triple-wall metal flue pipe

Insulation

Damper handle

Hearth

Air space

Firebrick

NOTE: A "Zero Clearance" metal fireplace depends on air circulation around the firebox to keep its outside walls cool. Do not let anything obstruct the air openings at the top and bottom.

TYPES OF DAMPERS

Raising the grate

To experiment, set the grate on bricks to raise the fire a couple of inches higher . . .

Sometimes a smoking fireplace can be fixed by raising the grate . . .

Sometimes it takes two bricks to get it high enough . . .

If this stops the smoking, raise the grate permanently by installing one or more additional layers of firebrick over the floor of the firebox.

Floors & Stairs

How to fix damaged sections and surface flaws; eliminate squeaks; and refinish wooden floors. How to remove burns and stains from carpets. How to patch floor tiles, and concrete and stone surfaces. How to repair banisters, treads and risers.

Replacing a Damaged Board in Wood Floor

If a board in your hardwood floor has been damaged to the point where a good patching job is not feasible, a replacement job awaits you. It's understandable if you are reluctant to tear into that lovely floor. The work is not particularly difficult but it has to be precise.

Most hardwood floors are tongue and groove, which requires more patience on your part than simple boards do. Use a square to mark the lines of your cuts.

If the floor board is wide enough, lower a power saw on the line to make most of the cut and then finish it with a keyhole saw. If this won't work on your floor, drill a series of large holes across the board just inside the line. Do as little damage to the subfloor as possible. Complete the cut with a wide chisel, holding the flat edge against the good board.

Now look over the piece to be removed. If there are countersunk nails, use a nail set to drive them as far through the board as possible. If there are screws covered by wooden plugs, chisel out the plugs and unscrew the board.

Because of the tongue and groove arrangement, you cannot easily pry that board out of there. With a thin chisel, cut off the tongue of the board to be removed and pry it out. Alternatively, split the board down the middle and remove.

Cut the replacement board for a precise and snug fit. Make sure the end of the cut floor board is smooth and square.

Repairing hardwood floor board

1. Mark the edge of the damaged section with a square.

2. Drill holes along the cross-cut line.

3. Split out the damaged board (see text) . . .

4. And clean up the drilled edge with a chisel.

5. Cut replacement board to fit, remove bottom side of groove, apply glue all around and slip it into place.

— Remove

6. Hammer it down snugly, nail, and finish to match the rest of the floor.

Fitting a replacement board into a tongue and groove floor requires a nice little trick. Turn the board over and use a chisel to trim off the lower half of the groove. Now coat the tongue, the half-groove and both ends of the replacement board with glue and slip into place. Use a rubber mallet or protective board when hammering it down snug.

For a more secure fit, the board should be nailed in place, particularly if it is a long one. To prevent splitting, drill pilot holes slightly smaller than the nails at both ends and along the sides if necessary. Put the holes in at opposing angles to give the nails a better grip in the subflooring. Countersink the nail heads, fill in the holes with wood putty, and then cover them and the board ends with a putty stick that matches the floor color. You can also use countersunk screws instead of nails. Fill holes with plastic wood. If by chance, some of the subfloor had to be removed — maybe you discovered some dry rot — the replacement piece will have to be supported at each end by the floor joists. Nail cleats on the side of the joists to fully catch the ends of the replacement piece.

Fixing Surface Flaws in Wood Floors

The President is about to arrive at your modest home for the night when you notice some flaws in your hardwood floors. A few of these you can

repair before the arrival; others may require the entourage to wait a bit.

Among the more common problems are minor surface scratches and white rings where someone put down a wet glass at the last party.

In many cases, rubbing the light scratches with a paste wax will make them nearly disappear. Or, if you happen to have some crayons around the house, find a color that matches and rub the scratches with that. It will probably last until you wax and buff the floors again; certainly until the dignitaries leave.

If your floors are shellacked, remove the wax and rub the scratches briskly with wood alcohol. This should soften the shellac and fill in the scratches.

For those white rings on the floor, caused by water and alcohol or something hot, try an old but proven trick. Rub the rings with a combination of cigar ash and a little saliva. If that doesn't do the job, rub them with very fine steel wool and some mineral or vegetable oil.

If none of these works, take your pick of the following (keep them in mind for wood furniture as well as floors): commercial cleaners, lighter fluid, benzine, undiluted ammonia. One last good trick: oxalic acid. You can obtain this at most paint stores. Mix ¼ cup of crystals to a pint of water. Incidentally, oxalic acid is also good for removing rust stains from porcelain or marble.

■ **Burn marks:** For quite minor burns, treat the spot with the mixture of oxalic acid. Lighter fluid may also work.

For deeper burns, carefully scrape out all the blackened wood with a sharp knife. If very little wood was lost, retouch the spot with crayon for an immediate repair. For a more lasting job, color the spot with a matching artist's oil paint. Use your finger to rub on a light coat, let dry overnight and then apply another one.

If you have a deep burn hole to repair, treat it as you would a gouge.

■ **Deep scratches and gouges:** If you have a shellacked floor deeply scratched, the easiest repair is made with a shellac stick. These are available in a variety of colors at most hardware stores.

The stick must first be softened with heat — from a gas burner, propane or even a cigarette lighter. Smooth it into the scratches with a flexible putty knife that has also been heated over a flame.

Gouges and deep scratches in wood floors are permanently repaired by filling them with plastic wood. This can be stained with oil paint for a nearly perfect color match. However, it is advisable to make two or three test batches and let dry to judge the color before applying it.

Fill the gouges or scars and smooth with a flexible putty knife. After the plastic has hardened and set, sand it smooth and refinish.

Such scars can also be repaired quite effectively by sawing up some of the same board material, if you have some, mixing the sawdust with glue and smoothing into the mark. When dry, buff with steel wool.

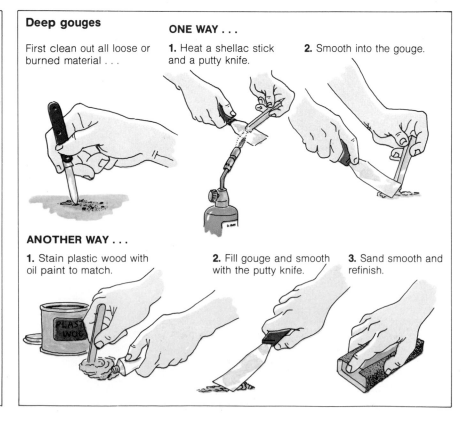

Burns

1. Scrape away all the blackened finish with a sharp knife.

2. Retouch the spot with a matching crayon or artist's oil paint.

Deep gouges

First clean out all loose or burned material . . .

ONE WAY . . .

1. Heat a shellac stick and a putty knife.

2. Smooth into the gouge.

ANOTHER WAY . . .

1. Stain plastic wood with oil paint to match.

2. Fill gouge and smooth with the putty knife.

3. Sand smooth and refinish.

Correcting Separated Floor Boards

Wood floors sometimes separate a little during long dry spells but return to normal when the humidity increases. If they don't, or if the boards are buckled or turned up at the corners, there are several efficient ways to correct the problem.

■ **Separated boards:** For relatively minor separations between boards, fill with a plastic wood. The plastic can be dyed in advance with a wood stain to match the color of the floor. Make a test batch before applying. If the plastic wood has shrunk below the floor level, apply another layer, then sand and finish when hardened.

For long, severe separations between boards, use a power saw to rip long shims from a new board to fill the gaps. Nail in place, fill the cracks with plastic wood, then stain and finish to match the adjoining floor.

Short, wide cracks in floorboards can be filled in the same manner, using short wedges of matching wood.

■ **Split, cracked floor board:** This may continue splitting unless stopped immediately. An excellent·solution here is to fill the crack with a mixture of glue and sawdust matching the floor. Work this into the split and then buff with steel wool when dry.

An alternative method is to drill through the board in several places alongside the crack and nail or screw it in place to stop the splitting. Put nails in at an angle for maximum holding power. Countersink them. Fill the crack and the nail holes to match the floor.

■ **Loose boards:** Work some glue along the sides and underneath the base board if possible. Drill holes at an angle and pull the board down with nails or screws. Countersink and fill the holes with matching putty stick.

If two adjacent boards are warped up along the edges, start the repair by cutting off the tongue of one board. Use a sharpened, stiff putty knife for this or, if the split between the boards is wide enough, a power saw set just to the depth of the boards.

Drill the boards at regular intervals over the warp and then use long wood screws sunk to the subfloor to pull the boards back down. This may not be possible to do all at once, so tighten the screws a little each day. Countersink the heads and top with plastic wood.

■ **Warped boards:** Minor protuberances can sometimes be sanded down, or even planed and sanded.

Otherwise, remove the wax and finish, and keep the boards under damp rags for 48 hours. Then pull into place with wood screws as described above.

Separated boards

1. Measure the width of the crack carefully. If it's tongue-and-groove flooring, remove the tongue that projects into the opening with a saw or chisel.

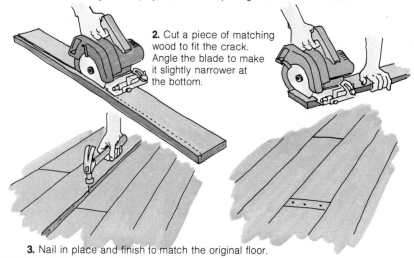

2. Cut a piece of matching wood to fit the crack. Angle the blade to make it slightly narrower at the bottom.

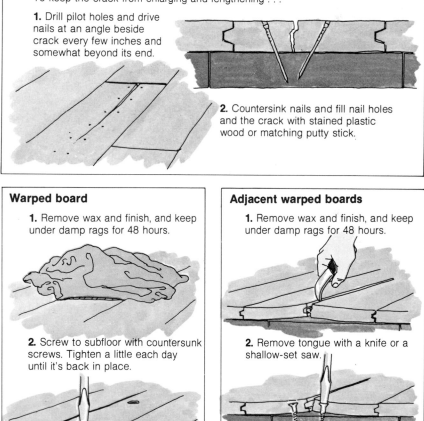

3. Nail in place and finish to match the original floor.

Split board

To keep the crack from enlarging and lengthening . . .

1. Drill pilot holes and drive nails at an angle beside crack every few inches and somewhat beyond its end.

2. Countersink nails and fill nail holes and the crack with stained plastic wood or matching putty stick.

Warped board

1. Remove wax and finish, and keep under damp rags for 48 hours.

2. Screw to subfloor with countersunk screws. Tighten a little each day until it's back in place.

3. Fill screw holes and refinish to match the original floor.

Adjacent warped boards

1. Remove wax and finish, and keep under damp rags for 48 hours.

2. Remove tongue with a knife or a shallow-set saw.

3. Screw to subfloor with countersunk screws. Tighten them a half turn or so each day until boards are flat.

4. Fill screw holes and refinish to match the original floor.

Refinishing Wood Floors

When you finally decide that you can no longer put off refinishing that floor, go to your local equipment rental shop and get a drum sander and a smaller disc sander. If possible, get them with vacuum bags attached to minimize the sawdust blown around the room. Explain your needs to the rental agency and have them show you how to change the sandpaper on both machines. Get enough rough sandpaper to remove the old finish and enough fine paper to give the raw floor a smooth finish.

Before you start, remove all furniture and pictures. Cover drapes or blinds with sheets to save on subsequent cleaning. Repair any loose or warped boards as explained on page 45. Check for protruding nails and drive them down with a nail set.

When you start the drum sander, tilt it back and up first, then lower it slowly to avoid scarring the floor. Sand with the grain and keep the sander in check; it will want to run away from you. Each time you complete a pass, overlap this by 50 percent on the next run. Do the entire floor this way and then go back over it again until you are down to bare wood.

When using the disc sander along the edges, carefully remove the shoe molding so you can work right up to the baseboard. Any scarring of the baseboard will be hidden when the molding is replaced. For corners and inaccessible areas, use sandpaper wrapped around a block of wood.

After the old finish is completely removed, pick up the dust with a dry dust mop, and change to the fine sandpaper for the finish sanding. Don't try to use worn-down coarse paper for this; it just doesn't work. Do the finish sanding in the same manner as the rough sanding. Be particularly careful to keep the sander moving at an even pace at all times. Never let it run in one place since it takes only seconds to round out a small valley in your floor. If there are still a few patches of the old finish left, work at them with hand-sanding.

■ **Refinishes for wood floors:** In considering how you want to finish the floor, decide whether you want a penetrating stain or a glossy surface covering.

The penetrating stain also seals

Use an electric drum sander with a sawdust bag for the main area of the floor; a small electric disc sander for the edges; and a handheld sanding block for the corners and inaccessible areas (see text).

Eliminating Floor Board Squeaks

Squeaks are caused by two boards rubbing against each other, and the solution is to stop that.

If the squeak comes from a loose board in the finished floor, screw or nail it tight against the subfloor. Use pairs of screw-nails or cement-coated finishing nails driven at opposing angles to each other for maximum gripping strength. Countersink the screws or nails and fill the holes with a matching putty stick. On hardwood floors, drill the nail holes to prevent splitting.

Alternatively, that pesky squeak can be fixed several ways from under the floor, if you can get under it.

With someone walking on the floor to locate the squeak for you, start by driving small wedges between the joists and subfloor.

If the squeak persists between the joists, nail a supporting block in there. Force the block up against the subfloor by toenailing at an upward angle.

Another effective method is to drill up just into the finish floor and pull the board down with a wood screw. Use a washer on the screw head and don't screw through to the surface of the finish floor.

Drive two nails or screws into the squeaking board at different angles. Drill pilot holes first.

Drive small wedges of shingle between the joist and subfloor: just enough to stop the squeak; don't raise the floor.

Nail a block between the joists. The toenailing will force it upward tightly, stopping the squeak.

Use a screw with a washer to pull a squeaky floor board tightly against the subfloor. Drill a pilot hole first.

the wood. It soaks into the floor and leaves the appearance of oiled wood. Some stains leave a more glossy finish than others, but all brighten up considerably after they have been waxed and buffed.

These stains come in a wide variety of colors. Since they penetrate directly into the wood with little surface gloss remaining, any scratches are made right in the wood and don't show up much.

Take note that these stains can be applied only to bare wood and not over a floor that has had only some of the wax removed. The old finish or seal must also be removed. To penetrate the wood evenly, the stain should be rubbed in vigorously by hand. Applying stain with a brush leaves brush marks. After letting the stain dry for 2

or 3 days, rub on a paste floor wax and bring out the gloss with a floor buffer. Two or three coats of wax will be needed to give the floor a deep luster.

For surface coatings that give a hard and glossy finish, there are three basic types to choose from:

Shellac, the old standby, gives a high gloss and dries very quickly — within an hour. So you can apply several coats in one day and be done with it.

Floor varnish takes longer to dry but is more resistant to spills and scuffs. Some varnishes tend to darken slightly with age.

Among the most popular glossy floor finishes today are polyurethanes, the plastic finishes. They dry quickly, and are extremely tough. Two or three

coats are generally recommended. They require no waxing to bring out the gloss.

In caring for the floors, whether waxed or glossy, clean them only with a dry dust mop. Water will lessen the sheen. If you have to move furniture, slip some old carpet scraps under the legs so you won't scratch the floor. Keep wide floor protectors under the legs of chairs or couches that are periodically pushed around.

These precautions help make your new floor something to enjoy, not worry about.

Rub penetrating stain deep into the wood by hand . . .

When stain is dry, apply paste wax by hand (see text for alternative finishes) . . .

Use an electric buffer to polish the wax after each coat.

Repairing Carpet Burns and Stains

If the burn in your carpet is superficial, snip off the charred ends and then scrub the area with liquid dishwashing detergent and water. After it's dry, wash again with white vinegar diluted with a little water.

For deep burns, cut out the damaged fibers down to the backing. If you can lift the rug or carpet, use a needle to weave matching fibers through from the back. When the hole is filled, put a spot of rubber cement on the backing and then trim the top of the fibers until flush.

If you can't get at the back of the rug, cut away the damaged area and then pull some fibers from under a chair or little used corner. Roll into a tuft, glue one end into the hole and trim the surface.

For grease stains, blot up what you can and scrape off any solid matter with a kitchen knife. Then, using a tablespoon of liquid detergent in a pint of water, blot at the stain. Don't rub. Keep repeating the process and use a hair dryer to speed the drying.

If that is not successful, repeat the same process with dry cleaning fluid or use special carpet cleaning detergents.

Superficial burn

1. Snip off charred ends.

2. Wash with liquid dishwashing detergent and water.

3. When dry, wash again with white vinegar.

Deep burn

1. Cut out the burned fibers down to the backing.

2. Make a tuft of matching fibers (see text) and glue into the hole.

3. Trim the tips to match the original fibers.

Repairing and Replacing Resilient Floor Coverings

Today's resilient floor coverings, whether asphalt tile or seamless vinyl, are generally covered with a long lasting, stain resistant finish. Even so, they can be stained, scratched, gouged or broken.

The hard finishes on these floors can be damaged if you use chemical cleaners to remove stains. In most cases, floor marks can be removed with items commonly found in the house. Try any of the following to remove stains: household bleach, ammonia and water, white vinegar, rubbing alcohol or lighter fluid. It's a

of waxing but this is not considered advisable. Because of specific movements in and around the kitchen, specific patterns of wear begin to show up. To correct this, the old acrylic or polyurethane finish must be completely removed, a difficult and tedious chore. Solvents cannot be used without risk of ruining the floor, so it all must be removed with fine steel wool.

However, if it is only the shiny finish on your vinyl floor that has turned dull, special finishes to recoat the floor are available from hardware stores and flooring dealers.

■ **Scratched, gouged flooring:** If you are putting down new flooring, be sure to put aside several extra tiles or large pieces of scrap. Sooner or later you are going to need them for some repair work.

cation of heat. One of the best sources is the household iron. With a piece of aluminum foil between the floor and iron, go back and forth over the tile, especially around the curled edges, until it is pliable. Other good sources of heat include a heat lamp or a propane torch. Floor tile does not easily burn, but keep the flame off the flooring itself.

When the curled edge is soft, pull it back slightly and scrape off all the old adhesive from the edge and the floor. Apply a thin layer of new mastic and press the corner back into place. Wipe up immediately any mastic that squeezes up. Put a weight on the tile overnight.

■ **Bubble in flooring:** This is generally caused by poor application in the first place or dampness in the sub-

---

Fixing gouges

1. Cut shavings from a matching piece of flooring . . .

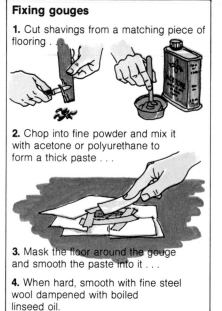

2. Chop into fine powder and mix it with acetone or polyurethane to form a thick paste . . .

3. Mask the floor around the gouge and smooth the paste into it . . .

4. When hard, smooth with fine steel wool dampened with boiled linseed oil.

Fixing curled edge

1. Warm the curled edge with an iron over aluminum foil (other warming methods in text) . . .

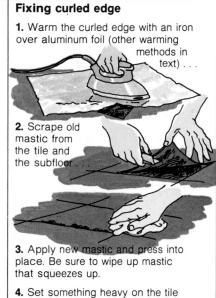

2. Scrape old mastic from the tile and the subfloor . . .

3. Apply new mastic and press into place. Be sure to wipe up mastic that squeezes up.

4. Set something heavy on the tile overnight.

Flattening bubbles

1. Heat the bubble and slit it down the middle. Check for dampness . . .

2. Clean under the edges of the slit and force some mastic in . . .

3. Wipe away excess mastic and weight down overnight.

---

good idea to test one of the above in an inconspicuous place on your floor first.

Some specific marks, such as those caused by heels, crayons or grease, can usually be removed by rubbing them with a clean rag dipped in bleach. If necessary, use fine steel wool also, but be careful about marring the floor finish.

For such choice items as paint or chewing gum stuck to the floor, first scrape up what you can with a table knife, then remove what remains with lighter fluid.

Sometimes, what appears to be a large stain is a buildup of wax that has become dirty and yellowed. This is best removed with a commercial wax remover. You can also try detergent with household ammonia added. In reapplying the wax, keep the coats thin and let the first dry thoroughly before applying the next.

Some people apply acrylic or polyurethane finishes to the floor in place

If you have a damaged floor and don't have a replacement piece around, see if you can find a match at flooring stores. If that fails, remove a piece from inside a closet or similar out-of-the-way location.

For deep scratches and gouges in unpatterned flooring, use a sharp knife to scrape the surface of a matching piece of tile. Chop or grind the scrapings into a fine powder and then mix with either acetone or polyurethane. It should be a thick, pasty concoction.

Now surround the gouge with strips of masking tape to protect the adjoining floor and smooth in the patching material with a putty knife or spatula.

When completely dry, remove the tape and smooth the patch with fine steel wool and some boiled linseed oil.

■ **Curled edges:** Before working on resilient floor tiles, you must soften them or they are likely to crack. The flooring is made flexible by the appli-

flooring. Heat the bubble with an iron or torch and then use a sharp knife to slit it down the middle. Inspect underneath for the cause of the problem. If the floor is damp there, you may want to wedge the slit open or even cut out some of the floor covering so that air can get at the damp patch. In any case, let it dry completely before continuing.

When ready, force some mastic under both edges of the bubble and press flat. Remove any excess and weight down overnight.

■ **Removing a broken tile:** If the hole or break in the tile is of any size, it's best just to remove and replace that tile. The trick here is not to damage the edges of any adjoining tiles.

Start by heating the entire tile with a torch or iron. If it gets quite soft, you may be able to slip your putty knife under one edge and work your way across. More likely, you will have to chisel and chip the tile out. For this,

Replacing a broken tile

1. Heat the tile, chisel and chip it out. Work from the center out when possible so as not to damage the edges of adjacent tiles . . .

2. Clean all the old mastic and debris from the subfloor. Patch any cracks or holes in the subfloor with plastic wood or spackling compound. Check that new tile will fit . . .

3. Spread mastic on the subfloor and set the tile. Flatten it evenly with, e.g., a rolling pin and wipe away any mastic that oozes up.

4. Weight down overnight.

---

make a cut in the middle and then, driving the putty knife with a hammer, chip your way to the outer edges.

After the square is removed, scrape off all the old adhesive from the floor so the new piece will lie flat and smooth. Inspect the subfloor carefully for any wide cracks or holes. Fill these with plastic wood or spackling compound before putting down the new tile or it will just break again.

When ready, see if the new tile fits exactly. If too large, sand it down by rubbing the edges back and forth over sandpaper laid on the floor.

Put down a thin layer of mastic on the floor with a special notched trowel available at hardware or flooring stores. Then carefully set the replacement tile in place. Do not slide it back and forth. Finally, use a rolling pin or bottle to flatten it evenly. Wipe up any adhesive that squeezes up between the joints.

■ **Holes in sheet flooring:** For this job you better have a matching piece of flooring. Otherwise, put down a contrasting piece and when guests gasp, call it a conversation piece.

Begin by taping the patching piece in place over the hole. It should be considerably larger than the hole and the patterns must line up exactly with each other.

Now, with a sharp utility or linoleum knife and a steel square to guide you, cut out a square around the hole. The cut must penetrate both layers of linoleum.

If the bottom layer hasn't been glued in place, it will simply lift out. Otherwise chip it out as you would a broken asphalt tile. Put the patch in place with adhesive.

Cover the patch with a piece of plywood before applying the weights so it is pressed evenly into place.

Be aware that despite your best efforts, this patch is going to be rather visible when completed unless you were lucky enough to be able to cut most of it carefully along the edges of patterns.

■ **Worn hallways, kitchens:** Because people tend to walk in repetitive patterns through the house, certain areas are worn faster than others. A good solution here if you have asphalt tiles is to replace a whole series of them along the worn area with colorful and contrasting pieces of tile.

If you have badly worn sheet flooring, the same effect could be gained by carefully removing a swath the width of two or three tiles and installing them.

Patching holes in sheet flooring

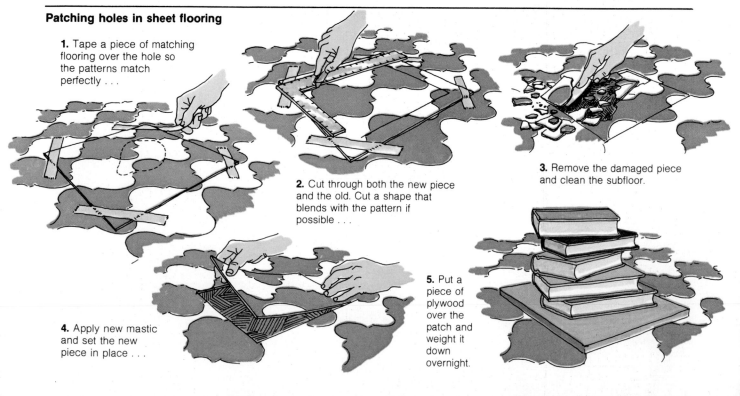

1. Tape a piece of matching flooring over the hole so the patterns match perfectly . . .

2. Cut through both the new piece and the old. Cut a shape that blends with the pattern if possible . . .

3. Remove the damaged piece and clean the subfloor.

4. Apply new mastic and set the new piece in place . . .

5. Put a piece of plywood over the patch and weight it down overnight.

Big Problems in Concrete and Stone

Making a success of repairs to concrete surfaces requires a good understanding of the mixing, bonding and curing process. A professional makes slight adjustments in the amount of aggregate, cement and water for each job. That fine tuning, however, comes only with experience and the more you get, the better you'll be. But for beginners, here are some of the basics. Keep them in mind and you will do good work even on your first attempt.

■ **Available types of concrete:** If you have a very large area to fill with concrete, the most efficient move is to have it delivered in a cement truck. This is also the most expensive method, and that much concrete is not usually required in repair work.

The second easiest method is to buy concrete already mixed and bagged. All you have to do is add water and mix. This, too, is relatively expensive but efficient for small jobs.

Finally, you can mix your own. If you have a lot to do, rent a mixer. Otherwise, you can mix all the necessary batches in your wheelbarrow.

The recipe for concrete calls for portland cement, fine aggregate (sand) and coarse aggregate (¾-inch gravel). For finer work, such as laying bricks or filling cracks, use masonry cement and fine sand only.

Concrete is mixed according to volume, not weight. Thus the standard combination of 1-2-3 means 1 part cement, 2 parts sand and 3 parts gravel. Most homeowners measure by the shovelful. However, a more precise way is to make a box that holds a cubic foot. Since one sack of cement holds a cubic foot also, you can go from there.

Cement from the bag should pour easily. Break any lumps up between your fingers. If you can't, screen them out.

Sand should also be screened if you dig your own from along stream beds, to keep out debris. Never take sand from the seashore because the salts therein will prevent the concrete from curing properly.

When mixing in a wheelbarrow, put all the dry elements in first and mix with shovel or hoe until you attain an even color. Then add water slowly and continue to mix. The final mix should be neither soupy nor crumbly. It should be smooth and plastic to work with.

■ **Basic tools:** Concrete work, even just repairs, needs a few special tools to do the job right.

First is a trowel to place the mortar. Use the trowel also to vigorously work concrete after it's in place so it will settle without any air bubbles.

A 4-foot carpenter's level is needed to check your work as you go, particularly when doing walls. A long, straight 2 by 4, called a strikeoff board, is used to scrape off any excess concrete. A wood float levels the surface and gives it a rough finish; a steel finishing trowel gives the concrete a smooth finish.

■ **Curing:** Concrete should be applied to damp surfaces. This keeps the old surface from too quickly drawing out the water in the new mix. Even so, that water is going to be lost through a combination of drawing out and evaporation. But it must go slowly and steadily so the concrete will set, or

Repairing hairline cracks

1. Brush out all loose material and caulk (see p. 14) . . .

2. Smooth off the excess.

Repairing cracks or holes

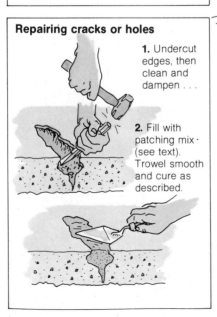

1. Undercut edges, then clean and dampen . . .

2. Fill with patching mix (see text). Trowel smooth and cure as described.

Replacing broken concrete

1. Break out the damaged area to an edge, an expansion joint or a solid unbroken area . . .

2. Undercut any edge of solid concrete . . .

3. Clean thoroughly of loose material. Build a form if necessary and dampen . . .

4. Fill with concrete mix; finish and cure as described in the text.

cure, properly. In normal weather — that is, neither near freezing nor extremely hot — allow concrete 7 days to cure. During this time keep it covered with polyethelene film or damp burlap bags.

■ **Large cracks and holes:** With a heavy hammer and cold chisel, and wearing goggles to protect your eyes, chip away a groove beneath the edge of the crack or hole. This gives the patch a ledge to lock into. Clean the hole and then dampen, but do not leave small pools of water. Fill it with a ready-mix concrete or make your own from 1 part portland cement, 2 parts sand and 3 parts gravel not larger than ¾ inch. Cure for 7 days.

■ **Cracked floor:** For cracks that are not hairline but not large either, and in areas of heavy traffic, make the repairs with your own mix. First widen the crack by undercutting it, clean it completely and then dampen it. Make a creamy mix of 1 part masonry cement and 3 parts fine sand. Work this into the crack and smooth off, leaving the surface about ⅛ inch higher than the floor to allow for shrinkage. After firming up overnight, sand the patch

smooth with coarse sandpaper until it's flush with the floor. Keep it damp for a week to cure.

■ **Concrete dusting:** This is a fine powder that keeps recurring on some concrete floors and makes it impossible to keep them clean. The best method to correct this is to clean and dry the floor thoroughly, then give it two coats of commercial concrete sealer.

You can also make your own solution from 1 part sodium silicate and 3 parts water. Give the floor three coats of this.

■ **Repairing flagstone:** A common problem connected with flagstone floors and walks is loose or crumbling mortar in the joints. To correct this, use a cape chisel or small cold chisel to chip out the loose and cracked mortar. Vacuum out all dust and debris.

Mix 1 part masonry cement and 3 parts fine sand into a creamy paste, and work into the joints. Smooth it down to match the other joints and wipe off any material that spilled onto the flagstones.

Flagstone is relatively easily split or chipped. When this happens, clean the

pieces, coat each matching surface with epoxy resin, and fit them together. If any of the resin gets onto the surface, wipe it clean immediately. Weight down the stone until the joint is dry.

If the stone itself is broken in half, remove it and glue together with epoxy resin. Before replacing it, make sure the base is level so it will not break again.

Treat a loose flagstone in much the same manner. Chisel it out and clean thoroughly. When replaced, fill the bonding space around it with a dry mix of 1 part masonry cement and 3 parts fine sand. Dampen this joint with a fine spray three times at 10 minute intervals to allow the water time for full penetration. Add more mix as it settles.

■ **Decayed stone:** This is not a common problem but if it should happen and you can't find a replacement stone, make your own.

Mix a batch of 1 part portland cement, 2 parts sand and 5 parts pea gravel or crushed stone.

Add mortar coloring to a test batch and let dry to compare with the existing stonework before completing your own stone clone.

Resetting a loose stone

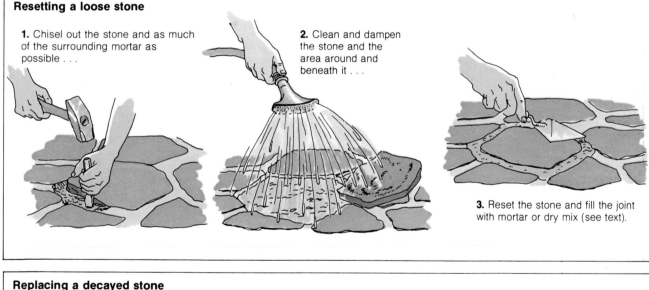

1. Chisel out the stone and as much of the surrounding mortar as possible . . .

2. Clean and dampen the stone and the area around and beneath it . . .

3. Reset the stone and fill the joint with mortar or dry mix (see text).

Replacing a decayed stone

1. Chip as much of the crumbled stone away as you can . . .

2. Make small test batches of concrete mix and mortar color to match the color of the existing stone . . .

3. Fill the cavity with the colored concrete and sculpt the surface to match the other stones as it is setting.

Repairing Ceramic, Plastic or Metal Tiles

Ceramic and plastic tiles are widely used on both floors and walls. Repairs are basically the same for all three types, regardless of their location.

■ **Ceramic tile:** Cutting these is easier than it appears. It just takes careful work. If you are doing a large area where many tiles will have to be cut, rent a tile cutter from the store where you bought the tile. Or, with the aid of a glass cutting tool, you can do the cutting.

Use a straight edge to guide you as you score the tile, once and firmly, then snap it over a length of dowel placed on the floor or over another tile's edge held between your knees.

To fit around pipes, split the tile and then mark out half the pipe size on each piece. Use the glass cutter to score the curve and then score a cross-hatch pattern inside the curve. Break this out piece by piece with pliers or tile nippers.

■ **Cracks between tiles:** If the old grout is coming loose, chisel it all out. Dampen the edges with water and then work in a new bead of prepared grout available at any hardware store. Use the end of a toothbrush or a roundheaded clothespin to smooth the grout. Quick repair work is important if the tile is in the bathroom where crumbling grout can easily allow water to penetrate behind tiles.

■ **Broken tile:** Break the tile more with a hammer and then chip out all pieces with a cold chisel or putty knife. Carefully remove all grout from edges of the adjoining pieces. Scrape off all the old adhesive from the floor or wall so

the replacement piece will lie flat. Coat the back of the tile with a silicone adhesive and press it firmly into the opening. Remove any of the glue that squeezes out around the edges. Keep the tile centered by slipping pieces of toothpicks or cardboard around the edges until it dries 24 hours later. Dampen the joints and fill with a commercial grout. Wipe up any mess you made and then round out the grout with a toothbrush handle or round clothespin head.

■ **Repairing broken soap dish:** If the extending part of a ceramic dish broke off, it's possible to repair it. Make sure both exposed edges are dry and then coat them with epoxy resin. Press firmly together, wipe off any excess, and then hold in place with several strips of tape.

If the whole piece must be replaced, proceed as you would for a broken tile. Tape it in place to hold it while the glue dries.

■ **Plastic tiles:** If the grout has come loose, work it all out with a nail and then replace with a special plastic adhesive available in hardware stores. If this mastic sticks to the face of the tiles, a special solvent for removing it is also available in hardware stores.

To cut plastic tiles, use a fine-toothed cross-cut blade for straight lines and a coping saw for curves.

To replace a plastic tile, remove it as you would ceramic tile and put in the replacement with a plastic tile adhesive.

■ **Metal tiles:** These are repaired and replaced just as ceramic tiles. However, resist any temptations you might have to install them in a bathroom for they do not easily survive moisture.

Metal tiles are best cut with a hacksaw for straight lines and a pair of tin snips for curves.

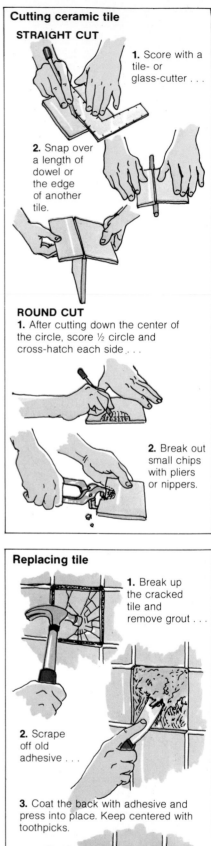

Cutting ceramic tile
STRAIGHT CUT

1. Score with a tile- or glass-cutter . . .

2. Snap over a length of dowel or the edge of another tile.

ROUND CUT

1. After cutting down the center of the circle, score ½ circle and cross-hatch each side . . .

2. Break out small chips with pliers or nippers.

Replacing tile

1. Break up the cracked tile and remove grout . . .

2. Scrape off old adhesive . . .

3. Coat the back with adhesive and press into place. Keep centered with toothpicks.

4. Next day, dampen joints and grout.

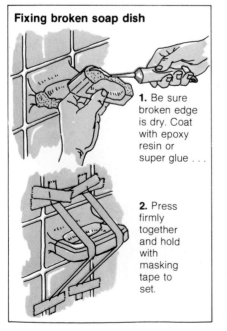

Fixing broken soap dish

1. Be sure broken edge is dry. Coat with epoxy resin or super glue . . .

2. Press firmly together and hold with masking tape to set.

Replacing grout

1. Chisel out old grout, then clean and dampen the joint . . .

2. Put in new grout, smooth and clean up.

Tightening Loose Banisters

Technically speaking, banister is a catch-all word for all the elements of a handrail illustrated here. One or more elements sometimes work loose.

■ **Loose handrail:** If the rail is separating from the baluster, the best solution is to pull it down tight again. Do this by drilling up at a 45 degree angle through the baluster into the rail. Squirt some white wood glue between the rail and baluster, then cinch them tightly together with a long wood screw. Countersink it and cover the hole with matching putty stick.

Alternatively, you can tighten the rail by driving a small glue-coated wedge between it and the baluster. Saw off any excess flush with the baluster.

■ **Loose baluster:** These uprights are either simply nailed to the top of the treads or they are notched and set into the treads. In the first case, they can be tightened with a long wood screw as at the top in the baluster. Drill at an angle and cinch the baluster to the tread.

Nails can also be used but they are not as effective. If you insist, drill pilot holes slightly smaller than the galvanized finishing nails you will use, to prevent splitting the wood.

If the balusters are fitted into slots, first remove the trim holding them there along the outer edge of the treads. Drill through the baluster and into the edge of the tread. Put white glue around the notch before tightening down with a screw.

■ **Loose newel post:** This post supports the base of the stairs and takes a beating. If it is only slightly loose, drill at an angle along the base

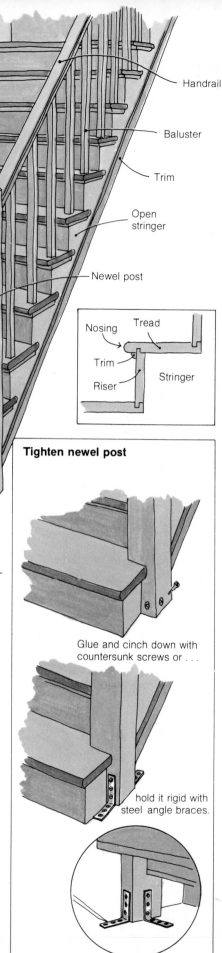

and run screws into the floor on four sides of the post. Before you tighten them, however, squirt some white glue between the post and the floor. Countersink the screws and hide with putty stick.

If this is not sufficient to stabilize the post, and it is possible to get under the stairs, drill through the stringer into the newel post and cinch it down with two lag screws.

Tighten newel post

Glue and cinch down with countersunk screws or . . .

hold it rigid with steel angle braces.

If possible put the braces out of sight beneath the stairs

Tighten handrail

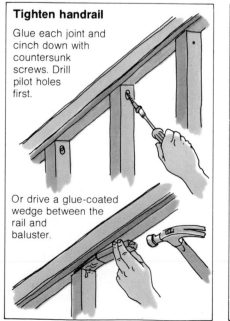

Glue each joint and cinch down with countersunk screws. Drill pilot holes first.

Or drive a glue-coated wedge between the rail and baluster.

Tighten baluster

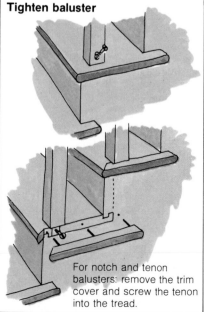

For notch and tenon balusters: remove the trim cover and screw the tenon into the tread.

Repairing Loose or Squeaky Stairs From Above

Squeaky stairs really aren't all that bad. You can tell when people are moving up and down, and this could be useful. Ancient Japanese rulers used to surround their sleeping quarters with specially designed porches and stairs that creaked loud warnings if anyone set foot on them.

But if you're still intent on making repairs, start by having a look to see how your particular stairs are put together. Some treads and risers are fitted together with simple butt joints. Other, better made stairs are put together with dado joints. You can check quickly by carefully prying off the narrow strip of molding that fits just under the nose of the tread.

■ **Lubricating stairs:** Squeaks are caused by two pieces rubbing against each other, so treat them just as you would a squeak in your car. Locate the problem and then use a small tube of graphite powder to shoot some lubrication in there. Talcum powder will also work for awhile. You might have to repeat the process a few times until the powder works its way in.

■ **Tightening loose treads:** Because of warps or settling of the house, the edge of the tread sometimes separates slightly from the riser. This can be tightened down by driving 4 to 6 finishing nails at an angle through the tread into the top edge of the riser. Narrow screws would hold even better. Make sure you are far enough back from the nose of the tread to hit the riser. Remove the molding underneath if necessary to check.

If the stairs are hardwood, it is better to drill pilot holes slightly smaller than the finishing nails, to minimize wood-splitting or bent-nail problems. Use a nail set to countersink the nails and hide the holes with matching putty stick. The nails should be cement-coated or screw-nails for better gripping power.

However, if you are going to drill pilot holes, you might as well put in wood screws for maximum strength. Three or four screws across the tread, countersunk and hidden with putty stick, should eliminate the squeak.

It's a good idea to have someone standing on the tread while you are doing this work, to make sure the tread and riser are pressed firmly together.

■ **Using wedges:** Squeaks can also be eliminated by driving small wedges between the riser and tread.

After locating the squeak, remove the molding under the nose of that

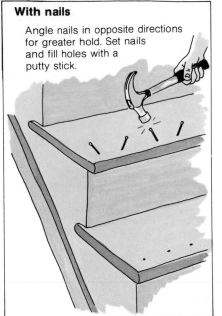

With nails

Angle nails in opposite directions for greater hold. Set nails and fill holes with a putty stick.

With screws

Drill pilot and counter-sink holes. Cinch screws down tightly and fill holes with a putty stick.

With wedges

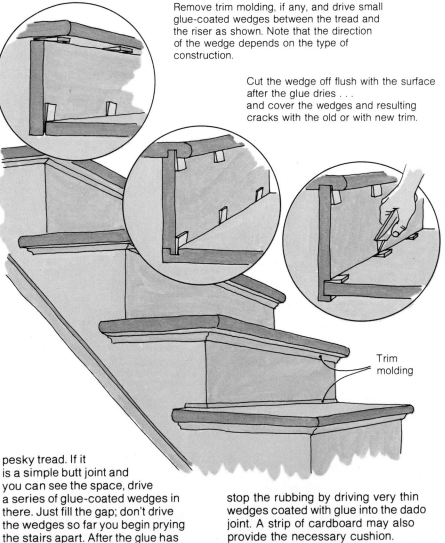

Remove trim molding, if any, and drive small glue-coated wedges between the tread and the riser as shown. Note that the direction of the wedge depends on the type of construction.

Cut the wedge off flush with the surface after the glue dries . . . and cover the wedges and resulting cracks with the old or with new trim.

Trim molding

pesky tread. If it is a simple butt joint and you can see the space, drive a series of glue-coated wedges in there. Just fill the gap; don't drive the wedges so far you begin prying the stairs apart. After the glue has dried, trim off the excess wood on the wedges with a fine-toothed cross-cut saw and replace the molding.

If the stairs are dadoed together,

stop the rubbing by driving very thin wedges coated with glue into the dado joint. A strip of cardboard may also provide the necessary cushion.

In some cases, the squeak is at the rear of the tread where it meets the riser. Again, insert glue-coated wedges and trim them off flush with the tread.

Repairing Loose or Squeaky Stairs From Underneath

If at all possible, make the repairs on your stairs from underneath. For one thing, heavier bracing can be done and any mistakes you might make are out of sight.

Here again it is useful to have someone on the stairs while you work, not only to force together any separations but to make sure you fix the right step.

■ **Warped tread:** If treads and risers are joined by a butt joint and are warped apart, several small wedges provide a quick solution.

Coat the wedges with glue and tap them carefully into the gap between the top of the riser and the tread. Space them about 4 to 8 inches apart. Be careful not to drive them so far that you widen the gap or knock off the molding on the other side.

Two or three shelf brackets are also efficient and easily installed as step supports from underneath. With the problem tread weighted down, come in one-third of the width of the step on each side and install the metal angle supports. Drill pilot holes for screws short enough not to go right through the tread or riser.

To make sure you do not drill too far, measure the thickness of the wood used in the steps. Reduce this measurement by $\frac{3}{16}$ inch and mark that length on the end of your drill with a piece of tape. Do not exceed that mark when drilling.

■ **Block support:** When dealing with several steps that squeak between the top of a riser and a tread, counterattack with wood blocks. With the tread unweighted, glue and screw a length of 2 by 4 or 2 by 2 across the back of each riser. The block should be forced up tight against the tread to keep it from moving when weighted down.

■ **Additional support:** When it seems your whole stairway sags and creaks when you walk on it, the best solution is to install a new central support underneath. If the underside of the stairs is sealed with plaster or drywall, remove it. If that sounds like a slightly awesome task, it is. But when you're done, instead of just recovering the back of the stairs, consider instead enclosing the entire space to make a closet storage room.

When the underside of the stairs is ready, run a 2 by 6 board on edge down the middle. The top end should be lag-screwed to a wall stud and the bottom end cut to fit flush on the floor. Now, from this middle support beam,

extend lengths of 1 by 6 up to fit tightly under each tread. These upright pieces should be glued and screwed to the support where they fit under each tread.

Additional supports can be run below each side of the steps if necessary.

While under there, check all the wedges that hold the steps firmly into the stringers down each side. Give them all a tap to tighten them slightly.

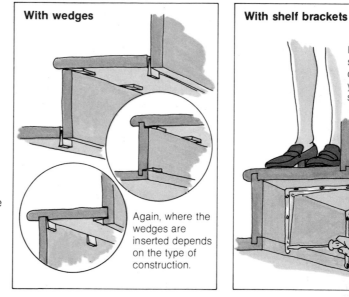

With wedges

Again, where the wedges are inserted depends on the type of construction.

With shelf brackets

If possible have someone stand on the tread as you install the shelf brackets.

With blocks

Force a glue-coated block tight against the tread and screw to the riser.

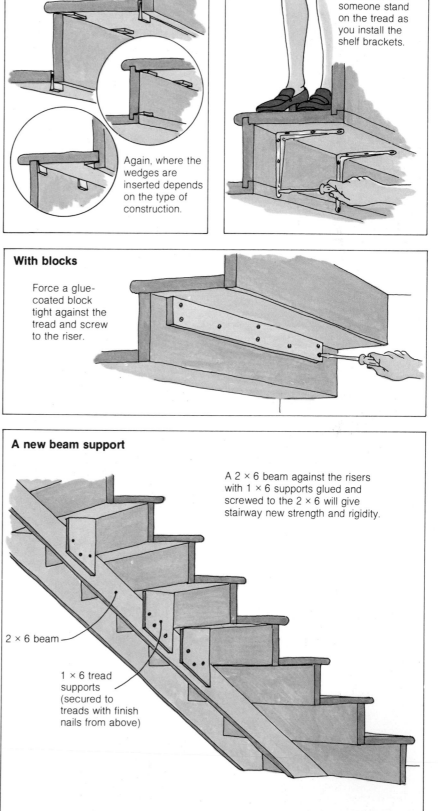

A new beam support

A 2 × 6 beam against the risers with 1 × 6 supports glued and screwed to the 2 × 6 will give stairway new strength and rigidity.

2 × 6 beam

1 × 6 tread supports (secured to treads with finish nails from above)

Repairing Treads and Risers

Treads may become deeply worn and the risers badly scarred. Either may require their removal for repair. In most cases the treads and risers can just be turned over and used again. If parts of the steps are split or broken in the removal process, save all the pieces to provide a pattern for the new element.

Removing parts of steps is a fairly ambitious project that requires patience and careful attention to detail.

The difficulty of your job will be determined by whether the stringers are open or closed. In the first instance, the stringers are cut sawtooth fashion and the steps are fastened directly to these edges.

In the closed style, the steps (risers and treads) are fitted into grooves cut in the side of the stringers. They are held in place by glue and wedges.

Closed stringers are more difficult to work on and generally require you to work from beneath the stairs. If your problems are further compounded because the back of the stairs is enclosed and you don't want to rip it out, call in a qualified carpenter. Repairs made from above on such stairs require considerable experience and expertise.

■ **Repairs from above:** In a case of an open stringer, you first remove the one or two balusters on the offending tread.

If the base of the baluster is just toenailed to the tread, pry the baluster up slightly and slip a backsaw under there to cut the nails. When free, twist the baluster back and forth a little. The top is normally just glued into the handrail and should come loose quite readily.

If the tread and balusters are notched and fitted together, you will first have to pry off the molding along the outer edge of the tread. The baluster may be nailed into the notch, in which case you must tap it loose enough to slip a hacksaw blade in there to cut the nail flush with the tread. Twist and remove the baluster from the handrail.

Now, carefully pry loose the molding beneath the nose of the troublesome tread. With a crowbar or straight-clawed hammer, pry up the front edge of the tread enough to get a hacksaw

Repairing treads and riser:

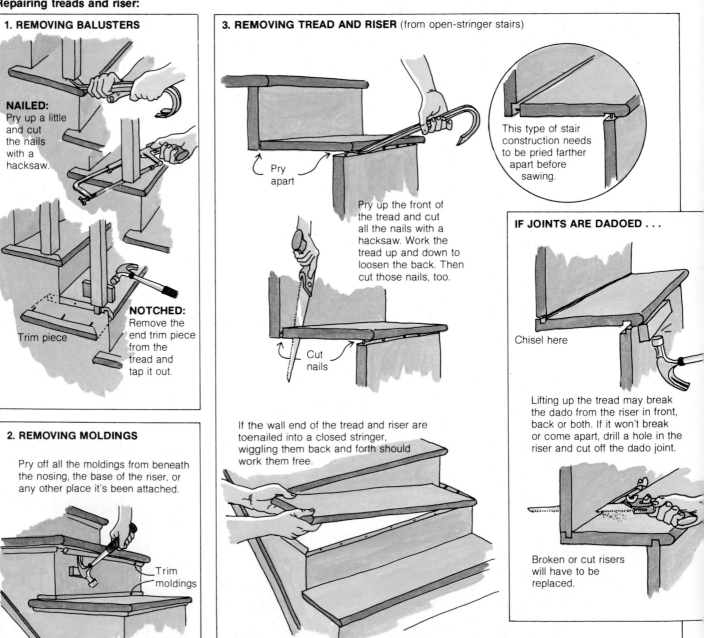

1. REMOVING BALUSTERS

NAILED: Pry up a little and cut the nails with a hacksaw.

NOTCHED: Remove the end trim piece from the tread and tap it out.

Trim piece

2. REMOVING MOLDINGS

Pry off all the moldings from beneath the nosing, the base of the riser, or any other place it's been attached.

Trim moldings

3. REMOVING TREAD AND RISER (from open-stringer stairs)

Pry apart

Pry up the front of the tread and cut all the nails with a hacksaw. Work the tread up and down to loosen the back. Then cut those nails, too.

Cut nails

This type of stair construction needs to be pried farther apart before sawing.

If the wall end of the tread and riser are toenailed into a closed stringer, wiggling them back and forth should work them free.

IF JOINTS ARE DADOED . . .

Chisel here

Lifting up the tread may break the dado from the riser in front, back or both. If it won't break or come apart, drill a hole in the riser and cut off the dado joint.

Broken or cut risers will have to be replaced.

or utility saw in there to cut the nails.

With the front end loose, carefully work the tread up and down to loosen it at the back from the bottom of the riser. If the steps are joined with butt joints, you should be able to slip a hacksaw blade through there to cut the nails driven from the back of the riser into the edge of the tread.

At this point you can see that a considerable number of nails have to be cut. If you are replacing several steps, it would save you time and frustration to rent a reciprocating saw with a utility hacksaw blade.

One end of the tread may be toe-nailed into a closed stringer along the wall. Wiggling the board should free it, however.

Well-made steps are joined with dado cuts. Should this be the case with your steps and you can't break the riser free, you may be able to chisel off the edge of the riser where it fits into the tread.

An alterntive method is to drill a hole in the riser flush with the back of the tread. Use a keyhole saw to cut across the riser and free the tread. That riser will then have to be replaced.

At this point, you have the tread and riser out. Turn the worn tread over and with a router, or more laboriously, a chisel, cut matching grooves on the other side.

Because there are so many slight variations in the way stairs are built, it is difficult to tell you exactly what cuts are required here. Essentially, you must use the old pieces as a model. If reversing the old tread won't work because of interfering notches, replace it.

When you've made the necessary angled cuts and bevels, fit the pieces back into place. The riser should be checked with a level. If necessary, use wedges or plane it to make it even.

Use finishing nails driven at an angle to put the front edge of the tread in place with the riser. From behind, drill pilot holes and screw the bottom of the new riser to the back of the new tread. Wood blocks screwed and glued along the back edges will give additional support.

■ **Repairs from below:** If your stairs have closed stringers where the steps are dadoed in between the stringers, most of the work must be done from beneath the stairs.

First remove any molding that is beneath the nose of the tread. Now, from behind, use a crowbar to pry the riser and tread apart enough to cut the nails with a hacksaw. Remove any wedges from the dado cuts on the stringers.

If the tread and riser are not jointed, pry apart the back of the tread and bottom of the riser, and cut those nails. If jointed, the easiest solution is to cut across the riser. From the front and using a block of wood to protect the tread, remove the riser by driving it back and out.

Now carefully cut the replacement pieces and fit them in place. A partially driven nail from the bottom of the riser into the back of the tread will hold the steps in place while you drive the wedges to lock them in place. Coat both surfaces with white glue before driving the wedges home.

Drill pilot holes and put 3 screws across the bottom of the riser into the back edge of the tread. Use finishing nails driven at an angle to hold the front edge of the tread to the next riser. If you're using hardwood, better drill pilot holes slightly smaller than the nails to prevent splitting.

■ **Loose stringer:** Because of settling and just old age in some cases, the stringer and steps may separate slightly.

With open stringers, place a protective length of 2 by 6 or 2 by 8 and then use a 10-pound maul to drive the entire stairway against the wall. Afterwards, tighten up any loose wedges or steps from underneath.

An alternative method to tighten the stairway is to drive wedges between the wall and the stringer. Put the wedges along the studs to keep from buckling the wall. Do not let the gap exceed ½ inch between the wall and stringer.

You can provide additional support for the stringer by drilling and putting in ½-inch by 5-inch lag screws through the stringers into the wall studs.

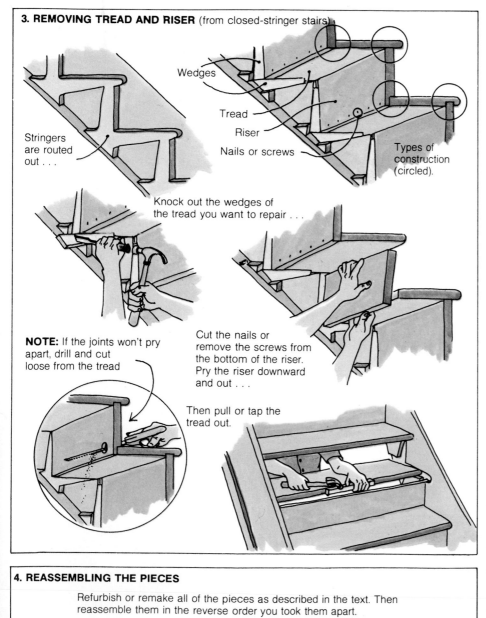

3. REMOVING TREAD AND RISER (from closed-stringer stairs)

Wedges

Tread

Riser

Nails or screws

Stringers are routed out . . .

Types of construction (circled).

Knock out the wedges of the tread you want to repair . . .

NOTE: If the joints won't pry apart, drill and cut loose from the tread

Cut the nails or remove the screws from the bottom of the riser. Pry the riser downward and out . . .

Then pull or tap the tread out.

4. REASSEMBLING THE PIECES

Refurbish or remake all of the pieces as described in the text. Then reassemble them in the reverse order you took them apart.

Electrical Systems

How to repair wiring, switches, outlets, lamps, ceiling fixtures, fluorescent units and door bells. How to understand and reset circuit breakers, and change fuses.

Electrical Safety

Electricians are fond of saying there are no careless electricians; just dead ones.

Don't let that maxim scare you out of doing your own electrical repairs. But keep it in mind when you are in a hurry and tending to get careless. Start by following these basic rules.

1. Before working on anything, from a fuse box to a light switch, make sure the power is off.

2. Learn how to turn off all power to the house and selected areas through the service box. Know whether you must push a handle down, remove a fuse block or push a breaker switch to "off."

3. When working with a service box, never stand on a damp floor. It's a good practice to keep two or three 2 by 4 boards on the floor near the box to stand on even when just changing a fuse.

4. Wear rubber gloves when working in the service box. A slip of a bare finger could put you in contact with a bare and "hot" wire, and with possibly fatal consequences.

5. Make sure the service box is securely screwed to the wall. Its unexpected movement could cause you to slip and touch a hot wire.

6. In the house, always grasp the plug and not the cord when disconnecting an appliance. Pulling on the cord may eventually expose wires at the edge of the plug and touching those could give you a very severe shock.

7. If you have small children in the house, keep receptacles covered with masking tape, or better, install wall plates with spring-loaded flaps that cover the holes.

8. Buy an inexpensive voltage tester and keep it in a handy place. It will quickly tell you if the power is on or off where you are working.

9. If an appliance gives you a shock or a spark pops while you're putting a plug into an outlet, make the repairs immediately before something more serious happens.

10. Think before you act.

Pulling on the cord, instead of the plug, will damage the cord.

When the floor is damp, always stand on a rubber mat or dry boards when doing any electrical work.

Circuit Breakers and Fuses

Electricity comes into your house in a manner similar to water. Just as water is pumped from a reservoir through pipes to your house, electricity is pushed through wires by a generator.

Once in the house, hot wires carry the electricity to each switch or outlet, just as water under pressure arrives at faucets.

The size of the wires carrying electricity is important, just as with water pipes. If the wires are too small to allow swift passage of the current being pushed through, they will grow hot and break. This open circuit diverts the flow, sometimes with dangerous consequences.

In working with electricity you will constantly come across certain terms. Familiarize yourself with these:

—Volts are the amount of "pressure" required to push electricity through your house. At an outlet, the usual voltage is 120 but it can range from 110 to 126.

—Amps, or more properly, amperes, are the measure of the volume of current flowing through the wire. It is actually the number of electrons passing through the wire and here's something for trivia enthusiasts: 1 amp represents 6,280,000,000,000,000,000 (that's

a billion billion) electrons passing a given point in a second.

—Watts tell you how fast an appliance or bulb uses up electricity. You find the amount of watts with this formula: volts × amps = watts (120 volts × 5 amps = 600 watts). Conversely, to find how much current is needed when you know the wattage, use this formula: watts ÷ volts = amps. Thus, if you have a space heater that uses 1200 watts, it requires 10 amps (1200 watts ÷ 120 volts = 10 amps).

—Ohms are the measure of resistance in wires. As noted, if there are too many volts (pressure) in a small wire, that can cause overheating and breaking. Some wires, however, are specially designed to resist and heat up — light bulbs, toasters and heaters. These items require more electricity than nonheating devices.

■ Circuit breakers and fuse panels: These panels are important safety devices in a house. If there is an overload or open circuit, the breaker switch trips or the fuse blows. The problem generally is an overload on that circuit. Take some of the load off before you replace the fuse or flip the switch back on.

There are two main types of service panels; circuit breaker switches and fuse boxes. In the first case, you can clearly see where the problem lies by the thrown switch. Make sure all lights

and appliances on that circuit are off and throw it back on.

In fuse boxes, you will see either a series of round glass-topped fuses or cartridge fuses, or both. Cartridge fuses are often in the back of plastic boxes in the panel. Pulling out the main fuse block will shut off all power to the house if there is not an off-on handle to do so.

Looking at the glass-topped fuses will tell you what kind of an electrical problem you're having. If the window is blackened, the fuse was blown suddenly by a short circuit. If the window is clear and the metal strip burned in half, it was done by an overload.

There is nothing visible on a cartridge fuse to tell you if it is good or bad. You can check by exchanging a suspect cartridge fuse with a known good one after shutting off the power. Or use a continuity tester to touch each end and see if the test bulb lights.

See the illustrations for more about the different types of fuses.

■ Changing fuses: It's a routine function that requires routine precautions: don't change fuses with wet or sweaty hands; don't do it while standing on a wet floor; wear a rubber glove for extra safety; use fuse pullers on cartridges.

And always replace a fuse with one of the same amperage. If a 20 amp

---

Types of fuses

PLUG FUSE: A metal strip that shows through the glass top completes the circuit. A break in the strip indicates overload; blackened glass usually indicates a short circuit.

DUAL ELEMENT FUSE: The metal strip is spring-loaded to allow a temporary overload—as when the motor in a washer or power saw starts.

CARTRIDGE FUSES: These give no indication when they have blown—you must replace them or use a circuit tester to find out. The flat-end type goes up to 60 amps. Over 60 amps they have knife-edge contacts.

Types of circuit breakers

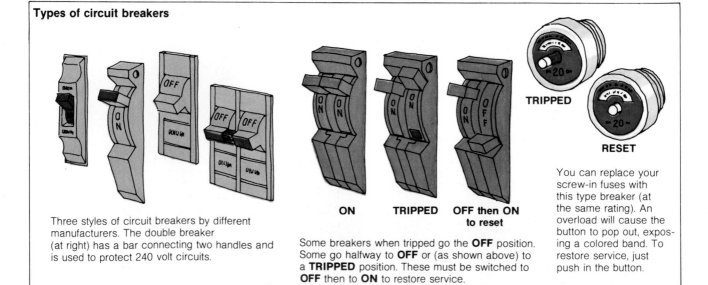

Three styles of circuit breakers by different manufacturers. The double breaker (at right) has a bar connecting two handles and is used to protect 240 volt circuits.

ON   **TRIPPED**   **OFF then ON to reset**

Some breakers when tripped go the **OFF** position. Some go halfway to **OFF** or (as shown above) to a **TRIPPED** position. These must be switched to **OFF** then to **ON** to restore service.

TRIPPED

RESET

You can replace your screw-in fuses with this type breaker (at the same rating). An overload will cause the button to pop out, exposing a colored band. To restore service, just push in the button.

KILOWATT HOURS

Meters register KILOWATT HOURS and run continuously from when they're installed. To tell how much is used in a month, take a reading at the first of the month, another at the end and subtract the first from the second. Some have a direct read-out as at the left. Most have dials as at the right. Read the lower of the numbers the needle is between. If the needle

KILOWATT HOURS

appears to be directly on a number, look at the next dial to the right. If that needle has not yet reached zero, the other needle has not yet reached the number.

Both of the meters shown above have the same reading, 54698.

---

have a ground wire system according to the National Electric Code.

If you are in doubt about your house, shut off power along one circuit of wall outlets. Unscrew the plate and look at the receptacle. If the house is ground wired, there will be 3 wires leading into the outlet: hot black, neutral white and a bare ground wire in the middle usually attached to a green terminal on the receptacle.

■ **Adapter plugs:** If your house is properly ground wired but the outlets do not have 3 prong openings, use an adapter for 3 prong plugs. This way, if a short occurs in the appliance you are handling, that loose electricity will be carried away through the ground wire, not you.

The adapters come with a small pigtail wire that must be clinched under the center screw on the outlet cover to be effective.

■ **Ground fault interrupter:** More commonly known as a GFI, this device can prevent fatal shocks. Many of your kitchen appliances have only 2-prong plugs and thus are not grounded. A short in that appliance could give you a severe shock. The GFI, which can be plugged into an outlet or wired to your breaker panel, senses a short in a split second and trips the breaker switch. You receive only a minor sting. Consider it a warning.

---

fuse blows, don't replace it with a 30 amp one so it won't happen again. That's like cementing down a safety valve — worse things can happen.

Round fuses simply unscrew. Touch only the glass while doing this and make sure the power is off first.

With cartridge fuses, pull down the lever to shut off power and open the box. If the fuses are in the back of the plastic box, pull it out and replace the bad one.

If the cartridge fuses are in brass holders and facing you, use fuse pullers to remove. Be sure the power is off before changing fuses with bare fingers.

■ **Grounded wiring and you:** Electrical work around the house normally involves you with three wires. The black one inside a cord or cable carries the electricity in and is hot.

The white one is neutral and does not carry electricity unless the switch is on. It then completes the circuit and allows the current to flow. Never connect a black and a white wire.

In most residential housing there is a third, or ground wire hooked into a switch or outlet. The exception here is in older houses or when the wires are housed in a metal sheath that serves as the ground wire.

The purpose of a ground wire is to safely carry away any leaking current. The ground wire connects back to the fuse or breaker panel which in turn connects to a pipe set in the ground, usually a water pipe.

■ **Checking your system:** If all the house outlets have 3-prong openings, that indicates they are already ground wired.

Any house wired after 1962 has to

Checking grounds

You can be pretty sure an outlet is grounded if, in addition to a black and a white wire, there is a bare copper wire attached to a green terminal on the receptacle (**A**); to a screw on the metal box of a two-prong receptacle (**B**); or if metal-armored cable is attached to the box with a clamp (**C**). See text.

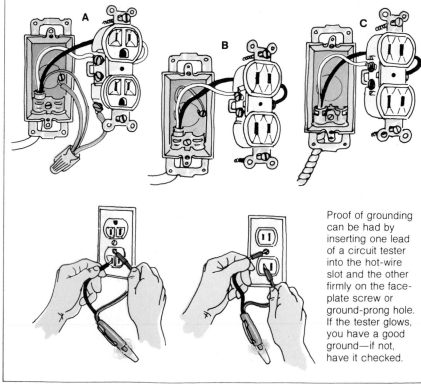

Proof of grounding can be had by inserting one lead of a circuit tester into the hot-wire slot and the other firmly on the face-plate screw or ground-prong hole. If the tester glows, you have a good ground—if not, have it checked.

Grounding adapters

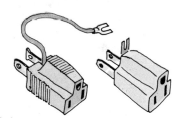

A three-prong plug can be used in a two-prong outlet with one of these adapters. Be sure the green grounding lug is attached securely to the face-plate screw and that the mounting yoke or receptacle box is properly grounded.

Ground fault interrupter

A GFI receptacle can be wired in to replace an existing outlet in the kitchen, bathroom, etc.

There are also portable GFIs that plug into any 3-prong outlet.

Wiring Repairs

Power arrives in most homes today in a 3-wire system that brings in between 14,000 to 24,000 watts. Exceptions to this are smaller homes built a few years after World War II that had only a 2-wire system bringing in less than 4,000 watts. This is totally inadequate by today's standards.

The service entrance wires run through the meter and into the circuit breaker panel or fuse box. One of the wires is white and neutral while the other two are black and hot. The black wires each carry 120 volts for most of the electricity you need in the house. However, inside the panel these wires are also joined at one place to raise the power to 240 volts for such heavy-demand appliances as stoves, heaters, dryers and air conditioners.

Outlets carrying 240 volts are purposely made different from the 120 volt outlets to prevent you plugging into them by mistake. These 240 volt outlets have three slots, and one of the slots may be L-shaped. These 3-slot outlets are not to be confused with the 2-slot plus 1-hole outlet for grounded plugs.

Power is distributed through the house by circuits. One series of circuits is called general and handles living rooms, bedrooms and bathrooms. It is usually protected with a 20 amp fuse or breaker. Special circuits handle areas of heavier electrical demand such as kitchens, laundry rooms and workshops. When wired properly they are covered under 30 amp devices and larger wires.

■ **Splicing, soldering:** As the illustration on page 63 shows, the smaller the wire the larger its identification number. The smaller the wire, the greater the resistance. Therefore, it's important to use the right wire for the right job.

Wire sizes 14 and 12 are standard

Soldered or tap splice

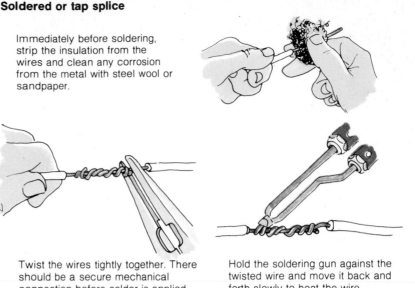

Immediately before soldering, strip the insulation from the wires and clean any corrosion from the metal with steel wool or sandpaper.

Twist the wires tightly together. There should be a secure mechanical connection before solder is applied.

Hold the soldering gun against the twisted wire and move it back and forth slowly to heat the wire.

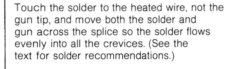

Touch the solder to the heated wire, not the gun tip, and move both the solder and gun across the splice so the solder flows evenly into all the crevices. (See the text for solder recommendations.)

Let the splice cool thoroughly before moving it. Wrap with electrical tape, overlapping one half on each turn. Go back and forth until the tape is as thick as the original insulation.

for house wiring on general circuits. Where more electricity is needed on the special circuits for such things as ranges and dishwashers, No. 10 wire is used. On circuits wired for 240 volts, No. 8 and No. 6 wire are standard.

House wiring is most widely done with plastic-sheathed cable that carries the black hot wire, white neutral and a paper-coated ground.

In removing this outer sheath, use a pocket or paring knife to slit through the slight indentations to expose the individual wires. Be careful not to cut the individual wire insulation.

To expose the tips of the wire for splicing or connecting, use a knife or

■ **Aluminum wire hazards:** More than 2 million homes have been wired with pure aluminum wire in an attempt to beat the rising cost of copper. It can be dangerous, resulting in fires and deaths, if improperly hooked to an outlet or switch.

The problem centers on two aspects of the wiring. In the first instance, aluminum wiring is often screwed to or fitted into a brass terminal on the outlet. Mixing two such dissimilar metals results in corrosion which increases resistance and can result in fires. Second, aluminum wire begins to oxidize when exposed to air and

this too increases its resistance.

However, aluminum wiring can be safe if put in proper outlets and switches. Shut off power along one circuit and remove a switch plate. If the wiring is aluminum rather than copper, it must be affixed to a receptacle or switch marked CO-ALR for 15 or 20 amp devices, or CU-AL for those with higher amperage. (See pages 64 and 66 on how to read switches and outlets.) Since aluminum easily contracts and expands, make sure all terminal screws are tight, or that the wires are pushed firmly in place. (See the illustration next page for two types of terminals.)

Continuity tester

A self-powered device that tests for malfunctions when the power is off. To test a switch, before it's hooked up, attach the alligator clip to one terminal and touch the probe to another.

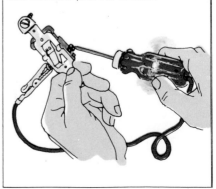

scissors blades (or an electrician's multipurpose tool). To prevent accidental grounding and short circuits, never expose more than the bare minimum of wire needed to make the connection.

Splicing wire is a common and safe practice, with two exceptions: never splice underground wires and never splice house wiring anywhere inside walls.

The fastest way to splice two wires is with wire nuts. These are commonly used in connecting wires after installing a new ceiling light. Strip off about ¾ inch of insulation, twist the wires together, push them hard into the wire nut and then twist the nut as far as you can. No wire should be exposed at the end of the nut. For added safety, secure the wire and nut with a couple wraps of electrical tape. Other common splices are illustrated here.

Soldering wire splices or taps makes a stronger tie and permits a better flow of electricity. For these jobs you basically need a soldering gun or iron and *resin* core solder. Always use solder with resin core, never acid core, on wiring jobs. Acid core can result in corrosion.

Make sure the tip of the soldering gun is clean, then "tin" it by applying a thin layer of solder which helps conduct heat from gun to wire. Move the gun slowly up and down the splice to heat the wire. Do not let the insulation begin to melt: if this repeatedly happens, your soldering tip is not powerful enough for the job.

When the wire is hot, touch solder to the wire near the gun. Don't touch solder to the gun tip. Move tip and solder slowly along the splice so the solder flows evenly into all crevices. If it does not flow smoothly, you are probably going too fast; if large droplets occur, you are probably going too slowly. After you finish, remove the gun

and solder, and let the soldered splice cool enough to touch before moving. If the solder is cracked before it cools, the connection may be poor. When cool, wrap with electrical tape back and forth, overlapping with half the tape on each wrap. Keep the tape tightly stretched. Continue wrapping until the thickness of the tape equals the insulation.

Wire sizes

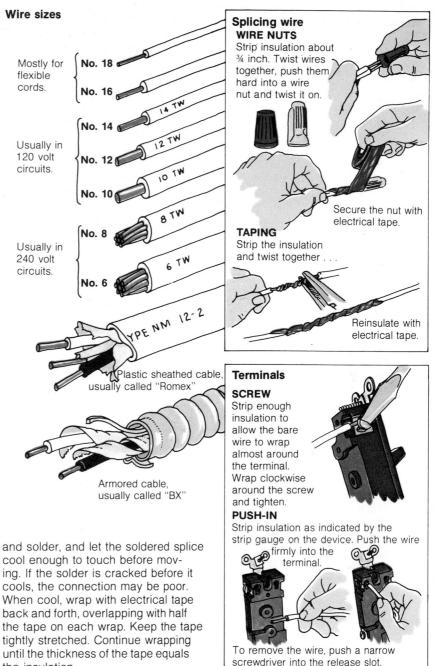

Mostly for flexible cords. { No. 18 / No. 16 }

Usually in 120 volt circuits. { No. 14 / No. 12 / No. 10 }

Usually in 240 volt circuits. { No. 8 / No. 6 }

14 TW
12 TW
10 TW
8 TW
6 TW

TYPE NM 12-2

Plastic sheathed cable, usually called "Romex"

Armored cable, usually called "BX"

Splicing wire
WIRE NUTS
Strip insulation about ¾ inch. Twist wires together, push them hard into a wire nut and twist it on.

Secure the nut with electrical tape.

TAPING
Strip the insulation and twist together . . .

Reinsulate with electrical tape.

Terminals
SCREW
Strip enough insulation to allow the bare wire to wrap almost around the terminal. Wrap clockwise around the screw and tighten.

PUSH-IN
Strip insulation as indicated by the strip gauge on the device. Push the wire firmly into the terminal.

To remove the wire, push a narrow screwdriver into the release slot.

Voltage tester

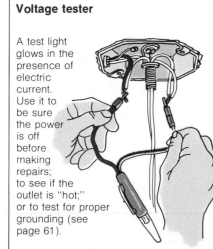

A test light glows in the presence of electric current. Use it to be sure the power is off before making repairs; to see if the outlet is "hot;" or to test for proper grounding (see page 61).

Stripping wire

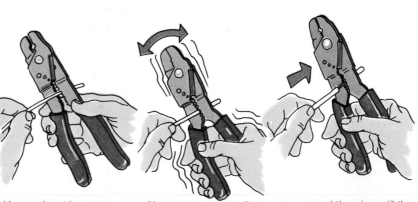

Use a wire stripper or a multipurpose tool if possible. Determine how much insulation must be removed . . .

Never remove more than necessary. Place the wire in the groove of proper size and rotate the tool back-and-forth

around the wire until the insulation is cut through and you are able to pull off what you've cut.

All About Switches

If every time you flip a switch, a fuse blows or a circuit breaks, plan on replacing that switch. That's one good reason. Other good reasons for replacing a switch are to save electricity, make lighting more dramatic and add convenience.

If you are changing a switch, be sure you match it with one of the four basic types illustrated here. They are not interchangeable.

Among the wide variety of switches available to you are dimmers that can pay for themselves soon in saved electricity. They are especially useful in dining and living rooms where you want to create moods. And when one partner would like a romantic candle-lit dinner but the other grouses about not being able to see the food, a compromise can be reached with a dimmer.

Other gadgets include mercury switches, which are silent and useful in children's rooms; neon-handle switches that glow in the dark; pilot-light switches that light up to remind you a basement or outdoor light is on; time-delay switches that keep the lights on an extra 45 seconds to give you time to leave the garage or basement; and time-clock switches that will turn lights and television or radio on and off while you are away, supposedly convincing strangers that you are still home.

■ **Replacing the common switch:**
The basic switch in your house is the common, or single-pole switch. Included in this variety are the old-fashioned push-button switches, tap switches and the silent mercury switches. Replacing them is not a difficult process.

Start by shutting off the power along that circuit first. Unscrew the cover plate and then loosen the two screws that hold the switch in place. You can now double-check that the power is off by using a voltage tester. Grasp the switch handle and pull it out a little. Now put one wire of the voltage tester on the metal outlet box and the other wire on each of the brass terminals, in turn. If it is a push-in switch, press the tester wire into the slot in the back. If the voltage tester glows, you don't have the power off.

When you're sure the power is off, pull the switch out of the box until the wires are extended. Now unscrew both terminals and remove the wires.

If the switch has push-in connections, you will see a small slot next to the wire. Push on this with a small screwdriver to release the spring-clip holding the wire and pull the wire free.

In hooking up a replacement switch that has screw terminals, make the wire loop curl in the same direction the screw turns to tighten. If it is a push-in variety, make sure the insulation on the wire is nearly flush with the back of the switch when connected.

To make sure you put the right wire with the right terminal, keep this color chart in mind:

Color of Wire	Color of Screw
Black	Brass
White	Silver
Green	Green (or dark color)
Bare wire	Electrical box (ground)
Red	Brass

To read a switch

Everything you need to know to choose the proper switch is either stamped into the mounting yoke or molded into the back of the plastic case. Study it all carefully.

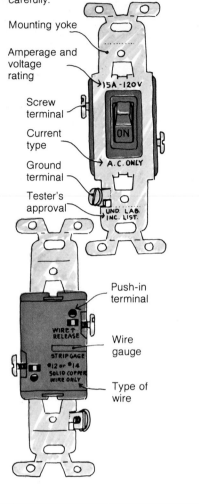

Mounting yoke

Amperage and voltage rating

Screw terminal

Current type

Ground terminal

Tester's approval

15A·120V

ON

A.C. ONLY

UND. LAB. INC. LIST.

Push-in terminal

Wire gauge

Type of wire

WIRE RELEASE

STRIP GAGE #12 or #14 SOLID COPPER WIRE ONLY

Basic switches

SINGLE-POLE
The most common switch, utilized for simple control of a light or outlet. It has an "OFF" and "ON" on the toggle. Both terminals are the same color.

3-WAY
Used in pairs to control a light or outlet from two locations. The toggle has no "ON" and "OFF" designations. One of the three terminals is a darker color than the others.

4-WAY
Used with other 4-way and 3-way switches to control a light or outlet from three or more locations. The toggle has no "ON" and "OFF" designations. All four terminals are of the same color.

DOUBLE-POLE
Usually used to control 240-volt appliances. It has four terminals, like a 4-way switch, but has "ON" and "OFF" designations on the toggle.

To save yourself doubt, connect each wire to the replacement switch as soon as you remove it from the old switch. Make sure you put it in so the switch handle is down when off. And adjust the switch so it is installed straight, even if the electrical box is crooked. The replacement switch may have little "ears" near the mounting screw for a different type of electrical box. If these are in the way, they will bend and snap off.

■ **Installing grounded switch:** Until recently, ground wires were connected only to the metal electrical box by a screw. That was considered sufficient. Now, better grounding is done through the switch itself and your replacement model should be this variety. The grounding screw is usually located near the bottom mounting screw and is identified by either a green ground screw or the letters GR.

To make this hookup, use two "jumper" wires or "pigtails" — short lengths of bare ground wire or insulated green wire. One short length is hooked to the back of the metal electrical box with a screw. The other is screwed into the ground terminal. Now connect the two jumper wires and the two ends of the ground wire by twisting them all together in a wire nut. As an alternative, the jumper wire can run from the ground screw connection on the switch to the screw on the metal electrical box. Both ends of the ground wire should then also be fitted

under that screw. This is sometimes difficult; the wire nuts make the hookup easier.

■ **Replacing dimmer switches:** To remove a malfunctioning dimmer switch, first remove the control knob. This may pull directly off or there may be a small setscrew along the edge that you need to loosen first. After that's off, remove the cover plate. If this or any other wall plate has been painted over, use a razor blade or sharp knife to slit along the edge of the plate first, to prevent cracking the paint.

Complete the hookup as you would for the common single-pole switch.

■ **Replacing combination switches:** These useful little devices combine outlets and switches. By using a neutral jumper wire, you can make the switch control the outlet or have the outlet "hot" all the time.

To do this the switch must be in the middle of a run: that is, there must be four wires entering the box—a hot and neutral wire from the service panel and two wires from the light fixture. If there are only two wires entering the box, they are part of a switch loop and there is no neutral wire. Therefore, a combination switch cannot be installed.

To start, attach a jumper wire to both neutrals with a wire nut and to the silver screw.

To have the outlet controlled by the switch, attach the black power wire to the copper screw and the black switch

wire to either brass screw.

If you want the outlet hot all the time, attach the black power wire to either brass screw and the black switch wire to the copper screw.

■ **3-way and 4-way switches:** A 3-way switch controls a light from two different locations; a 4-way switch is hooked up between the 3-way switches to control the light from three different spots.

These switches are hooked up essentially the same as the common single-pole switch, only there are more wires. If you are replacing a defective 3-way or 4-way switch, make it easy on yourself by tagging all wires with tape and paper to keep them straight. When pushing the switch back into the box, make sure no bare wires are bent enough to touch each other.

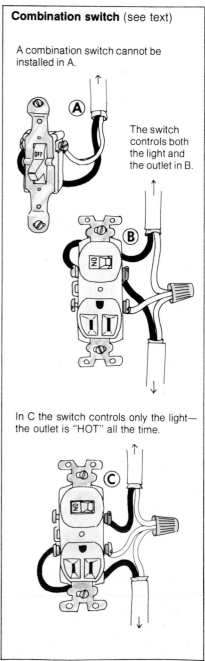

Combination switch (see text)

A combination switch cannot be installed in A.

The switch controls both the light and the outlet in B.

In C the switch controls only the light—the outlet is "HOT" all the time.

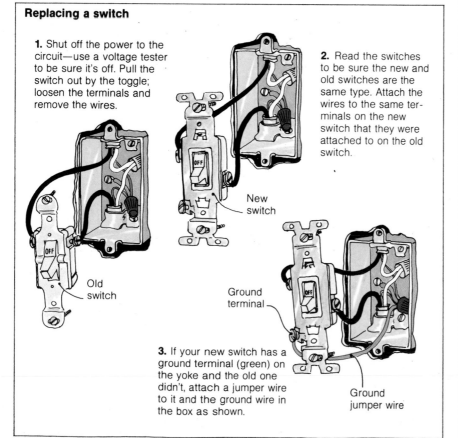

Replacing a switch

1. Shut off the power to the circuit—use a voltage tester to be sure it's off. Pull the switch out by the toggle; loosen the terminals and remove the wires.

2. Read the switches to be sure the new and old switches are the same type. Attach the wires to the same terminals on the new switch that they were attached to on the old switch.

New switch

Old switch

Ground terminal

3. If your new switch has a ground terminal (green) on the yoke and the old one didn't, attach a jumper wire to it and the ground wire in the box as shown.

Ground jumper wire

All About Outlets

When installing new outlets, consider using any of the many specialized varieties. Some optimize safety and some convenience in the receptacle.

If you have small children around the house, for instance, consider safety outlets. One variety of these has spring-loaded covers that snap shut over the outlet. Another type has a twist cover that must be turned to expose the receptacle. The spring in this one is usually stronger than small exploring hands and will keep the child from pushing a bobby pin or nail in the hole just to see what happens.

In terms of convenience, there are outlets that can be installed in floors and covered with handsome brass caps; twist-lock outlets that will prevent a plug from pulling free; and even recessed outlets that will hide the cord of a wall clock.

Also note that the push-in type of outlet is widely sold. Instead of carefully bending wires and fitting them under screws, you can just trim off about ⅜ inch of insulation to expose the wire, push it in the right slot in the back of the outlet, and be done. They are completely interchangeable with the screw-type terminal outlets.

■ **Caution:** As outlined in detail on page 62, some houses have been wired with aluminum instead of copper as a cost-cutting measure. Aluminum wiring is safe if done correctly; if not, fires can and have resulted. If you have aluminum wiring, the outlet or switch must state on it CO-ALR for 15- and 20-amp devices or CU-AL for higher ratings. See the illustration on this page for details on how to read an outlet.

■ **Replacing an outlet:** Like all of us, outlets eventually succumb to old age, become worn down, perhaps hiss and make strange noises. A common malady is a worn receptacle that no longer firmly holds plugs in place. Even bending the plug's prongs farther apart will eventually be of no use. Occasionally, one of the wires inside becomes loose and this also can cause partial or total malfunction. If every time you plug something into an outlet you hear your radio sputter, take that as an indication of a loose wire.

On the other hand, you can be sure the outlet is faulty if every time you plug something in there, a fuse blows or a circuit breaker trips. You can double-check by plugging in a lamp that you know works. If it doesn't go on, plan on replacing the outlet.

The task is quite straightforward. Start by shutting off all power along that circuit. If the outlet is not properly functioning and you're not sure

the power is off there, pull the main switch and cut off power throughout the house. Alternatively, you can use a voltage tester. This inexpensive tool is a definite asset even if you do very little electrical work around your house.

With the power off, remove the center screw on the wall plate. If the cover has been painted over, cut around the edges with a razor blade or sharp knife before pulling it free. Next, remove the two screws that hold the outlet in the electrical box. Once free, pull the outlet straight out to extend the wires.

At this point, wiggle the wires on each screw terminal. If one is loose, you may have found your problem. Tighten it back down, replace the outlet and wall cover, and then try it again.

If that was not the problem, shut off the power again and pull the receptacle out again.

At this point, determine whether this outlet is somewhere in the middle of the circuit or at the end. If it is in the middle of the "run" and the house is wired with plastic sheathed wire, you will see a black, white and ground wire coming up from the bottom of the box, hooking into the outlet, and the same wires going out the top of the box to the next outlet. If it's at the end of the run, there will only be wires coming up from the bottom of the box.

Whatever the case, hook the replacement outlet up exactly like the old. Remember, the black wire coming up from the bottom of the electrical box is the hot wire. Attach it to the

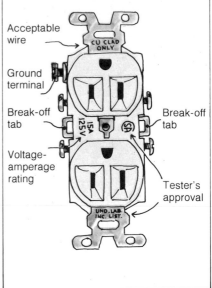

To read an outlet

Everything you should know about an outlet is usually on the front—stamped on the metal yoke or molded into the plastic case.

Acceptable wire

Ground terminal

Break-off tab

Voltage-amperage rating

CU CLAD ONLY

15A 125V

Break-off tab

Tester's approval

UND. LAB. INC. LIST.

bottom brass screw on the outlet. Hook the other black wire (if any) to the top brass screw. Similarly, attach the incoming white neutral wire to the lower silver screw and the outgoing neutral wire to the upper silver screw. The ground wire attaches to the green screw terminal. For further details on proper grounding methods, refer back to page 61.

If there are only two incoming and two outgoing wires, look carefully and

The outlet

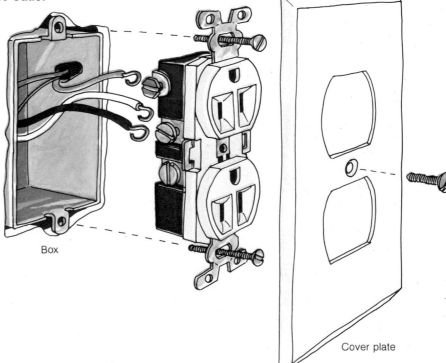

Box

Cover plate

you will probably see the wires are encased in metal. This is known as BX cable and is required by code in some parts of the country. In this case, the metal casing on the wire serves as the ground and the circuit is completed in the outlet by a jumper wire from the outlet to the back of the metal electrical box.

■ **Hooking the wire properly:** This is a matter of practice makes perfect but there are a few basic steps to keep in mind.

First, with a knife or multipurpose tool, remove ⅜ inch of insulation from the end of the wire. With a pair of needlenose pliers, bend the wire into a small loop. Now slip it around the

screw so that the loop is running in a clockwise direction, the same way the screw tightens down.

Once around the screw, use the pliers to tighten the loop, then tighten the screw. The two important things to remember here are: no excess wire should be exposed, and the loop should tighten with the screw.

To replace an outlet (see the text for step-by-step procedure)

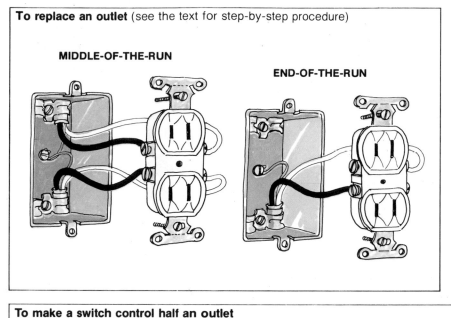

MIDDLE-OF-THE-RUN

END-OF-THE-RUN

Replace a simple outlet with a grounded one

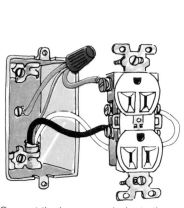

Connect the bare ground wire to the receptacle and the box with short lengths of green wire and a wire nut.

To make a switch control half an outlet

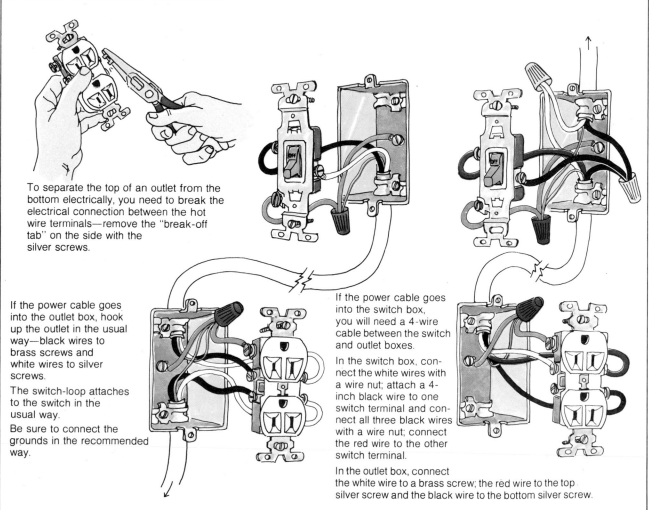

To separate the top of an outlet from the bottom electrically, you need to break the electrical connection between the hot wire terminals—remove the "break-off tab" on the side with the silver screws.

If the power cable goes into the outlet box, hook up the outlet in the usual way—black wires to brass screws and white wires to silver screws.

The switch-loop attaches to the switch in the usual way.

Be sure to connect the grounds in the recommended way.

If the power cable goes into the switch box, you will need a 4-wire cable between the switch and outlet boxes.

In the switch box, connect the white wires with a wire nut; attach a 4-inch black wire to one switch terminal and connect all three black wires with a wire nut; connect the red wire to the other switch terminal.

In the outlet box, connect the white wire to a brass screw; the red wire to the top silver screw and the black wire to the bottom silver screw.

Repairing Plugs and Lamps

There are a wide variety of plugs on the market, a type for any need. Some are very easily connected by just slipping the cord, insulation and all, into the plug and pressing down on a clamp that sends small pins into the wire. These, however, are not particularly sturdy. The old standby models with screws to hold the wires are best.

It's not the plug that usually wears out, it's the cord, and that may mean getting a new cord and wiring a plug to it. Do this immediately if you see cracked or broken cord. Also, watch that there is no exposed wire just where the cord enters the plug.

In removing an old plug, first pry off the insulating cap that slips over the prongs. Now loosen the 2 or 3 screws (3 screws for a 3-prong plug), free the wires and remove the plug. If plug and cord are sealed together, just snip off the plug.

If the old cord is still good beyond the damaged section, just cut that part away.

If the cord has an outer insulation, remove that 2½ inches back from the end of the cord. If the cord is molded, slit it back about the same length. In either case, don't cut through the inner insulation. Now remove ½ inch of insulation from the end of each wire. If it is stranded wire, twist it tightly. Even better, put a light bead of solder on each wire to keep the strands from separating later and touching each other, perhaps causing a short circuit.

Slip the wires into the plug and tie the underwriter's knot as illustrated here. Pull the knot firmly back into the plug and loop the exposed wires clockwise and tightly under the screws. It doesn't matter under which screw — except with 3-prong plugs, where the bare or green wire goes to the green or darkest screw terminal. Replace the insulation cap.

■ **Repairing lamps:** If your favorite lamp flickers all the time, do yourself a favor before you dismantle it: make sure the bulb is in tight. Unplug it.

If the bulb is broken, remove the base by balling up a couple sheets of newspaper, pushing the wad down on the jagged edges and unscrewing it.

If there is no sign of damage to the cord, you will only have to replace the switch. If your lamp has a "harp" curving over the bulb to support a shade, remove it by slipping up the slides at the bottom and then squeezing the base of the harp together.

Press in at the base of the brass or aluminum outer shell of the socket and pull it free. The insulated shell inside will pull right out. Now simply loosen the two screws on the old switch, remove the wires and then attach them to the new one. If there isn't already an underwriter's knot in the wire, tie one first.

If the switch is in the base of the lamp, use a knife to peel back any felt cover on the bottom. The switch is normally held in place by a single nut. Remove that and the wires, and install the new switch.

■ **Replacing cord in a lamp:** First remove the top part of the lamp as described above. Now pry off the protective felt cover on the bottom. You will see a nut that secures the tube running up the center of the lamp through which the cord runs. Unless you are going to replace the tube, don't bother with that nut. Cut the cord below the knot and pull through the tube. Before pushing the new cord in, tie a knot by the hole in the base as added protection against jerking the connecting wires loose.

Now run the wire up the tube, tie the underwriter's knot and complete the hookup as described above.

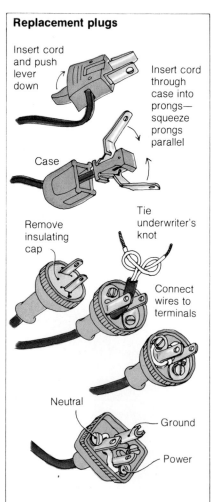

Replacement plugs

Insert cord and push lever down

Insert cord through case into prongs— squeeze prongs parallel

Case

Remove insulating cap

Tie underwriter's knot

Connect wires to terminals

Neutral

Ground

Power

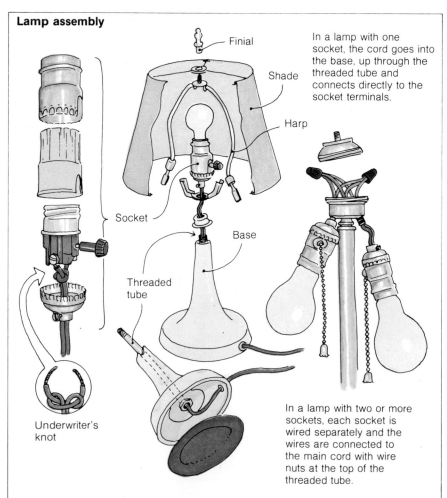

Lamp assembly

Finial

Shade

Harp

Socket

Base

Threaded tube

Underwriter's knot

In a lamp with one socket, the cord goes into the base, up through the threaded tube and connects directly to the socket terminals.

In a lamp with two or more sockets, each socket is wired separately and the wires are connected to the main cord with wire nuts at the top of the threaded tube.

Repairing Ceiling Fixtures

If your ceiling fixture doesn't work and you've checked the bulb, then the fault is probably in the socket(s). You can replace the sockets, but first give some thought to replacing and modernizing the entire fixture.

How to remove the decorative cover to get at the bulbs on some fixtures can be baffling. There may be a single cap nut in the center or several screws around the edge.

Before doing anything beyond changing the bulb, make sure the breaker switch for that fixture is off or the fuse is removed. Simply turning the wall switch off is no guarantee.

With the power off, remove the one or two screws holding the fixture in place. Don't let it hang by the wires but instead support it with a hooked piece of coat hanger.

The wires from the sockets will be connected to the incoming wires with wire nuts. Make sure these are twisted tightly. If one is loose, tighten it and try the fixture before proceeding further.

If it is a simple one-light fixture, black wire hooks to black wire and white to white. If there are two sockets, it's still the same principle: all the black wires fasten together in one wire nut and all the white in another (see illustration).

If you are not replacing the entire fixture, then just remove the old sockets. In some cases the wires are permanently attached while in others they are held by screws. In the first case, free the socket by unscrewing the wire nut holding the wires above; in the second, loosen the screws and remove the wires.

Take the old socket with you when buying the new one. If it already has wires attached, trim off about ⅜ inch of insulation from each end and twist the wires together again, black to black, white to white. Make sure no bare wire is exposed at the base of the wire nut. For added protection, give it a couple of wraps with electrical tape.

If the wires are not already attached to the new socket, hook them back as they were before, black to the brass screw and white to the silver screw.

■ **Installing new fixture:** The electrical aspects of putting up a new ceiling fixture are generally no more complex than in fixing an old one. Getting the right hardware can be time consuming.

Look carefully at the electrical box after removing the fixture. It either has a central threaded stud or not. On the edges of the box will be two holes through which small bolts can be run as another way of hanging the new fixture.

If your new fixture is supposed to hang from the central stud but doesn't fit, ask your electrical supply store for a *reducing nut* and *nipple* of the proper size.

If the new fixture must be mounted by two screws along the outer edges rather than by the center stud, buy a *strap* and *locknut*. This strap is screwed onto the center stud and then the fixture is hung from it. If there is no center stud, the strap can be attached to the electrical box through the two holes on the edges, and the fixture then hung.

How they're attached

Here are three of the most common types of ceiling fixtures and the ways they are usually attached to the electrical box.

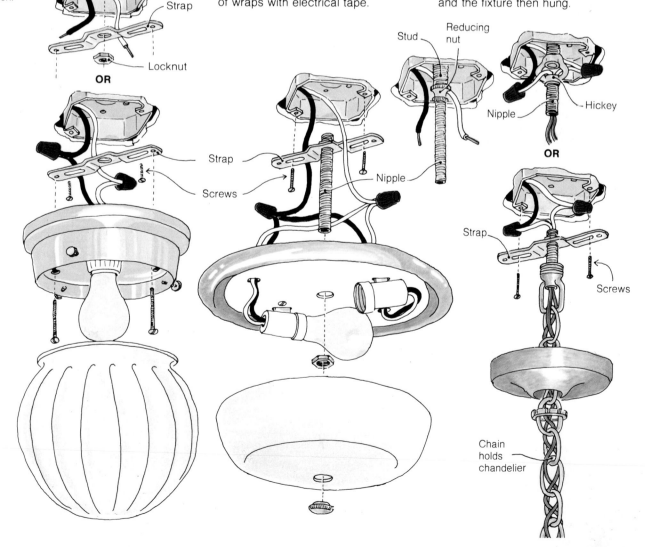

Stud

Strap

Locknut

OR

Strap

Screws

Nipple

Stud

Reducing nut

Nipple

Hickey

OR

Strap

Screws

Chain holds chandelier

Fluorescent Light Units

Fluorescent lights may cost you more to install than incandescent bulbs but in the long run you save money. A 40-watt fluorescent tube will last five times longer than an ordinary 40-watt incandescent bulb and put out six times more light. The chief problem is that many people don't like the generally harsh, cold light. However, some new types of fluorescent bulbs, particularly the deluxe warm white, are quite similar to incandescent bulbs.

The two basic types of fluorescent units are the straight tube and the circular. They are equipped with either a replaceable starter unit or a rapid-start system built into the ballast. If you have to replace either the starter or ballast, take it with you to the store so you get exactly the same type.

If you have a problem, try to pinpoint it with the following checklist:

■ **Troubleshooting fluorescent lights**

1. *Tube won't light:* First check fuse or circuit breaker. If tubes are black at both ends, replace. Otherwise, replace starter. As last resort, replace ballast (see below for details).

2. *Light blinks on and off:* Remove tube, straighten and sand tube pins, then reseat tube. If it still blinks, shut off power and sand contacts in light unit. If problem continues, replace starter; if the surrounding air goes below 50°F (10°C) use a cold-weather starter. As a last resort, replace ballast.

3. *Light flickers:* Normal in new tube. If tube old, first replace it, then starter if necessary, and finally ballast.

4. *Humming noise:* Tighten ballast wire connections, or replace ballast with low-noise variety.

5. *Discolored tube:* Brown at ends is normal. Black ends on old tube indicate it's burned out. If ends blacken on new tube, replace starter. If tube discolored down one side, turn over and keep using. If one end in new tube darkens, turn tube end for end.

■ **Replacing a tube:** Give the tube a quarter-turn either way and slip it out. The new one goes in the same way: just slip into the slot and give it a quarter-turn to set it properly.

For circular lights, carefully pull the tube back out of the socket and free it from any retaining clips. Just reverse the process to put in the new one.

■ **Replacing a starter:** From the diagram, you can quickly tell if your unit has a starter. If it does and the starter needs replacing, just give it a quarter turner counterclockwise and remove. There are no wires to worry about here.

■ **Replacing a ballast:** After removing the tube, start disconnecting all the wires from the ballast. Make it easy on yourself by labeling each wire as you unhook it. Remove the mounting screws and pull the ballast free. If you haven't already got a new ballast, take the old with you to the store to get the exact same thing. A useful variation would be a low-temperature ballast if the light is in a room that's cold in winter.

Put the new ballast in place with the mounting screws and then reconnect all the wires and replace the tube. If it still doesn't work, refrain from kicking the wall and go through the troubleshooting checklist again.

Two types of starters

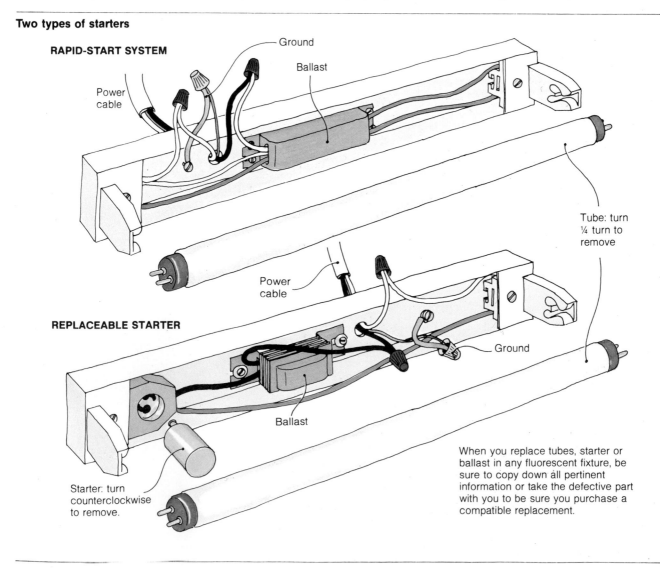

RAPID-START SYSTEM

Ground

Ballast

Power cable

Tube: turn ¼ turn to remove

Power cable

REPLACEABLE STARTER

Ground

Ballast

Starter: turn counterclockwise to remove.

When you replace tubes, starter or ballast in any fluorescent fixture, be sure to copy down all pertinent information or take the defective part with you to be sure you purchase a compatible replacement.

Repairing Doorbells

Doorbells are operated through a transformer that reduces 120 volt house current down to 20 volts or less. Thus it isn't necessary to turn the power off unless you must work on the transformer. Then pull the main power switch since the transformer is probably not on a general circuit.

Doorbells, chimes and buzzers are connected with small 18 or 20-gauge wires that can break or work loose. These must be checked over carefully, from the chime system to the bell push or buttons.

Problems often originate in the button by the door because it is exposed to the elements and dirt. You can make a quick test here if the bell doesn't ring by unscrewing the mounting plate and pulling out the button and wires. Remove the wires and then, holding them by the insulation, touch them together. If the bell rings, it means the contact on the button is bent or corroded. Straighten

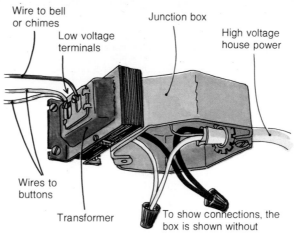

Wire to bell or chimes
Low voltage terminals
Junction box
High voltage house power
Wires to buttons
Transformer
To show connections, the box is shown without its cover

and clean the contact and try it. If it doesn't work, replace the button.

If the bell works but makes a dull or incomplete sound, the problem is likely in the sound mechanism. You can generally remove the plate by pulling it off. If it has been painted, cut around the edges with a sharp knife to free it. Then check that all the wires are tightly connected and that none is corroded.

If the mechanism is in the kitchen, the problem may be a buildup of grease and dirt on the striker plates,

TRANSFORMER
Somewhere in your attic or basement, usually by a junction box, is a transformer that reduces your house current to the low voltage needed to operate the doorbell. The wire from the bell or chimes connects to one terminal; the wire from the button to the other terminal. If you have more than one button, more than one wire will be connected to the same terminal.

the plunger or the connections.

If any of the moving parts or strike plates are dirty, clean them thoroughly. Now lubricate with some powdered graphite. Don't use any oil, which will only attract more dirt.

If you remove wires in the sound device, be sure to hook them back in the same manner. This is particularly good advice if you have different-sounding bells for the front and back doors. It could save you from repeatedly opening the wrong door.

CHIMES
When the front door button is pressed, current energizes the top electromagnet, pulling the top striker to hit the high-note chime. Releasing the button breaks the circuit, the spring pulls the striker back to the low-note chime. When the back door button is pressed, the sequence is the same except that the back-door striker is not allowed to ring the low-note chime when it springs back: on some units there is a padded screw in the way; on others the end of the striker is padded so it hits the bar, but makes no noise.
If you hear "ding dong," you answer the front door. If you just hear "ding," answer the back.

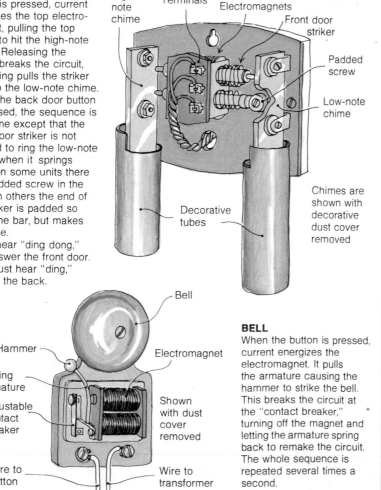

High-note chime
Terminals
Electromagnets
Front door striker
Padded screw
Low-note chime
Chimes are shown with decorative dust cover removed
Decorative tubes

Bell
Hammer
Spring armature
Adjustable contact breaker
Electromagnet
Shown with dust cover removed
Wire to button
Wire to transformer

BELL
When the button is pressed, current energizes the electromagnet. It pulls the armature causing the hammer to strike the bell. This breaks the circuit at the "contact breaker," turning off the magnet and letting the armature spring back to remake the circuit. The whole sequence is repeated several times a second.

Doorbell wiring

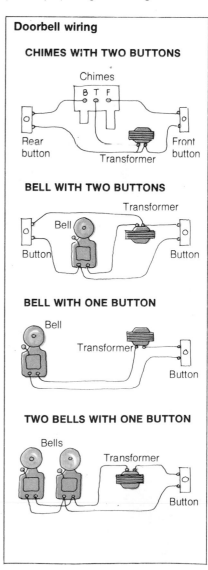

CHIMES WITH TWO BUTTONS
Chimes
B T F
Rear button
Front button
Transformer

BELL WITH TWO BUTTONS
Transformer
Bell
Button
Button

BELL WITH ONE BUTTON
Bell
Transformer
Button

TWO BELLS WITH ONE BUTTON
Bells
Transformer
Button

Outdoor Lighting

If you have already replaced some switches or outlets inside the house, you can use this knowledge to install outdoor lighting around your house. There's no difference in the basic process: it's just that outdoor wiring requires special hardware — including conduit to keep the wires dry — and some hard work on your part to complete the project. If you've forgotten how much fun it is to dig ditches, here's your chance to learn again.

Outdoor lighting can add both dramatic beauty to your grounds and at the same time increase your security. Law enforcement officials agree that good lighting around a house is a deterrent against prowlers and burglars.

The first step is to draw a scale model of your house and grounds on graph paper, using one square per square foot. Draw in the trees, steps, walkways, patios or pool areas you will want lighted.

Now stop and carefully consider some basic precautions:
—if you are planning to wire in or around a swimming pool, leave it entirely to a professional. One little short circuit here can electrocute anyone who touches the water;
—check your local codes to see what type of wire you must use and whether it must be encased in metal or plastic conduit;
—bury all wires at least 18 inches to prevent accidentally cutting them with a shovel; better yet, run wires through galvanized pipe;
—when doing any repair work on outdoor wiring, even changing a bulb, make sure the power is off. If you insist on working around electricity with damp hands while standing on damp ground, your survivors or the

■ **Ground fault interrupters:** This life-saving device has been mentioned before in this book but where outdoor wiring is involved, it's worth repeating. Besides, it's required by law on all outdoor wiring.

Essentially, this device monitors and compares the flow of electricity. It measures the number of amps flowing out through the hot wire and makes sure the same amount is coming back through the neutral wire. If there is less coming back, it means a leak has developed — and it might be going through you. The GFI senses this and shuts off all power in less than 1/40th of a second, before any harm can come to you. Be sure you have one.

Here are some ideas for outdoor circuits that might fit in at your house. One starts with a GFI receptacle behind a living room outlet on the front of the house (**1**); it then goes under the lawn to a light beside the walk (**2**) and on to a post lamp controlled by an electric-eye (**3**).

The second circuit begins at the existing light above the back door. It drops down to a GFI receptacle

beside the back door (**4**), then proceeds under the lawn to garden lights at the edge of the deck (**5**) and finally to an outlet beneath the tree (**6**).

Another idea is the floodlight in the eaves to illuminate the service yard (**7**).

new owners may have to finish the project.

■ **Planning details:** The power for the outside lighting will come from the house. If you are installing just a few lights outside, perhaps one under the eaves and another near some steps, you can safely tie directly into another circuit. For any type of elaborate lighting system, install a separate circuit so it is protected with its own fuse or circuit breaker.

Plan exactly the number of outdoor lights you will have and how many outlets will be required. Use No. 14 wire and buy 10 to 20 feet extra to allow for the loops, bends and hook-ups.

When digging a trench across your lawn, first cut and remove the sod with a spade and set it roots down on the grass. On the other side lay strips of plastic sheeting to hold the dirt. Dig a section, lay in the wire, replace the dirt and sod, then move on to the next section.

■ **Installing a fixture on an outside wall:** The easiest way to do this is to go through the wall directly behind an indoor fixture. Start your project by turning off power to that circuit. Unscrew the cover from the inside wall and remove the two screws holding the fixture in the electrical box. Pull it out so you can see in the box. On the back you will see one or two circles that are called knockouts. Punch one of these out with a screwdriver and hammer. You are now ready to drill through the outside wall.

The size of the opening on the outside wall will depend on whether

you are installing a surface mounted box or a flush mounted box. If surface mounted, you need only drill a hole large enough for a ½-inch piece of metal conduit. For a flush mounting, cut a hole the size of the box. At a hardware store, buy a threaded length of pipe long enough to connect the two electrical boxes plus two threaded bushings.

On the inside fixture, connect a length of wire as detailed on page 67 for installing outlets. Put black wire to brass screw, white wire to silver screw and connect the ground to the green screw terminal. In most cases there will be a screw available in the inside fixture for these hookups but if not, put the new wire right under the screw that already has a wire of the same color.

Push the wire through the conduit and complete your hookup to the outside fixture in the same way, black to brass, white to silver and the ground to both the metal electrical box and to the green screw on the fixture. (See the illustration on page 61 for more details on proper ground connections.)

The outside electrical box should have a weatherproof cover plate with a rubber gasket under that plate. Apply a generous bead of oil-base caulking between the box and the wall.

■ **Tapping existing source:** If you already have one outdoor light, you can tie into that for your outdoor wiring if the original fixture is alone on a circuit. For this job, you need an outdoor extender box.

Tapping an inside outlet

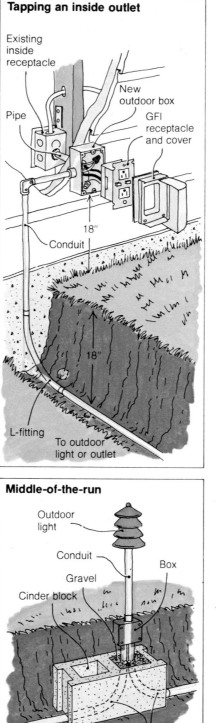

Existing inside receptacle

Pipe

New outdoor box

GFI receptacle and cover

18"

Conduit

18"

L-fitting

To outdoor light or outlet

Tapping a porch light

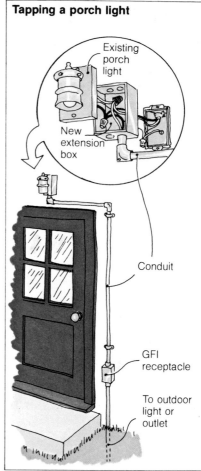

Existing porch light

New extension box

Conduit

GFI receptacle

To outdoor light or outlet

With the power off, remove the fixture and disconnect the wires. Onto the bottom of the extender box, screw a short nipple and an elbow if you are going to have to run the conduit pipe around and past a door frame. Otherwise, run the conduit straight down the side of the house and hold it in place with pipe straps. Stop about two feet short of the ground. If you are running metal conduit underground, the underground length must be bent with a rented conduit bender and fitted to the pipe on the wall with a threadless connector.

Before joining the pipes, run wire up the wall conduit and into the outlet. Connect the wires to the power source and reinstall the light and cover plate.

You now have wire ready to run underground. A note of warning here: Remember the wire you are working with is hooked to the light and power source. If the job is going to take longer than one day to finish, don't connect the outside wiring into the power source until all the rest of the work is completed.

■ **Extending underground wiring:** As you work your way along the ditch, connect each length of metal conduit with the threadless connectors. If you want a light or power source in the middle of a run, use a T-fitting. At the end of a run use an L-fitting or bend the conduit into a 90 degree angle.

For stabilizing short light fixtures or outlets where they extend above ground, run the pipe through a cinder block and then pack it with gravel and cover.

Middle-of-the-run

Outdoor light

Conduit

Box

Gravel

Cinder block

L-fittings

End-of-the-run

Outdoor receptacle

Conduit

Cinder block

Gravel

Bend or L-fitting

Floodlight beneath the eaves

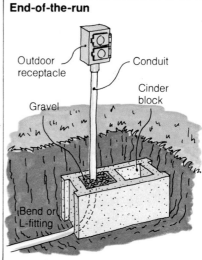

Although these floodlights are outdoors beneath the eaves, all the wires are within the house or attic, and the switch is indoors. Except for the outdoor light fixture, it's installed just like an indoor light.

Plumbing Systems

How to repair and join pipes, fix leaks and faucets, unclog sinks, tubs, drains, and garbage disposals. How to repair and replace toilets. How to check a water heater.

Plumbing Emergencies

Before you have an emergency, learn where the main water valve is. If you have a serious leak that can't be stopped near the source, close the main valve to stop the supply of water throughout the house. If you haven't already located it, the main valve should be near your water meter or near where the water enters your house. Turn it clockwise to close it.

Except in dire situations, you won't have to use the main valve; there are several other key valves around the house to shut off water, and you should learn where they are also.

Hot water can be shut off throughout the house by turning the handle on top of the water heater. Sometimes there is a handle also on the cold water supply.

■ **Sink:** If you have a leaky faucet or handle on a sink, there are shut off valves below the sink. Both bathroom and kitchen sinks have these valves. Again, turn the handle clockwise to shut it off.

■ **Toilet:** If the water persists in running into the tank, remove the top and jiggle the float (see page 86 for details) until the water stops. If you are unsuccessful, stop the flow of water by closing the valve beneath the tank.

If the bowl fills and won't drain, use a plumber's helper, sometimes called a rubber force cup. It should have a protruding narrow cup at the end designed for use in toilets. Press firmly into the drain hole and then work it up and down rapidly for a dozen thrusts. If that doesn't work, add water to the bowl to keep it more than half full, then work away for another 15 minutes. Rest for an hour, by which time the clog may have softened and be ready to break free. Do not attempt to flush the toilet until the water has drained from the bowl.

■ **Overflowing washers:** If either your dishwasher or clotheswasher overflows, turn off the supply. In the case of a dishwasher, this may be between the sink and the washer, since they are sometimes tied together.

The water supply valve for a clotheswasher is usually on the pipes behind the washer. If you are unable to pull it out from the wall to get at the valve, shut off the main valve.

Consider, first, if the drain has been plugged by lint, grease or dirt. If water keeps flowing after the control panel indicates it should be off, the electrical panel may be at fault. Turn off the current to that circuit by removing the proper fuse or throwing the breaker switch to off, and then pull the electric plug.

■ **Leaking pipes:** For a pinhole leak, push a toothpick in the hole and break it off. The wood will swell and slow the leak. Wrap it several times with electrical tape.

A larger leak can be temporarily stopped by wrapping it with a piece of rubber, such as an old inner tube or a kitchen glove, then compressing it between two pieces of wood with a clamp. A C-clamp does the best job.

These are only emergency repairs. For a proper job, you must turn off the water and drain the pipe. Details on how to "sweat" copper pipes are given on page 77; more details on pipe repairs are given on page 78.

■ **Thawing frozen pipes:** Open a faucet or spigot closest to the frozen section and then do all the thawing work between the open valve and the frozen section. This will allow steam from the melting ice to escape rather than being trapped between ice and water and possibly breaking the pipes. Thaw the pipe with rags and hot water, a heat lamp, hair dryer or propane torch.

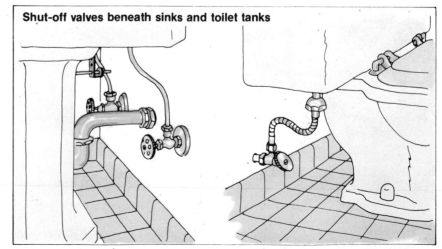

Shut-off valves beneath sinks and toilet tanks

All About Pipes

Your supply of fresh water enters the house under pressure. One pipe leads away from the main water line and runs through the water heater. Incoming fresh water is usually carried in copper pipe because it is easy to work with and resistant to internal corrosion that can impede the flow of water. Galvanized steel, plastic and occasionally brass are also used. In older houses, cast iron pipe may carry the water in.

Used water is carried away through a drain system that operates by gravity flow. Drain systems must also be connected to vent pipes to carry off excess air and gas. This whole system is known as the drain-waste-vent, or DWV system. Drain pipes in older homes are often made from cast iron. Some houses use copper but most houses in recent years are fitted with plastic drain and vent pipes.

The type of pipe used is controlled by local codes. Before undertaking any major job that involves replacing pipe, see what the code requires. If you are just making a repair, such as fixing a leaky faucet or pipe, you do not have to have a building permit first. If you are replacing a fixture such as a sink or toilet, you probably should, but not if it's considered

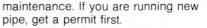

maintenance. If you are running new pipe, get a permit first.

■ **Cast iron pipe:** If you have to repair cast iron pipe, the work will appear formidable. It's not easy but it's not impossible.

First, note whether the pipe is fitted together with built-in hubs (one end is bellshaped, the hub, and the other end has a slight ridge, the spiggot, that fits into a hub) or whether each section is joined with a neoprene sleeve and stainless steel clamp. This style is easy to work with: just loosen the clamp, slip the sleeve off, and remove or replace that section of pipe.

Hub pipes are joined by packing each joint with fibrous oakum and then pouring a 1-inch seal of lead around the top. To remove a section, chisel out the soft lead and pull out the oakum.

If your local code permits, use no-hub pipe (sleeve and clamp) for all replacement work.

Cast iron pipe comes in 5-foot lengths and is broken rather than cut to fit. To cut standard weight pipe, rent a cast iron pipe cutter or cut a groove ⅛ inch deep around the pipe with a hacksaw where you want to sever it. Support one side on a 2 by 4 and rap on the other side with a hammer to break it on the scored line.

For heavier pipe, mark the cutting line and then work your way around it with a cold chisel.

■ **Steel pipe:** For plumbing purposes, this is troublesome pipe to work with. Each joint must be threaded and screwed together rather than just slipped together like copper or plastic. It is also subject to buildups of corrosion that will impede the flow of water.

If you must work with it, rent the necessary equipment. This will include a pipe cutter, which is much faster and easier to use than a hacksaw; proper size dies and die stock; and a pipe reamer.

Cut the pipe to the desired length, but be sure your measurement runs from *inside* to *inside* of each pipe fitting or you will be too short.

In cutting threads on a pipe, use liberal amounts of oil as you work to minimize wear on the die. Always ream out the steel burrs inside the pipe after cutting.

If you remove just a short section of pipe in the middle of a run, you will have to use a coupling on one end of the replacement piece and a union joint on the other end. Union joints are also commonly installed where pipes may have to be disassembled occasionally, as around a water heater.

■ **Plastic pipe:** Three types of plastic pipe commonly used in or around a home are ABS, PVC and CPVC. Al-

Supply line pipe

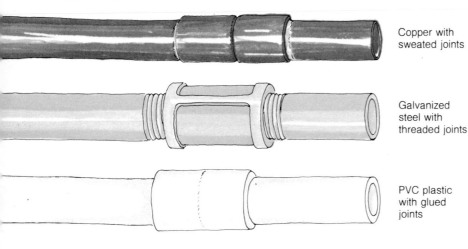

Copper with sweated joints

Galvanized steel with threaded joints

PVC plastic with glued joints

Drain and waste pipe

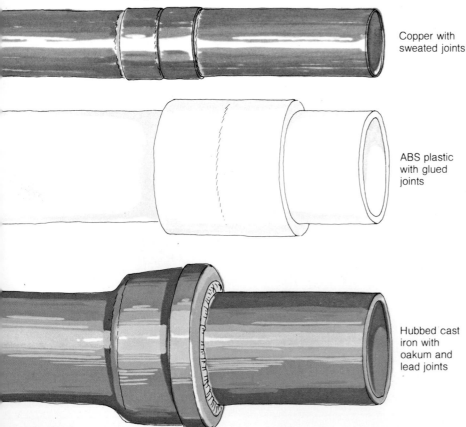

Copper with sweated joints

ABS plastic with glued joints

Hubbed cast iron with oakum and lead joints

though not permitted by code everywhere, ABS is used widely in homes for the drain-waste-vent system. This black plastic is strong, easily cut and fitted together, and impervious to corrosion that can attack metal pipes.

PVC and CPVC are similar except that only the latter can handle hot water. Use of these pipes to carry water inside the house is still widely restricted by local codes. CPVC is rated to handle temperatures only up to 180°F (82°C) and 100 pounds of water pressure. If you are using this pipe, be sure the pressure relief valve on your water heater does not exceed this.

Plastic pipe is easy to work with. Make all cuts with a hacksaw and then clean out the burrs with sandpaper or a pocket knife. It's also advisable to sand off the gloss where the pipe is going to be glued into a fitting. (In working with CPVC, you must always use a special cleanser before applying the glue.) Swab a moderate layer of glue both inside the fitting and on the pipe, push firmly together and then give a quarter turn. Turn the fitting exactly where you want it the first time because the glue sets in a matter of seconds.

Let all joints set 12 hours before running water under pressure through the system. Any joint that leaks must be cut out and replaced.

■ **Copper pipe:** This is the favorite pipe of most plumbers for carrying supply water throughout your house. It's expensive but it goes together rapidly and is strong, corrosion resistant and long lasting. It comes in rigid and flexible tubing. Rigid pipes are joined in a soldering process called "sweating" and flexible tubing is joined with flare fittings.

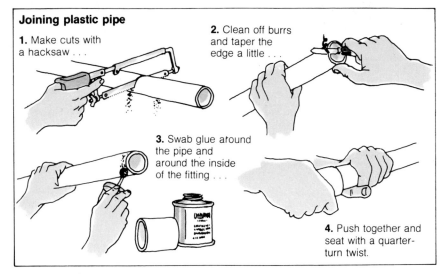

Joining plastic pipe

1. Make cuts with a hacksaw . . .

2. Clean off burrs and taper the edge a little . . .

3. Swab glue around the pipe and around the inside of the fitting . . .

4. Push together and seat with a quarter-turn twist.

Sweating copper joints properly is a matter of practice but there are basic steps to keep in mind.

Preferably, cut the pipe with a tube cutter; it's faster and smoother than a hacksaw. File off any burrs and then use emery cloth to polish the outside of the pipe and the inside of the fitting until bright.

At this point make sure there are no dents in the pipe or fitting. The solder may not fill them and leaks will result. Now apply a thin layer of flux to the pipe and fitting to keep the copper from oxidizing when heated. Slip the fitting on the pipe and make sure it faces the way you want. With a propane torch, heat the fitting and not the pipe. When the temperature is just right, the solid-core solder will melt when you touch it to the joint and be immediately drawn up into and around the joint. For a perfect sweat, only a narrow line of solder should be visible around the joint.

If more than one section of pipe fits into the joint, sweat them all at once. If this is not possible, keep the joint already sweated wrapped with a wet rag to keep it from melting while you do the other side.

In removing a fitting, heat it completely and then rap it lightly with a hammer to break it free from the solder. The pipe must be dry because any water inside, even just a little, will keep the fitting from getting hot enough to break free. Drain pipes by opening the lowest valve in the house after shutting off incoming water.

Flare joints are used to connect smaller, flexible copper tubing. If you are going to be doing much of this work, it's best to buy a flaring tool for precise control. Always remember to slip the flare nut over the tube before making the flare; and be careful you do not cross-thread the fittings when joining them. If you do, throw it away, for a leak will result there. And always use two wrenches to tighten the fittings.

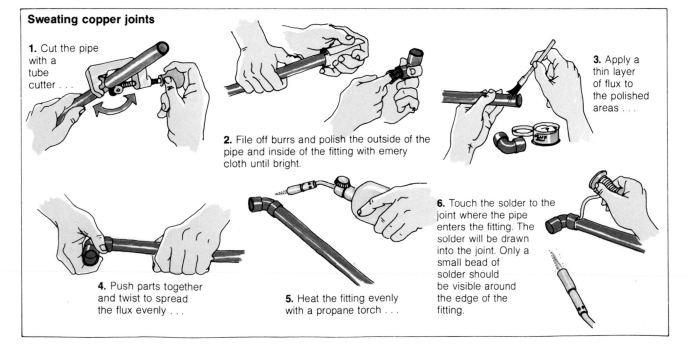

Sweating copper joints

1. Cut the pipe with a tube cutter . . .

2. File off burrs and polish the outside of the pipe and inside of the fitting with emery cloth until bright.

3. Apply a thin layer of flux to the polished areas . . .

4. Push parts together and twist to spread the flux evenly . . .

5. Heat the fitting evenly with a propane torch . . .

6. Touch the solder to the joint where the pipe enters the fitting. The solder will be drawn into the joint. Only a small bead of solder should be visible around the edge of the fitting.

Unclogging [Sink, Tub, Shower and Main] Drains

There are two tools that should be required in all households: the rubber plunger cup, or plumber's helper, and the trap-and-drain auger. Neither is very expensive but even if they were made of platinum, they might still cost less than bringing in a plumber for the time needed to free a clogged drain. Keep both tools handy and be willing to attack any clogging problem with them.

■ **Clogged sink:** Since it is difficult to tell where the stoppage is, start by removing the sink strainer and cleaning it. It removes by either prying up or loosening two small screws. With a bent coat hanger, reach down the pipe and see if you can hook something.

If there is a stopper in the way, it can usually be removed by giving it a quarter turn either way and pulling out.

Do not try a chemical drain cleaner until you have tried mechanically moving the blockage. The drain cleaners are caustic and may burn you if you later have to drain the pipes. Instead, go to work with a plumber's helper. Plug the overflow drain and keep the sink about half full of water. Pump the plunger rapidly to keep the water hammering at the blockage. If, after 10 or 15 minutes, you have made no progress, go to work under the sink.

If the P-trap has a cleanout plug, place a bucket under it, remove it and drain the water. Now push a coat hanger with a small hook bent on one end through the trap both up to the sink and down the drain pipe. Hook and remove what you can.

If this doesn't work, the obstruction is farther down. Wrap the nuts at each end of the P-trap with cloth to protect their chrome finish, then use a wrench to loosen and remove. Now run the auger through the branch drain toward the main drain. If you still hit nothing, the clog is in the main drain pipe — go to the next page.

■ **Clogged tub:** A tub sometimes doesn't drain properly because the adjusting nut on the linkage for the plug has loosened. To adjust this, unscrew the plate on the overflow drain and pull the linkage out. Tighten the nut on the threaded screw to keep the plug free of the drain. See page 81 for a detailed drawing of the linkage.

If this wasn't the problem, remove the linkage and pop-up plug, if it exists, and go to work with the plunger. Keep several inches of water in the tub both to minimize splashing and to develop more pressure. Also, keep the overflow drain plugged with rags to increase pressure.

The next stage is to run the auger down the pipe. Insert it down the overflow drain for a little easier access to the P-trap below. Keep pushing and cranking slowly clockwise as the auger descends. When you hook something, keep cranking into it as you begin withdrawing the auger.

If your bathtub has a drum trap located in the floor near the tub, rather than a P-trap, free the drain with a different approach.

With an adjustable wrench, remove the plug and then run the augur through the lower pipe back toward the tub. If there is no obstruction there, the auger should work its way up to the overflow drain.

If that isn't the solution, guide the auger down the upper pipe toward the main drain, slowly twisting it clockwise as it moves.

Again, if the auger moves into the

Unclogging a sink

First, plug the overflow drain with a wet rag and, with the sink about half full of water, pump the plunger up and down rapidly . . .

If the plunger doesn't work and the trap has a cleanout plug, remove it and try to get the clog with a hooked piece of coat-hanger wire . . .

The next step is to remove the trap and go down the branch drain with a trap-and-drain auger.

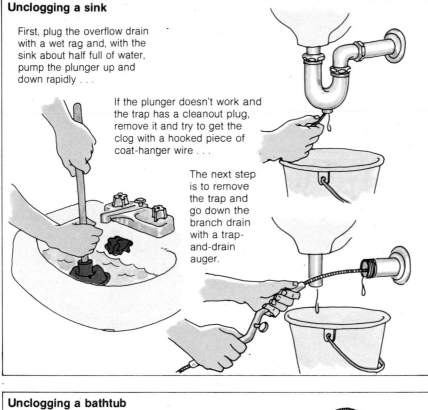

Unclogging a bathtub

Remove the stopper linkage (see page 81) if there is one. Stuff the overflow drain with a wet rag and use a plunger quickly . . .

If the tub is still clogged, run your snake down the overflow drain . . . or down the drum trap if your tub has one—the cover will be apparent near the side of the tub.

Drum trap

main drain line without hitting an obstruction, the clog is much farther along. See below for details on freeing clogged mains.

■ **Clogged shower drain:** These can be difficult to clear with a plumber's helper, but give it a try. Coat the bottom of the suction cup with some petroleum jelly for a tighter suction.

If the plunger doesn't work, the best solution is a length of hose pushed into the drain. If you can't reach a garden spiggot with the other end, buy an adapter at a hardware store and hook it to the bathroom sink faucet. When the hose is in place, pack the space between the hose and drain with rags, and turn on the water.

An even more effective device for this kind of work is an inexpensive rubber nozzle that inflates when the water is on to seal the drain while at the same time shooting a narrow, high pressure stream of water against the obstruction. These can also be used in clearing sinks — but be careful that the pressure doesn't blow the P-trap off the bottom of the sink.

■ **Main drains:** When you — or worse, your guests — start sniffing the air in your house and wondering aloud about the strange, malodorous atmosphere, it's probably a clog in the stack vent. Foul air that should be moving up and out the vent is trapped and making its way slowly into the house.

Before you go to work on it, make sure it isn't in one of the branch drains. If several sinks and a tub are not draining properly, that's a good indication that the main stack is blocked.

Rather than trying to run an auger around numerous pipe bends, work straight down the vent from its opening on the roof. Position yourself securely on the roof, using a hooked ladder (see page 5) or safety rope if it's not a flat roof. Use a trap-and-drain auger that is long enough to reach the bottom of the vent. Turning the auger clockwise, work it down the vent until it hits and engages the clog.

If you can't reach it with your own auger, consider renting a 50-foot powered auger, particularly if you have a two-story house.

If working down the stack vent doesn't open the pipes, you will have to go under the house to the cleanout on the main drain. This Y fitting will be at the bottom of the main stack. You'll need a large adjustable wrench to unscrew the cover plate.

Before you do this, however, remember there may be several feet of waste water backed up in that pipe. If possible, run no water in the house for several hours and some or all the water will seep through the blockage. At any rate, have several buckets, newspapers and mops ready to clean up the mess when you open the cover.

Work the auger down the drain toward the sewer pipe. Again, if you have a long pipe run, rent a powered auger for the job. When the obstruction is cleared, flush the pipe with water from a hose. When replacing the cleanout cover, coat the threads with joint compound.

Some houses are equipped with a U-shaped house trap, evidenced by two adjacent cleanout plugs. It's usually located near where the main drain leaves the house. In working from here, always first unscrew the plug closest to the sewer. Do it slowly, with newspapers and a mop handy. If little or no water runs out, the obstruction is most likely between the house trap and the main cleanout. Work the auger slowly back up the pipe and when you hit something, try to open just a small hole. Recap the house trap and let the trapped water drain through before removing all the clog.

Unclogging shower drain

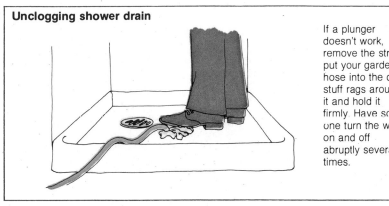

If a plunger doesn't work, remove the strainer, put your garden hose into the drain, stuff rags around it and hold it firmly. Have someone turn the water on and off abruptly several times.

Unclogging main drain

Y-FITTING ON THE MAIN DRAIN STACK
Remove the clean-out plug with a monkey wrench and run your trap-and-drain auger down the pipe.

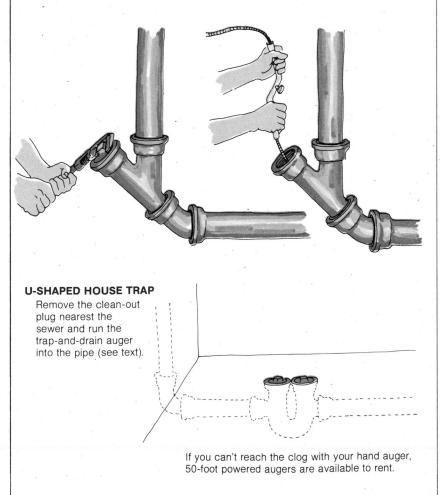

U-SHAPED HOUSE TRAP
Remove the clean-out plug nearest the sewer and run the trap-and-drain auger into the pipe (see text).

If you can't reach the clog with your hand auger, 50-foot powered augers are available to rent.

Repairing Leaks

Leaks can occur almost anywhere, from the White House (where they are known as usually reliable sources) down to that wretched P-trap under your sink. Some leaks are reasonably obvious while others may leave a little-noticed damp spot in a far corner. If that damp spot is on a ceiling or wall and it hasn't rained recently, suspect a leak in the pipes behind the walls.

If you harbor such suspicions, conduct a simple test. Turn off all the water in the house and then, using a felt-tip pen, make a line directly over the 1-cubic-foot scale on your water meter (if you don't have this scale, make the mark over the 10-cubic-foot scale.) Check the meter for the next hour or two. If it moves at all, you have a leak. If it moves rather rapidly, you have a big leak and you should immediately shut off the main water valve until you find and repair it.

If you have no water meter, put your ear to the main incoming pipe and listen for a telltale gurgle or hiss if there is a leak.

■ **Leaky P-trap:** The P-trap, that U-shaped device under your sink, is designed always to contain water to keep sewer gases from coming back up the pipe. But that constant water also tends to rust out P-traps or rot the rubber washers, either of which results in leaks. If water leaks from around the slip nuts, first try tightening them. If that is not sufficient, replace the washers. If the piping leaks, repair it as already described.

There are two types of P-traps — swivel and fixed. Both are held by slip nuts at each end of the trap. If they are chrome, wrap them with tape to protect the finish before loosening with a wrench. Be sure you have a bucket under the trap to catch the water. Then turn the nuts counterclockwise to loosen.

Inspect the rubber washers in all the slip nuts. Unless they are still soft and pliable, replace them.

Take the old P-trap with you to the plumbing store to get the right washers. To put it back in place, just hold it firmly and screw the slip nuts back together.

■ **Leaky cleanout:** This is rarely a problem, but may occur after you have unscrewed a long unused and partially rusted cleanout cover. Remove the cover and use a steel brush to clean out any rust particles lodged beween the threads. Now give the threads on the cover a liberal dosing of pipe joint compound and screw back down tightly. The compound will help seal the opening and keep the cover from rusting shut again.

Reading a water meter

Water meters register CUBIC FEET and run continuously from when they are installed. To tell how much is used in a month, take a reading at the beginning and end of the month and subtract. Some have a direct readout like a car odometer; most have dials as shown here. Read the lowest number the needle is between and put a zero as the unit digit. The sweep needle (or "ONE FOOT" dial) is to detect leaks only. This meter reads 371,940.

■ **Clearing frozen pipes:** Life is much easier if you never allow your pipes to get frozen in the first place. If a sudden cold snap arrives and you know the pipes aren't that well protected, keep a trickle of water running from each faucet during the night: moving water is much slower to freeze. If possible, put several 100-watt bulbs near exposed pipes or put a small heater down there for the cold spell.

For a more permanent cure, wrap all the pipes in special pipe insulation that comes with tape to keep the insulation neatly and tightly in place.

In areas where even more protection is needed, pipes can be wrapped with electrical heating wires designed just for this purpose. Some are equipped with thermostats to turn on the heat automatically when required.

However, if you're muttering that it's too late for precautions and you need instant cures, there are several good solutions.

First, always open the faucet nearest the leak or frozen place so vapor from the melting ice will have an escape vent, and not make a new one through the middle of your pipe. Then work from the faucet back along the pipe to the frozen area.

Grandmother's frozen-pipe cure — wrapping the pipe in rags and pouring boiling water over it — still works but is slow and messy. A heating pad wrapped around the pipe or a heat lamp aimed at it will work well. So does a hair dryer. The fastest cure, however, is a propane torch equipped with a flame spreader on the end. Never let the pipe get too hot to touch

Leaky P-trap

(See the text for the steps to take.)

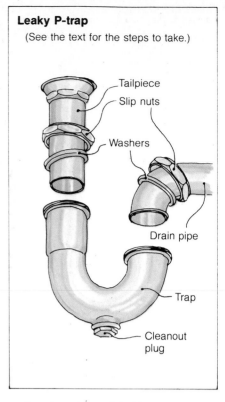

Tailpiece
Slip nuts
Washers
Drain pipe
Trap
Cleanout plug

and protect the wall behind with some sheet metal.

■ **Curing noisy pipes:** Loud noises in the pipes when the water is running are usually caused by loose pipe hangers. The pipes are simply vibrating as the water stops and starts. Track down the noise and then tighten the clamps against the pipes.

In some cases it may be easier to slip wedges between the pipe and clamp to stop the chattering. If there is a long run of pipe with no supports to hold it against the joists, add some.

If the rattling is coming from behind walls and you don't feel up to tearing out the wall, first try wedging the pipes tight both where they enter and come out the wall.

A water hammer is a different problem. It is easily recognizable by a slamming sound every time you shut off the water. It's caused by the flow of water being stopped suddenly and, having no other place to go, it vibrates the entire pipe. In properly plumbed houses, this is avoided by air chambers installed on the pipes near each faucet to cushion the impact of the water.

Air chambers are normally installed behind the walls but there are a few ways to avoid tearing out your walls to add more. Most plumbing stores carry copper coil air chambers that can be installed under a sink with a T-fitting and a couple of nipples.

If the plumbing is exposed, as in a basement or laundry room, a capped length of pipe can be added to provide the necessary cushion.

Sometimes, even with air chambers

Leaky cleanout

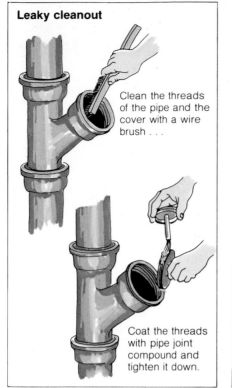

Clean the threads of the pipe and the cover with a wire brush . . .

Coat the threads with pipe joint compound and tighten it down.

Thawing frozen pipes

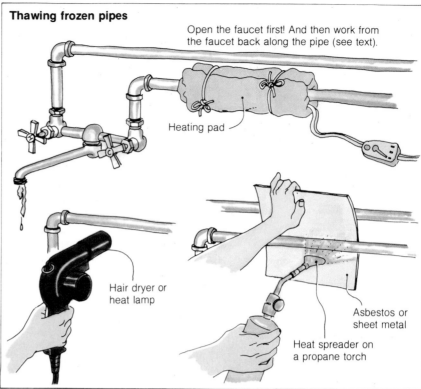

Open the faucet first! And then work from the faucet back along the pipe (see text).

Heating pad

Hair dryer or heat lamp

Asbestos or sheet metal

Heat spreader on a propane torch

installed, water hammering starts. In this case, the air chambers have usually become filled with water. To cure this, all pipes in the house must be drained. First shut off the main water line and then open all faucets in the house. Next, drain your hot water heater (this should be done every few months anyway) to let air move through the pipes and into the cham-

bers. Now, close the faucets and open the main valve to refill the system.

■ **Bathtub drains:** Excluding the good old rubber plug, there are two main types of plugs on bathtubs: the pop-up and trip-lever. Both are controlled by a locknut on a threaded rod. Repeated opening and closing can cause that nut to move, which results in either leaks or slow drainage.

■ **Trip-Lever drain:** In this type of drainage arrangement, the plug works by dropping straight into the seat at the base of the overflow pipe. If the nut has worked its way up, the plug will not fit tightly in the seat and water will leak through. If the nut has worked down the threaded rod, the plug will not lift completely clear of the drain when opened.

To adjust the lever assembly, unscrew the lever plate and pull it out. Usually it will not take much adjustment of the nut to correct the problem. That is done simply by trial and error.

■ **Pop-Up drain:** The linkage here is similar to the trip-lever drain. The pop-up stopper in the drain is attached to a rocker arm that is controlled by the trip-lever linkage.

If tub drainage is slow, do not attempt to correct it by removing the plug. It is designed to stop small objects from being swept into the drain where they can cause stoppages.

To adjust this drain, first unscrew the trip-lever plate and pull out the upper linkage. Now pull out the pop-up section if you want to check and clean it. Look for accumulated hair on the linkage and check the rubber washer around the stopper; if it isn't soft and pliable, replace it. In putting this section back in the drain, make sure the rocker arm is facing down.

Note the spring at the end of the threaded rod on the trip-lever linkage. When this presses down on the rocker arm, the plug pops up. Thus, if you want the stopper to rise higher, length-

Adjusting bathtub stopper

Remove screws and lift the mechanism out by the overflow plate. Adjust the lock nut. Check condition of cotter pins.

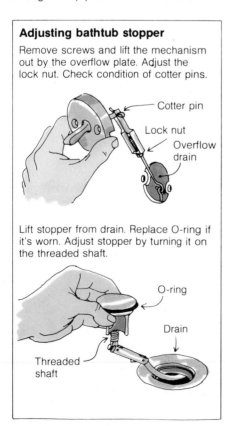

Cotter pin

Lock nut

Overflow drain

Lift stopper from drain. Replace O-ring if it's worn. Adjust stopper by turning it on the threaded shaft.

O-ring

Drain

Threaded shaft

Adjusting sink stopper

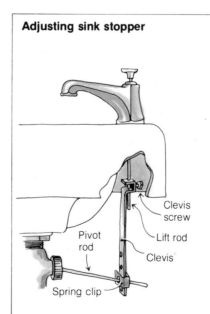

Clevis screw

Lift rod

Clevis

Pivot rod

Spring clip

Small adjustments are made by loosening the clevis screw and sliding the clevis up or down the lift rod. Larger adjustments require squeezing the spring clip and resetting the pivot rod in another clevis hole.

Sink strainers

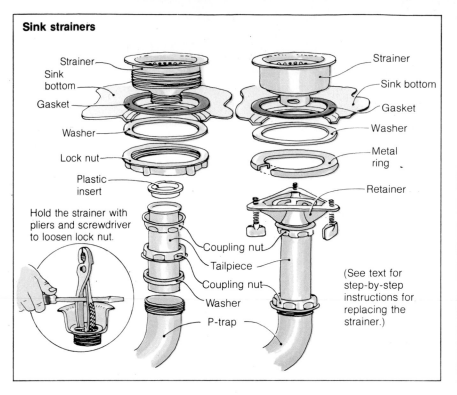

Strainer
Sink bottom
Gasket
Washer
Lock nut
Plastic insert

Strainer
Sink bottom
Gasket
Washer
Metal ring
Retainer

Hold the strainer with pliers and screwdriver to loosen lock nut.

Coupling nut
Tailpiece
Coupling nut
Washer
P-trap

(See text for step-by-step instructions for replacing the strainer.)

Copper pipes

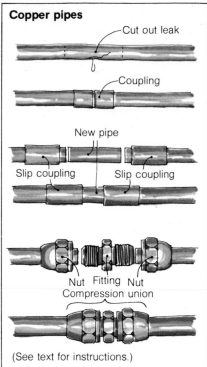

Cut out leak
Coupling
New pipe
Slip coupling   Slip coupling
Nut Fitting Nut
Compression union

(See text for instructions.)

en the rod; to make the plug fit tighter, shorten the rod.

■ **Leaking sink strainers:** Leaks sometimes develop around the drains in kitchen sinks because the sink strainer and its parts have corroded away. Check under the sink to see if your strainer is held by three screws in a plastic retainer or by a single locknut on the strainer.

In either case, loosen the slip nuts

Plastic pipe

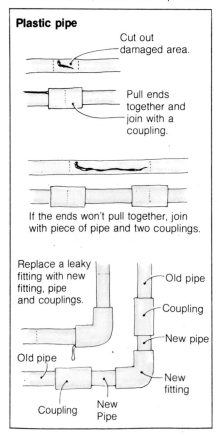

Cut out damaged area.

Pull ends together and join with a coupling.

If the ends won't pull together, join with piece of pipe and two couplings.

Replace a leaky fitting with new fitting, pipe and couplings.
Old pipe
Coupling
New pipe
Old pipe
New fitting
Coupling   New Pipe

holding the tailpiece between the sink and P-trap, and slide it down into the P-trap. Remove the retainer screws or loosen the locknut by turning it counterclockwise. If you don't have a pipe wrench big enough, drive it open with a hammer and a piece of wood wedged in one of the notches on the nut. With a screwdriver, pry the strainer out from the top. When installing the replacement, make sure the sink is completely dry and then coat the underlip of the strainer with a thick bead of plumber's putty. Press the strainer firmly in place and then replace the retainer or nut underneath. In tightening the nut, the strainer can be held in place by slipping the handles of a pair of pliers through the strainer and then slipping a screwdriver between the handles to apply counter force.

■ **Repairing leaky copper pipes:** For repairs of a pinhole leak in the middle of the pipe, shut off all water and drain the pipe. Clean the area around the hole with emery cloth, apply a coat of flux, heat the pipe with a propane torch and then apply a dab of solder to the hole. This solution is satisfactory only for a small hole, especially if reinforced with a pipe clamp. Water pressure will pop the solder out of a larger hole.

For larger breaks, cut the pipe on each side of the hole. If the pipe can be bent or moved enough, clean and flux the ends of the pipe and join them with a common coupling. Sweat it in place as detailed on page 77. If the pipe cannot be moved, cut out the break and join the two pieces of pipe with couplings or compression unions.

For leaks around joints in copper pipes, drain them and then heat the joint until the solder melts. Remove the joint, clean it with emery cloth and then sweat it back in place. If the leak is quite small, try fixing it first by smoothing a bead of epoxy paste around the joint when dry.

■ **Repairing plastic pipe:** For a pinhole leak, drain the pipe and let dry for several hours. Force some plastic pipe glue or epoxy cement into the hole and then wrap tightly with electrical tape.

If you can bend or move the pipes, cut out the holed section and rejoin the pipes with a coupling for a better repair job. If they won't bend, use a plastic union joint.

For a leaking joint, you can try smearing more epoxy pipe glue around it but this usually doesn't work. The best solution is to cut the pipe several inches away from the joint on both sides and install a new one, using couplings to rejoin the severed pipe.

■ **Repairing steel pipe:** As outlined in the Plumbing Emergencies section on page 75, a small leak in the middle of a pipe can be temporarily fixed with a piece of rubber and ordinary clamp. For a permanent repair, use a regular pipe clamp available at plumbing stores.

For small leaks around joints, shut off the water, drain the pipe and make sure the joint is dry. Pack the hole with epoxy paste and let dry before turning the water back on.

If the leak persists, unscrew the pipe, clean the threads with a wire brush and make sure they haven't rusted out. Clean the threads in the joint and then lay a thick bead of joint compound around the pipe threads and retighten.

If the break in the middle of the pipe is too large for a clamp, cut the pipe with a hacksaw and remove that section. Measure the amount of new pipe needed, allowing for the amount of pipe that has to go inside each joint so you won't come up short. Have a plumbing supply shop cut and thread this amount of pipe for you. If it is a short length, you can probably buy enough nipples and couplings at any hardware store for the job. Join the segment with a union coupling in the middle.

■ **Repairing cast iron pipe:** Leaks in cast iron are rare because the pipe is so massive. If a pinhole leak occurs in the middle of the pipe and you can't find a clamp large enough to fit the pipe, pack the hole when it has dried out with epoxy paste, then wrap it with a length of rubber inner tube and cinch this down by twisting strands of wire around it.

If the leak is around a hub, you can try tamping lead into the joint with a hammer and chisel. But you will probably have to pull out the old lead and oakum, pack it with new oakum and then pour in another layer of lead. Try "lead wool," which does not need melting. If the leak is from a horizontal hub of cast iron pipe, you must use a joint runner and clip to hold the molten lead in place. The joint runner, clip and ladle for the lead may be rented from a rental shop or a plumbing supply house.

For leaks around hubless pipe gaskets, tighten the clamps on the neoprene sleeves, or replace if necessary.

■ **Sizing pipe:** Pipe is measured by the inside diameter opening. If you can't measure this, it is often difficult to tell what size of pipe you need. This chart will aid you. Tie a knot in a piece of string, wrap it around the pipe and measure from the knot to where the other end came around and touched the knot.

Copper Pipe:

String Length	Pipe Size
$1\frac{9}{16}''$	$\frac{3}{8}''$
$2''$	$\frac{1}{2}''$
$2\frac{3}{8}''$	$\frac{5}{8}''$
$2\frac{3}{4}''$	$\frac{3}{4}''$
$3\frac{7}{16}''$	$1''$
$4\frac{5}{16}''$	$1\frac{1}{4}''$

Steel Pipe:

String Length	Pipe Size
$2\frac{3}{16}''$	$\frac{3}{8}''$
$2\frac{5}{8}''$	$\frac{1}{2}''$
$3\frac{1}{4}''$	$\frac{3}{4}''$
$4\frac{1}{8}''$	$1''$
$5\frac{1}{4}''$	$1\frac{1}{4}''$
$6''$	$1\frac{1}{2}''$

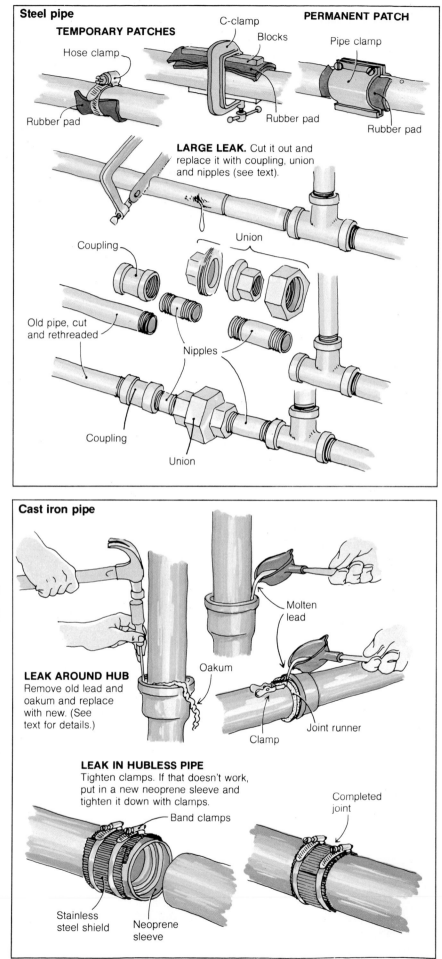

Steel pipe

TEMPORARY PATCHES

PERMANENT PATCH

Hose clamp

C-clamp

Blocks

Pipe clamp

Rubber pad

Rubber pad

Rubber pad

LARGE LEAK. Cut it out and replace it with coupling, union and nipples (see text).

Coupling

Union

Old pipe, cut and rethreaded

Nipples

Coupling

Union

Cast iron pipe

LEAK AROUND HUB Remove old lead and oakum and replace with new. (See text for details.)

Oakum

Molten lead

Joint runner

Clamp

LEAK IN HUBLESS PIPE Tighten clamps. If that doesn't work, put in a new neoprene sleeve and tighten it down with clamps.

Band clamps

Completed joint

Stainless steel shield

Neoprene sleeve

Repairing and Replacing Faucets

If the faucet giving you problems has separate handles for hot and cold water, it is known as a washer-type or compression faucet. That's because, when you turn the handle off, a washer is compressed into the opening to stop the water.

In the washerless, or noncompression faucet, a single handle controls both the flow of water and the amount of cold and hot water.

Repairing the compression faucet is a fairly straightforward process, but with the noncompression types you may have difficulty in finding replacement parts. There are a great many different varieties on the market and there is no standardization. Therefore you must buy the same make, but that isn't always a solution because your particular model may have gone off the market. If that's the case, you're better off to buy a modern new faucet. Then, of course, you'll have to remodel the entire bathroom to go with the new faucet.

■ **Compression faucets:** Before going further, your chief complaint may be that the faucet doesn't seem to put out as much water as it used to. In this case, it may only be a clogged aerator in the nozzle of your faucet. If you can't loosen it by hand, wrap some tape around it for protection and turn it counterclockwise with a pair of pliers. Clean it and put back in place.

■ **Leaking spout:** The problem here is almost always a bad washer or valve seat that allows water to slip past. The correction is made through one of the handles. If you have two handles and one spout, find which one is leaking by first turning off the water under one of the faucets. If the leak stops, that's the handle to repair; if it doesn't, it's the other one.

The handle screw is right on top of the handle but it may be hidden under a decorative cap. If so, unscrew or pry that off with a screwdriver and remove the screw. Now remove the handle. Beneath this is the packing nut that is removed by turning it counterclockwise. Protect chrome finish with tape.

With the packing nut loose, lift out the entire assembly and look at the bottom. A brass screw holds a washer in place. Remove the screw and if it's worn or bent, replace it. Replace the washer with the same kind, either flat or cone shaped. Remember that the cone always faces down when you reinstall it.

For this kind of repairs, plumbing and hardware shops sell small packages that contain a wide variety of washers, O-rings and a couple of brass screws, which saves you running back and forth to the store.

Now inspect the valve seat where the washer fits. If it is chipped or rough, it must be either replaced or refaced.

■ **Valve seats:** A gouged or roughened valve seat means the washer can't fit properly and you have a leaky faucet. To determine if the valve seat can be replaced, see if it has a hexagonal or round hole in it. If hexagonal, slip an Allen wrench in and unscrew it. If it is round, it must be refaced.

For this job, buy an inexpensive refacing tool at a plumbing shop. Now, with the faucet dismantled, slip the refacing tool through the packing nut, tighten the nut down, then screw the refacing tool down until you can work it back and forth to smooth it.

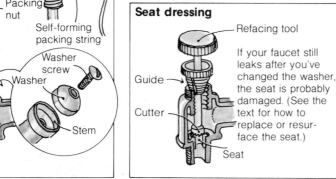

Washer faucet

Screw · Decorative button · Stem · Handle · Packing washer · Packing nut · Washer · Self-forming packing string · Stem · Washer screw · Washer · Stem · Valve seat

Seat dressing

Refacing tool

If your faucet still leaks after you've changed the washer, the seat is probably damaged. (See the text for how to replace or resurface the seat.)

Guide · Cutter · Seat

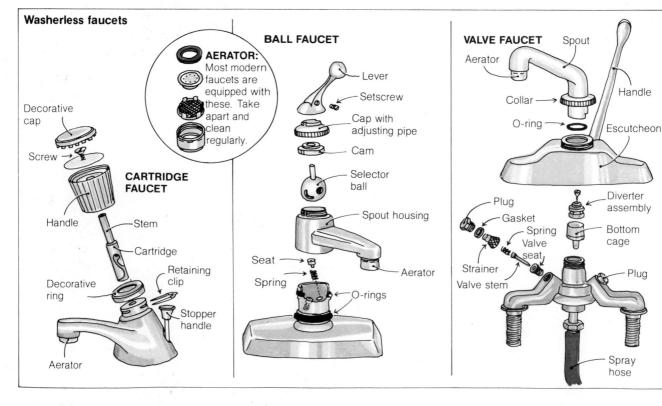

Washerless faucets

AERATOR: Most modern faucets are equipped with these. Take apart and clean regularly.

CARTRIDGE FAUCET

Decorative cap · Screw · Handle · Stem · Cartridge · Decorative ring · Retaining clip · Stopper handle · Aerator

BALL FAUCET

Lever · Setscrew · Cap with adjusting pipe · Cam · Selector ball · Spout housing · Seat · Spring · Aerator · O-rings

VALVE FAUCET

Spout · Aerator · Collar · O-ring · Handle · Escutcheon · Plug · Gasket · Spring · Valve seat · Strainer · Valve stem · Diverter assembly · Bottom cage · Plug · Spray hose

■ **Leaking handle:** Remove the handle as described above and then loosen the packing nut and lift out the stem. Under the packing nut, on the stem, you will see either a rubber O-ring (on newer faucets), a packing washer or some packing string. If it is an O-ring, work it off with a screwdriver and roll on the new one. It must be the same size.

For packing, buy a new packing washer, some graphite-impregnated string or Teflon packing string at a plumbing shop. Wind it clockwise around the stem until thick enough to be compressed — usually four or five turns — then tighten down the packing nut and replace handle.

■ **Noncompression faucets:** These faucets, with a single handle for control, come in three basic types: *cartridge*, *valve* and *ball*. In most cases, the manufacturers do their devious best to hide the screws and nuts necessary to dismantle them. Some are under snap or screw caps on top of the handle; sometimes there's a nut at the base of the spout; or there may be a setscrew located under the handle. On some cartridge types, the setscrew is found by pushing the handle all the way back and looking under it. After removing that, remove the two screws under the spout and then disconnect the pop-up stopper under the sink.

■ **Cartridge faucets:** These come in two basic varieties — the metal sleeve with a screw holding it from the top, and the newer ceramic disc.

Disassemble the metal sleeve style by removing the screw, then pushing a screwdriver down the hole to keep the stem in place while you pull off the handle and cover. Now unscrew the retaining nut and remove the spout. The faucet body is now exposed and you can see two O-rings, at the top and bottom. These are probably the source of your leaking spout.

Remove the retainer clip at the top of the faucet body, lift it off the stem and replace the rings. Reassemble in the opposite manner.

The ceramic disc cartridge is removed by shutting off the water and then tilting the knob all the way back to expose the setscrew. Remove it and the two screws under the spout, and then disengage the stopper mechanism under the sink. A cartridge held by two brass screws is now revealed. Replace it with the exact same model.

■ **Valve faucets:** Unscrew the collar at the base of the spout and pull free. If your only problem was a leak around the spout at this point, replace the O-ring at the base of the spout and reassemble.

Otherwise, with the spout off, lift off

the faucet body cover (escutcheon). On each side of the faucet you can now see a plug. Remove them by turning counterclockwise and pull out the gasket, strainer, spring, stem and valve. If any part is worn or chipped, replace it.

The seat will have to be removed with a seat removal tool or an Allen wrench that fits. In a pinch, put a screwdriver in the hexagonal hole to turn it. After the necessary parts have been replaced, reassemble the faucet. Before replacing the cover, however, adjust the screw at the base of the handle to firm up the handle movement.

■ **Ball faucets:** Loosen the setscrew at the base of the handle, then loosen and remove the cap at the base of the handle, having wrapped it with tape to

protect it from the plier teeth. Pull the ball and cam assembly out. Underneath, in the base of the faucet, you will see two rubber valve seats. If you have a leaking faucet, this is the problem. Pull them out with needle-nose pliers and replace.

See that the ball is not corroded or gouged, then slip it back in place. A slot in one side of the ball must line up with the metal projection on one side. The plastic cam assembly now slips on, its tab lining up with the slot in the faucet body.

Before putting the handle back on, turn on the water and open the faucet. If there is a slight leak around the stem, tighten the adjusting ring just inside the cam assembly by putting a small screwdriver in the slot and turning the ring.

Replacing faucets

If you don't like your old faucets, replace them with some new ones. It's not much harder than fixing the ones you have.

To replace them with a new unit, you must find one that fits the holes in your sink. Measure the space between the center of the holes. Draw a diagram to take with you to the store.

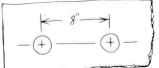

If your old sink's holes don't match any single-lever unit you can find, buy some modern individual faucets as replacements. DO NOT try to adapt your old sink to a unit that won't fit. It's just not worth it.

There are chrome-plated escutcheon caps available to cover extra unneeded holes.

1. Turn off the water at the shut off valves.

2. Use a basin wrench to loosen the upper and lower coupling nuts. Remove the supply tubes.

3. Remove the lock nuts and washers. Lift off the old faucets.

4. Set in the new faucet assembly and secure it with the washers and lock nuts.

5. Reconnect the supply tubes with the coupling nuts and turn the shut off valves back on.

6. Remove the aerator and run both hot and cold water full blast for a minute or two to clean out the pipes and to check for leaks.

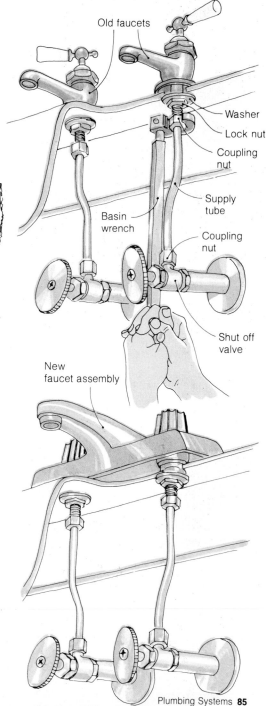

Old faucets

Washer

Lock nut

Coupling nut

Supply tube

Basin wrench

Coupling nut

Shut off valve

New faucet assembly

Repairing Toilets

Think how rich that English gentleman, Sir Thomas Crapper, would be if he and his heirs had received just one penny every time someone used his great invention, the flush toilet. Despite all this use, the mechanism of the toilet remains largely a mystery to many and when there is trouble, they have to call a plumber. These mysteries are now about to be revealed.

When you press down on the handle, a lever lifts a ball or flapper from a hole in the bottom of the tank, allowing the water to run into the bowl. As the water in the tank drops, a float ball drops with it, opening an intake valve in the ballcock assembly that lets in fresh water. At the same time, the ball or flapper falls back in place over the drain hole. As the water rises in the tank, so does the float ball until, at a certain level, it closes the intake valve.

Problems with toilets usually center on this mechanism. There is, however, a new unit on the market that has fewer moving parts, better water control, and eliminates several of the strange sounds associated with toilet tanks.

One of the most common problems with a toilet is water continuing to run into the tank when it should have shut off. First, remove the cover from the tank and place it carefully in a secure place. It can be easily broken.

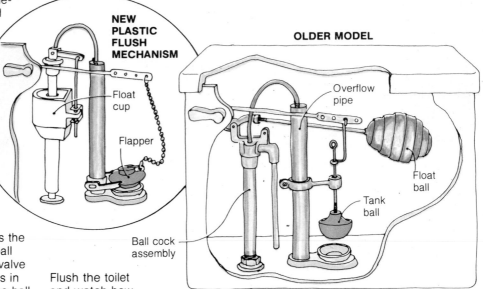

NEW PLASTIC FLUSH MECHANISM

Float cup

Flapper

OLDER MODEL

Overflow pipe

Float ball

Tank ball

Ball cock assembly

Flush the toilet and watch how the mechanism works.

As the tank refills, you will see that the water begins flowing into the overflow pipe and doesn't shut off. This is because the float ball hasn't risen far enough to shut off the intake valve. The ball may have water in it and not be floating properly. Unscrew it from the end of the rod and shake it. If it has water in it, replace it with a new one. If that wasn't the problem, replace it and then bend the rod down in the middle. Bending it down about ½ inch should make the water stop about ½ inch from the top of the overflow pipe.

If this doesn't correct the problem, it lies in the intake valve. Rather than trying to replace that, install a new self-contained plastic flush mechanism.

To install a new mechanism with an adjustable float cup for more accurate water control, first close the shut off valve on the water line beneath the tank. Flush the toilet to empty the tank. Slip an adjustable wrench or pair of locking pliers over the nut at the bottom of the ballcock assembly. With another wrench, loosen the nut under the tank that holds this assembly. Before tightening down the new assembly, be sure the washers are not cracked or too hardened to

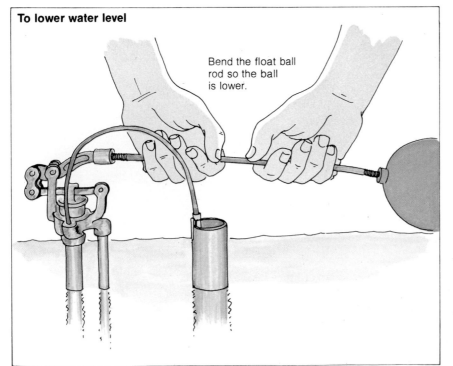

To lower water level

Bend the float ball rod so the ball is lower.

Replacing float ball

Remove float ball assembly with locking pliers inside the tank and adjustable wrench outside (see text).

be effective.

Another common problem with toilets is the tank ball or flapper on the end of the trip wire not seating properly in the drain. An irritating gurgle results.

To correct this, flush the toilet to drain the tank and then keep the float ball held up with a coat hanger bent under it and hooked on the sides of the tank. Unscrew the tank ball from the guide rod, clean the valve seat, and screw on a new ball.

A better solution is to replace the tank ball with a flapper, which is considered less prone to misalignment. The flapper, available in plumbing and hardware shops, clips around the base of the overflow valve and then hooks to the pull chain.

■ **Sweating tanks:** Condensation may build up on tanks when cold water flowing in cools the porcelain so much in a warm room that the "sweating" occurs. This can be more than a nuisance: the moisture dripping on the floor can loosen the tiles, soak the subflooring and result in rot.

The easiest solution, and effective unless the incoming water is very cold, is to line the tank with a layer of insulation. Half-inch thick styrofoam or foam rubber works well. Drain the tank and wipe it completely dry. Then use epoxy resin to affix the insulation to all four sides. It should reach well above the water line and not interfere with any of the mechanism. Let the glue dry before refilling.

If the tank still sweats, you will have to tap into an existing hot water line nearby and mix it with the incoming cold. Seek a plumber's assistance on this project.

■ **Unclogging a toilet:** If you notice a toilet not flushing completely, start working on it right away. It's much easier to clear now rather than when completely stopped.

First, work with a plumber's helper as an emergency treatment (see illustration at right).

If that fails, use either a closet auger designed for toilets or a trap-and-drain auger. Both can usually be rented but even if you have to buy one, it's cheaper than calling in the plumber.

When using the closet auger, put the curved tip of the tube into the drain hole. Now, pushing and turning the crank, feed the auger into the drain. Always turn in the same direction and when you hit the obstruction, keep turning the same way as you pull it out.

If the auger will not feed through the toilet's built-in trap far enough to reach the obstruction, and no amount of plunger work will free it, take two aspirin and admit to yourself that you should call a plumber — or pull the toilet.

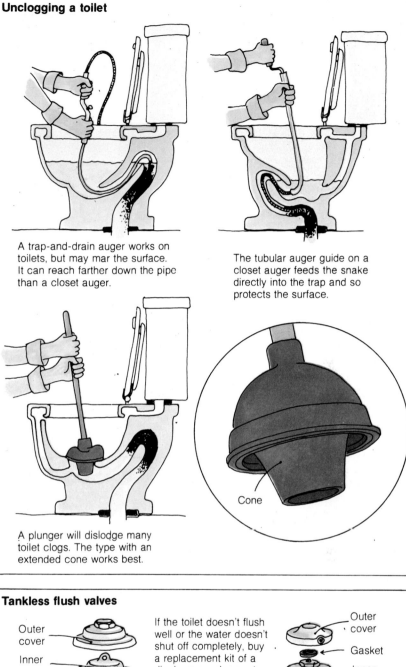

Unclogging a toilet

A trap-and-drain auger works on toilets, but may mar the surface. It can reach farther down the pipe than a closet auger.

The tubular auger guide on a closet auger feeds the snake directly into the trap and so protects the surface.

A plunger will dislodge many toilet clogs. The type with an extended cone works best.

Cone

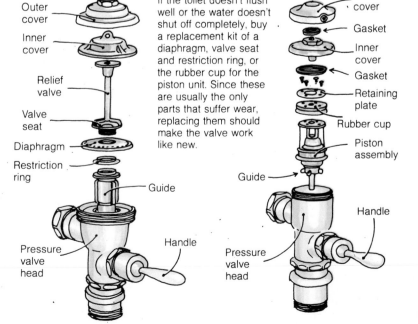

Tankless flush valves

If the toilet doesn't flush well or the water doesn't shut off completely, buy a replacement kit of a diaphragm, valve seat and restriction ring, or the rubber cup for the piston unit. Since these are usually the only parts that suffer wear, replacing them should make the valve work like new.

Outer cover
Inner cover
Relief valve
Valve seat
Diaphragm
Restriction ring
Guide
Pressure valve head
Handle

Outer cover
Gasket
Inner cover
Gasket
Retaining plate
Rubber cup
Piston assembly
Guide
Handle
Pressure valve head

Replacing a Toilet

If you have to remove a toilet to clear a blockage, you might consider replacing it with a newer model. There are three basic types of toilets and three basic mounting styles. When purchasing a new one, consider these differences in making your selection.

The older style, **wash-down** model is relatively noisy and has only the basic trap-sealing protection. However, it costs less than other styles.

The **reverse-trap** model is a step up in both money and efficiency. It's quieter, more elongated for comfort and has a deep trap.

The **siphon jet**, the most expensive and most efficient of the three, is identifiable by a ⅝-inch hole below the water line. It uses less water than the others.

In addition to the different types, toilets are mounted in different styles. The older style has a wall-mounted tank with an elbow connecting it to the bowl. A more up-to-date style has the tank mounted on the back of the toilet, and the very latest style is a single-unit toilet. There is also the wall-mounted bowl with the tank hidden in the wall. Installing one of these, however, requires extensive new plumbing.

■ **Removing the old toilet:** Replacing a toilet is more time consuming than complicated. Allow yourself 4 to 5 hours for the job.

Start by turning off the water under the tank, then flushing the toilet. Use a sponge and can to remove as much water as possible from both tank and bowl. Use a wrench to disconnect the water supply line. If this is a rigid pipe with no turnoff valve, plan on installing a valve and using a flexible pipe for the new toilet.

If the tank is wall mounted, remove the spud pipe, or elbow, connecting it to the tank. Unscrew the nuts on the hanger bolts inside the tank and lift it out of the way.

If the tank is mounted to the toilet, remove the two bolts holding it to the back of the bowl.

Before removing the bowl from the floor, measure the "rough in" distance — from the wall to the two bolts at the base of the bowl. If there are four, measure to the back ones. It is normally 12 inches but if different, explain this to the plumbing shop clerk so that you will get the proper replacement.

Unscrew or pry off the caps over the bolts and remove the nuts from these hold-down bolts. Now straddle the bowl and rock it gently from side to side to break the wax seal loose. When free, lift the bowl straight up to

Wash-down toilet

Reverse-trap toilet

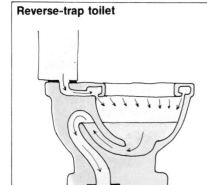

Siphon-jet toilet

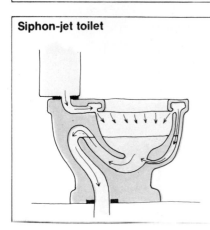

Steps in removing an old toilet

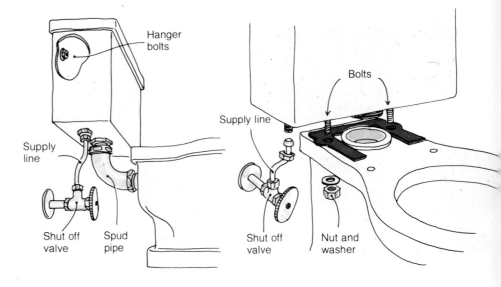

Hanger bolts

Supply line

Shut off valve

Spud pipe

Bolts

Supply line

Shut off valve

Nut and washer

Steps in installing a new toilet

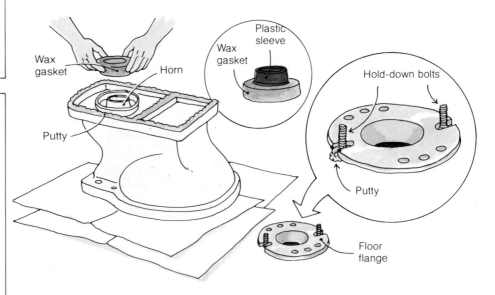

Wax gasket

Horn

Putty

Plastic sleeve

Wax gasket

Hold-down bolts

Putty

Floor flange

keep from spilling the water in the trap and set it carefully outside.

With a putty knife, remove all wax from the flange in the floor. Do this job thoroughly to avoid a leak around the new wax gasket.

Now turn the new bowl upside down on a bed of newspapers to keep it from scratching, and install the new wax gasket. Press it firmly and evenly over the horn, with the taped side fitting against the base of the toilet. If the floor flange is recessed in the floor, get a wax gasket with a plastic sleeve attached that fits down into the flange.

Slip new hold-down bolts into position in the flange and, if necessary, use plumber's putty to keep them upright. Put a thick layer of plumber's putty around the base of the bowl.

After double-checking that there is no packing paper left in the bowl, turn it over and set it smoothly and even-ly in place. Twist it back and forth slightly to smooth out the putty and then sit on it to force the gasket down.

Check the toilet with a level. If necessary, slip some thin metal shims under the base to even it up or to eliminate any rocking. Once level, tighten the nuts on the hold-down bolts. But be very careful here, for if you overdo it, you will crack the bowl. Double-check the level.

If the tank is to be mounted to the bowl, place the rubber cushion on the bowl so it lines up with the two bolt holes. Push the cone-shaped rubber gasket over the tank's flush outlet and then bolt the tank down.

All that remains now is to hook up the water supply line. However, if the new tank is lower and too close to the water pipe stub-out, put an elbow on the stub-out, drop down 4 to 6 inches with a nipple, then come out again with another elbow and nipple. Screw a valve onto the end of the nipple and connect that to the tank with a flexible water line. If the stub-out is copper, you will have to sweat on a brass adapter.

■ **Replacing a toilet seat:** The only occasional problem here is breaking loose corroded bolts holding the seat to the bowl. If they don't easily come loose, squirt some penetrating oil all around them and leave overnight. If they still won't budge, even using a socket wrench, saw them off with a hacksaw and tap them out. Put some cardboard between the saw and the bowl so you won't damage the porcelain.

In selecting a new seat, you need the dimensions of the bowl. Either carry the old seat jauntily with you or put a stiff piece of cardboard over the bowl and trace its outline.

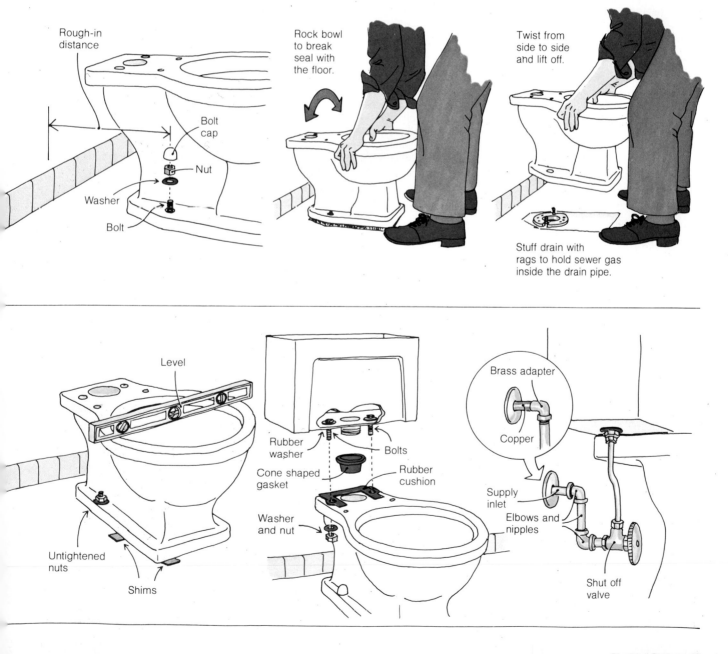

Rough-in distance

Bolt cap

Nut

Washer

Bolt

Rock bowl to break seal with the floor.

Twist from side to side and lift off.

Stuff drain with rags to hold sewer gas inside the drain pipe.

Level

Untightened nuts

Shims

Rubber washer

Cone shaped gasket

Washer and nut

Bolts

Rubber cushion

Brass adapter

Copper

Supply inlet

Elbows and nipples

Shut off valve

Garbage Disposer Repairs

One of the most common problems with a garbage disposer is jamming. This can be caused by overloading or feeding it some of your silverware. Large bones aren't helpful down there, either.

If your disposer jams, the cutting teeth will stop and you will hear only a humming sound. An overload protector built into the unit will shut the motor off by itself in about 30 seconds if you aren't nearby.

When a disposer jams, turn the switch to off and let the motor cool 5 or 10 minutes.

Since there are many different models, it's handy at this point if you have the manufacturer's instructions.

Some units have a switch that makes the disposer blades run in reverse to free themselves.

If yours doesn't, the standard way to handle these machines is to use a stick — perhaps the end of a broom handle — to force the cutting blades back in the opposite direction. Make sure the power switch is off before you do this. Once the blades are free, use a flashlight to see what jammed it. Never put your hand down there. If you see a fork or bone, use a pair of pliers to pull it out — but not before you've turned off the power to this circuit at the electric supply box.

Once the blockage is free, turn the power back on, push the red reset button on the unit and try it again. If it still doesn't run and you are sure the blades are free, you may have a defective motor that will need replacement or professional repair.

Some other problems:

Unit won't start: check that it is plugged in, the fuse on that circuit is good, and that the outlet is working properly. Also, push the reset button as a check that the overload protector hasn't been tripped.

Disposer too noisy: turn it off and see if silverware or large bones are down there. Or the mounting screws may be loose, the flywheel may be

Garbage disposal

To unjam, force blade backwards with a broom handle.

Reset button

broken or the motor may be defective.

Disposer drains poorly: First try running more water while cutting. If that doesn't help, turn off the power supply and use a bent coathanger to probe for a dishrag caught in the blades or below. Finally, you may have to clear the sink trap and drain it as described on page 80.

Fixing a Dishwasher

A basic maintenance procedure on a dishwasher is to clean the water jets on the sprayer. Unscrew the nut holding it, lift out, and use a piece of wire to pick out any food particles wedged in the holes.

Before doing any of the other repairs outlined below, make sure there is no power to the machine. If it is portable, unplug it. Otherwise, cut the power by removing the fuse or pushing the circuit breaker to off in your electric supply box.

■ **Washer won't run:** The door must close properly and tightly to activate the door switch. Wait a few moments: the machine may just be between cycles. Otherwise, open the door and make sure nothing is jammed against the spray arm. Then check the fuse or breaker for the circuit. If there is a red reset button on your model, push that, close the door tightly and try again. If it still doesn't work, call for a professional repair.

■ **Dishwasher overfills:** Most dishwashers are protected against this by a float switch. A float connected to this switch rides and falls with the water to control the amount being let in. If your tub is overfilling, jiggle the float located in the tub to make sure the arm is free.

If that isn't the solution, having shut off all power to the dishwasher, disconnect the leads, unscrew the float

switch and replace it with a new one.

■ **Washer won't drain:** Some dishwashers are drained by the motor reversing itself and instead of spraying water in, it pumps the waste water out. Other models have drains. First check if yours has drains and see that they are not plugged. If you have a reversible pump, better call for repairs.

■ **Dishwasher leaks:** First check that the gasket around the door is in place and is not cracked or broken. If it is, replace it. Also check the water supply hose. Tighten the clamps.

■ **Cycle and timer switches faulty:** This is usually a job for a professional.

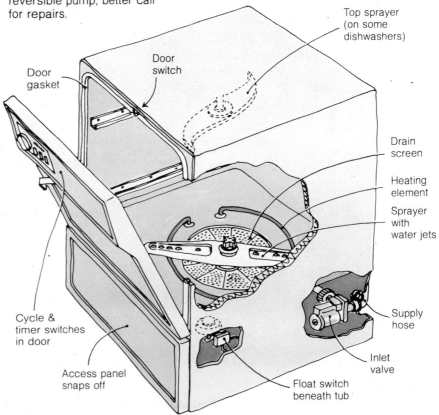

Top sprayer (on some dishwashers)

Door switch

Door gasket

Drain screen

Heating element

Sprayer with water jets

Cycle & timer switches in door

Access panel snaps off

Float switch beneath tub

Supply hose

Inlet valve

Water Heaters

The water heater is one of the biggest energy users in the house. Proper care and maintenance will save you money by keeping it efficient.

Make a standard practice of draining off a dishpan full of water from the heater every few months. This keeps sediment from building up in the bottom and reducing the heating efficiency.

And for safety reasons, once a year push down (or up, as the case may be) on the handle of the pressure relief valve to make sure it is working. This should be connected to an overflow pipe so that in the event water is forced out here, it won't spray all over the room, possibly scalding someone. If the heater doesn't already have an overflow pipe, you can quickly put one on yourself. Buy a threaded nipple long enough to reach 2 inches beyond the edge of the tank, a 90 degree elbow, and another threaded piece of pipe long enough to reach within 18 inches of the floor. Apply joint compound to the threads and tighten together with two wrenches.

Energy savings can also be realized by wrapping the heater with a layer of insulation. Fiberglass house insulation will do or you can buy prefabricated insulation covers.

In addition, keep the temperature setting on the thermostat down. Many families waste money by keeping the water hotter than they need.

All late model water heaters have an energy cut-off device that automatically stops power to the unit if the water becomes dangerously hot. It prevents the water from boiling, building up steam and possibly exploding the tank. If you find on repeated occasions that the water becomes hotter than normal just before the heat supply goes off, you probably have a defective heater thermostat. Call in professional service to replace it.

A rumbling sound in the heater is another indicator that the thermostat is defective and allowing the water to reach the boiling point. Shut off the heater immediately. Check first that you didn't have the thermostat setting pushed up to the maximum. If not, call for a professional.

If you start getting rusty water from the hot water tap, it indicates either corrosion in the tank or possibly in your main water source. Drain the water heater by attaching a hose to the spigot at the base and letting it run outside. If the water runs clear after this, you've removed a buildup of sediment or rust in the tank but it may return. If there seemed to be a lot of rust, start budgeting for a new heater.

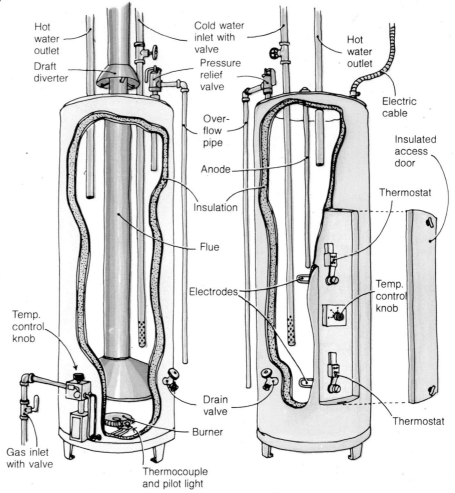

Hot water outlet — Draft diverter — Cold water inlet with valve — Pressure relief valve — Overflow pipe — Hot water outlet — Electric cable — Insulated access door — Thermostat — Anode — Insulation — Temp. control knob — Flue — Electrodes — Temp. control knob — Drain valve — Temp. control knob — Thermostat — Gas inlet with valve — Burner — Thermocouple and pilot light

■ **Replacing a water heater:** Shut off the water and fuel supply. Drain the tank through the spigot at the base and remove the flex hoses for the hot and cold water.

On oil and gas fired units, remove the collar linking the tank to the vent pipes.

Unless you have had any indication of problems, the pressure relief valve on the old tank is still good. Remove the overflow piping and unscrew the valve to use on the new unit.

When the new unit is in place, the fittings may not line up with the previous pipe hookups.

If the unit is too low, raise it onto stout wood blocks. Otherwise, use flex-pipe that will bend and reach the new connections.

Pressure relief valve

To check, pull up or push down on handle—styles vary.

Drain valve

Drain off sediment every few months.

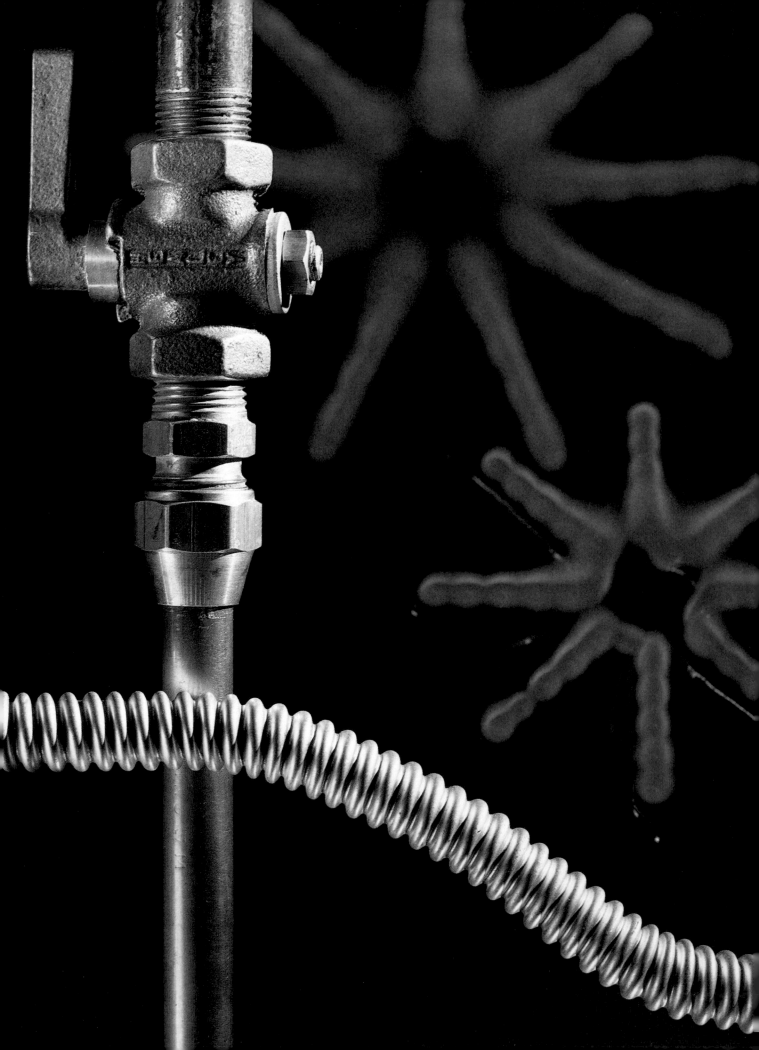

Natural Gas

How to clear gas nozzles, clean contact points,
and light a typical pilot light. How to troubleshoot laundry units
and kitchen ranges.

Pilot Lights and Thermostats

A pilot light can go out on a gas furnace because a strong down draft through the flue blows it out or because an energy-conscious person turns it off.

Next to a pilot light is a small device called a thermocouple. As long as it is kept warm by the pilot light, it will keep the main gas line open. If the pilot light goes out, the thermocouple shuts off all gas to prevent leaks.

Directions for relighting a pilot light should be on the unit, whether a furnace or water heater.

If you suspect any problem with the pilot light, turn off the fuel according to directions. Ream out the pilot nozzle with a fine piece of wire to make sure it is clean. Next, set the thermostat at the lowest setting and turn off the electric power to the furnace. Now turn the fuel supply valve to the pilot light setting only and light it. Let it run for 1 minute — more, if the directions say so — then turn the valve to open the main fuel line also. Turn the furnace power back on and move the thermostat up to the normal setting.

Thermostats can sometimes give you problems. There are two types — contact and mercury vial. Remove the cover on your thermostat by pulling it straight away from the wall.

If yours is a mercury vial variety, it must be perfectly level to work. Place a carpenter's level on the thermostat and adjust it until it is level. If it still does not work when level, replace the unit.

The more common type of thermostat has two contact points. Because different types of metal expand or contract differently as temperature changes, these differences cause the contacts to open or close according to the setting. Occasionally, they become too dusty to make a proper contact.

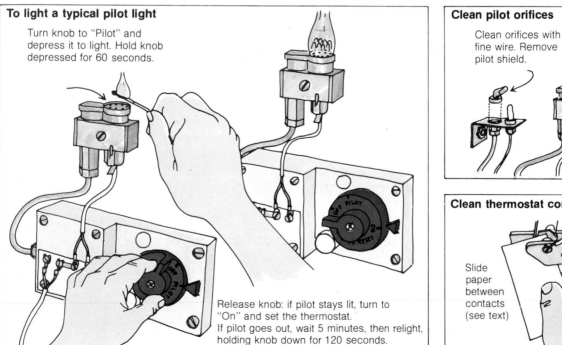

To light a typical pilot light

Turn knob to "Pilot" and depress it to light. Hold knob depressed for 60 seconds.

Release knob: if pilot stays lit, turn to "On" and set the thermostat.
If pilot goes out, wait 5 minutes, then relight, holding knob down for 120 seconds.

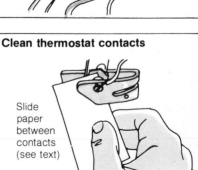

Clean pilot orifices

Clean orifices with fine wire. Remove pilot shield.

Clean thermostat contacts

Slide paper between contacts (see text)

Clean them periodically by running a piece of bond paper, a business card or a crisp new dollar bill between the contacts while closed. Never use emery cloth or a nail file because you will scratch and may damage the contacts.

Note also that for proper operation, a thermostat should never be attached to an outside wall or be in the way of a draft. It should be 4 or 5 feet off the floor — in a dining or living room — and on a wall where there are no heat ducts or hot water pipes behind it.

Dryers

Dryers, whether gas or electric, operate essentially the same except that the heating unit on one type is gas powered rather than electric.

With a gas dryer you must, for safety, close the gas shut-off valve immediately if you ever smell gas around the dryer. In addition, never smoke or use a lighted match when working around the dryer.

NOTE: These drawings are typical of dryers in general. The details of yours may vary. See your owner's manual.

If you feel the gas dryer is not doing its job properly, the problem may lie in the fuel adjustment to the burner. This is usually located at the bottom of the dryer. To get at it, pull out the bottom panel. On some models you may have to depress a release spring in the panel first.

With the dryer running, check the flame. If the flame has yellow tips it is receiving too little air; if it light blue and seems to be roaring, it is receiving too much air. In either case, the dryer is not providing maximum heat.

To adjust this, turn off the burner and let it cool. Loosen the small thumb screw on the heating element and adjust the air vents. Turn them to one extreme and then the other, and then settle for the place that gives a steady blue flame with no roaring sound.

Another problem with dryers is that they just won't start. The rotating drum,

even on a gas dryer, is powered by electricity, so make sure it is plugged in. Is the door completely closed? It must be to engage the door switch that is a safety device to keep the dryer from running with the door open. Finally, check the fuse or circuit breaker on the dryer's circuit.

Be sure to keep the lint screen clean. This is usually located on top of the cabinet. Simply pull it out and clean.

If the drum rotates but there is no heat, it could be too much lint in the screen, a faulty thermostat or the gas burner is out. If the pilot light is out, follow instructions on the panel for relighting and try again. If it still doesn't work, try cleaning it (see page 93). Then call for a professional.

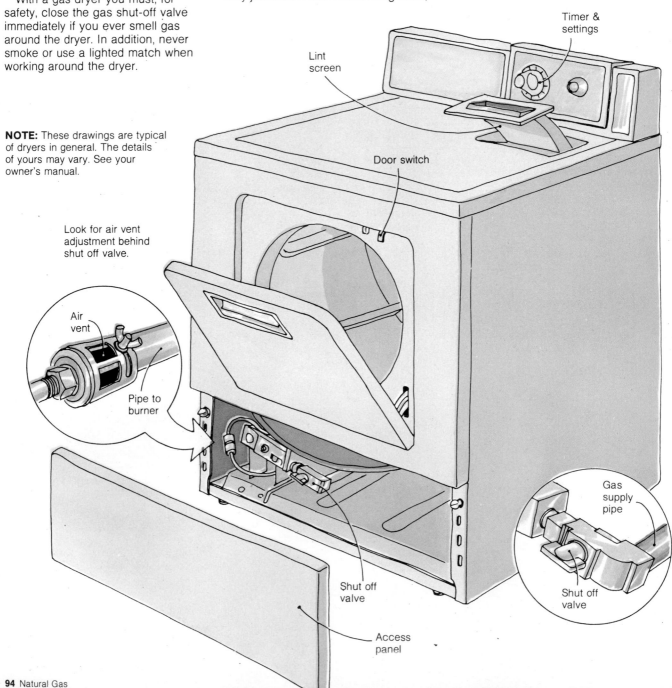

Look for air vent adjustment behind shut off valve.

Air vent

Pipe to burner

Lint screen

Door switch

Timer & settings

Shut off valve

Access panel

Gas supply pipe

Shut off valve

Gas Kitchen Range

Before you can repair a gas range, you need to know how to gain access to its vital parts.

On newer models of gas ranges, there is often an electric control panel on top. This may contain lights and a clock. If the lights are burned out, shut off the electric supply, then remove the retaining screws on the front of the panel and lift it clear. Replace the bulbs with new ones of the same wattage.

Rarely are knobs screwed in place. Most can be removed by pulling straight out. If you can't get a tight grip on a knob, slip a dishtowel behind it and then pull it free.

The top of the range usually lifts up from the front, but on some models you may have to push the top to the rear first to release it. With it open, you can do any necessary work around the burners or pilot light.

You should always locate the gas shut-off valve on your stove. On some models it is near the bottom of the stove and you may have to remove the broiler drawer to reach it. On other models the valve is under the top near the burners. When the small handle is in line with the pipe the valve is open; at right angles to the pipe, it's closed.

Here are some common problems and solutions for gas ranges:

■ **Burner doesn't light:** If your model has a pilot light, remove the top and see that it is still lit. If not, light it and if necessary, adjust the flame with the screw located on the small pilot supply line. The flame should reach about ⅛ inch above the pilot shield.

If the pilot light does not go on, turn on one burner and hold a match to it. If it and the other burners do not light, call the gas company — having checked first that the supply shut-off valve is open. If the burners do light, the problem is in your pilot light. Clean it out with a soft copper wire.

■ **Burner operating poorly:** If the pilot light is operating properly but the burner won't light or burns with a ragged flame, the flame holes have become clogged with dirt and grease. To remove it, lift the burner right out

or, if necessary, remove any retaining screws first from the support.

Wash the burner in hot sudsy water, scrape the holes clean with a piece of wire, rinse well in clean hot water and allow to dry well.

Another factor that influences burner performance is the proper mixture of gas and air. If there is too much air, the flame will be all blue and there will be a roaring sound; if too little air, the tips of the flame will be yellow. Adjustments are made on the air shutter below each burner on the gas line. Having shut off the gas supply, loosen the retainer screw and then open or close the shutter until you get a flame that is a steady, even blue.

On some models, there is a simmer adjustment screw hidden under the

control knob. Remove the knob by pulling it off and then with a screwdriver adjust the screw until the flame burns as low as possible without blowing out in a draft.

■ **Oven pilot light:** The pilot light in a gas oven is often at the bottom rear and it is necessary to pull out the bottom drawer to get at it.

On many models there is a boxlike ignition assembly with a pilot light adjustment screw on one end. If the pilot light is working but the oven doesn't light, the pilot light may be set too low. With a screwdriver, adjust the screw for a higher flame and then try again. Other models have a flame switch that can be tested with a volt-ohm meter set to the RX1 scale. Be sure all power to the range is off first.

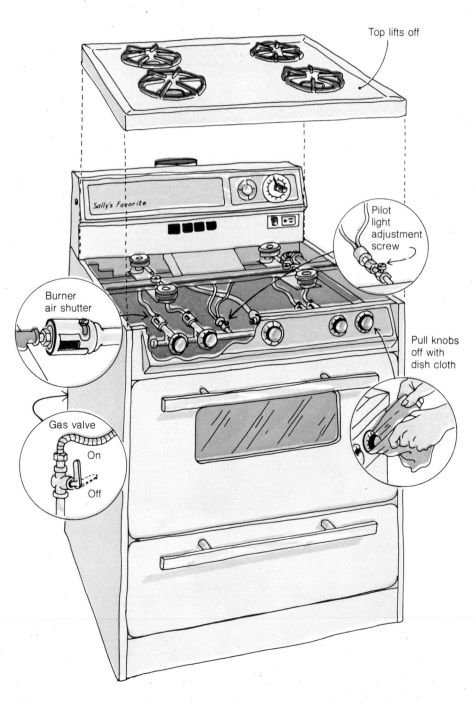

Top lifts off

Pilot light adjustment screw

Burner air shutter

Pull knobs off with dish cloth

Gas valve

On

Off

Sally's Favorite

Tools & Hardware

The home repair center. Basic and advanced tools to keep on hand.
Complete guide to nails, screws and hardware.

The Home Repair Center

This book deals mostly with the repair of things and systems that are integral parts of the house. Since this kind of work is usually accomplished "on location," right at the site of the malfunctioning part or system, a workshop is not really necessary. However, anyone who enjoys basic home repairs will discover that other kinds of projects arc fun, too. Then a place to keep the tools, hardware and other supplies — a home repair center — soon becomes desirable. Furniture repair and refinishing, even the construction of simple cabinets, tables, stools and all sorts of garden furniture are relatively easy for the beginner. These as well as hobby and craft projects of the family all benefit from a comfortable place to work.

Of course, an ideal workshop is the dream of many do-it-yourselfers but it's surely not necessary. The items most essential in a repair center or workshop are good light, sufficient electric power, a place to store tools, materials and supplies, and a serviceable workbench.

For storing hand tools nothing seems to work better than peg boards and the specialized accessory hooks that hold the tools to them. An old kitchen cabinet or Hoosier hutch is also very useful to store tools, hardware and other supplies if building a special cabinet is not in the offing.

A good workbench is a stable workbench. No matter if it's large or small, to be really satisfactory it should be as rigid and as heavy as possible. Ready-made workbenches are available, but

expensive. If you would like to build one yourself, designs and plans for really good workbenches are to be found in woodworking books everywhere. A good and portable work surface can be set up almost anywhere with a plywood panel and two sawhorses.

The location of the work center usually depends on where the space is available. A basement, garage, spare room or attic are all possibilities. Easy access to the outside — so you don't have to carry lumber and pipe through the house — is preferable but not absolutely necessary.

If there really isn't space in your house or garage, you can still have a work center — a very compact or portable one. We have suggestions for a couple of these.

> ■ **Caution:** Respect all sharp edged tools. And remember that they can be more dangerous if you let them get dull: then, you're tempted to apply more pressure on the wood chisel, say, and it may jump out of the wood and prove that it's still sharp enough to bite you.
>
> It's often a good idea to wear some kind of protective glasses or goggles — plastic, not glass ones. Even a little wood chip can damage an eye; more dangerous are the chemicals in some wood preservatives and finishes. If you're going to wear gloves, they should fit as closely as possible while still letting your hands have freedom.

Compact Work Center

This work center has been conceived especially for those who have no space for a workshop. Because of its compact design, it can be set up in a garage, on a back porch or in a basement. Overall, it is 6 feet high, 4 feet wide and 1 foot deep. When not in use it presents a neat and narrow profile. When it's open all your tools and hardware are handy and you have a small, but sturdy workbench resting firmly on the open lower doors.

Other features include a tall compartment for saws, steel square, etc., and a wide shelf for power tools. The 13¼-inch shelf in the middle area is the right size to hold a utility cabinet with 24 little plastic drawers. These are available almost everywhere and keep order in the ranks of screws, nuts and bolts, washers, etc. And there is a place for a peg board to hold your hand tools within easy reach.

■ Steps in construction:

1. Cut the two plywood panels as shown in the diagrams, and a 48 by 72-inch piece of hardboard or of ¼-inch plywood.

2. Glue and screw the tops (A) and the sides (B) together to form a box.

3. Nail on the hardboard panel. Be sure the corners of the box are square and it fits precisely to the edges of the hardboard.

4. Turn the box over and install the shelves and dividers with glue and screws. Start with the two shelves (C). There should be exactly 30 inches from the bottom of the box to the top of one shelf and exactly 18 inches from the top of the box to the bottom of the other. This leaves precisely 24 inches between the two shelves.

Next, the vertical dividers (D), (E) and (F) go in, and finally the shelves (G), (H) and (I). These shelves can be made adjustable if you think that's desirable and want to go to the trouble.

5. Attach the top and bottom doors and the workbench with hinges. Be sure the bottom doors are flush with the bottom of the cabinet and with the bottom of the lower wide shelf. When the workbench is hinged to the top surface of the bottom shelf, there should be a ¾-inch gap between the bottom of the bench and the doors.

6. To keep the lower doors from being kicked out from under the workbench while you're working, drill ⁷⁄₁₆-inch holes in the outer corners of the workbench and the top edge of each of the doors so they line up. Drop in short lengths of ⅜-inch dowel.

7. Attach the magnetic catches and door pulls.

8. If you opt for the pegboard, attach it to the back of the large middle compartment with the ⅛-inch bolts and ¾-inch spacers you've made from plywood scrap. This allows room to insert the tool holders into the pegboard.

■ Materials list:

2 sheets ¾″ × 4′ × 8′ plywood

1 sheet ¼″ × 4′ × 6′ hardboard or plywood
1 box 1½″ #10 wood screws
Wood glue
11 2½″ butt hinges
2 ⅜″ dowels
6 magnetic catches
5 door pulls

Optional

1 piece 20″ × 30″ pegboard
6 ⅛″ × 1¼″ bolts with washers and nuts
Your choice of assorted pegboard tool holders.

Compact work center

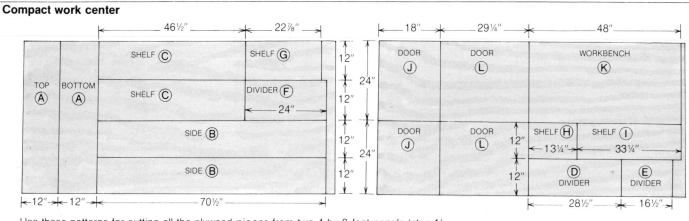

Use these patterns for cutting all the plywood pieces from two 4 by 8-foot panels (step 1).

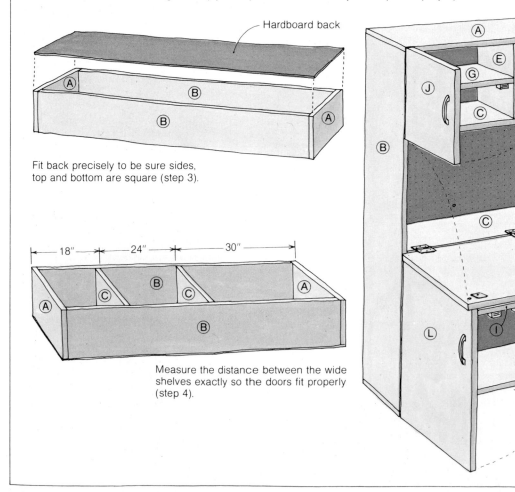

Hardboard back

Fit back precisely to be sure sides, top and bottom are square (step 3).

Measure the distance between the wide shelves exactly so the doors fit properly (step 4).

Sawhorse Work Center

A sawhorse is an indispensable part of any workshop. This one, however, is also a portable work center — at least, it has a storage place for a few tools and, when the door is open, a place to put things while you're using the top for sawing.

■ Steps in construction:

1. Cut a piece of 2 by 6 for the top, 36 inches long. Notch the four corners of the top and drill and cut the hand-hold in the middle.

2. Cut the four legs also from 2 by 6 stock. Our drawing shows them 30 inches long — when attached to the top at an angle, these legs make the sawhorse about 29 inches high. If you'd like your sawhorse higher or lower, adjust the leg length to suit.

3. Attach the legs to the top with glue and lag screws. Start by drilling two $\frac{3}{16}$-inch pilot holes through the legs into the top and drill a $\frac{3}{4}$-inch countersink hole so the lag screw head pulls against a flat surface. Offset the screws slightly so they can't meet. Apply the glue, insert and tighten the lag screws snugly. Do not overtighten the screws or you risk a compression fracture of the leg ends.

4. Cut all the plywood as shown.

5. Nail the ends, back and bottom in place.

6. Hinge the front to the bottom and attach the chains at the sides to hold it level when it's open.

■ Materials list:

1 piece 2 × 6 × 36″ fir or pine
4 pieces 2 × 6 × 30″ fir or pine
1 piece ½″ × 3′ × 4′ plywood
1 pair 2½″ butt hinges
2 magnetic catches
2 pieces 18″ light chain
8 ⅜″ × 3½″ lag screws
8 ⅜″ washers

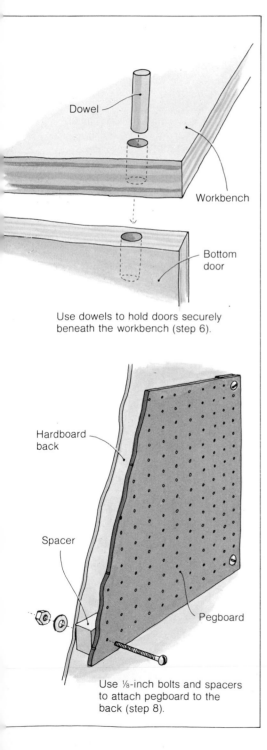

Use dowels to hold doors securely beneath the workbench (step 6).

Hardboard back

Spacer

Pegboard

Use ⅛-inch bolts and spacers to attach pegboard to the back (step 8).

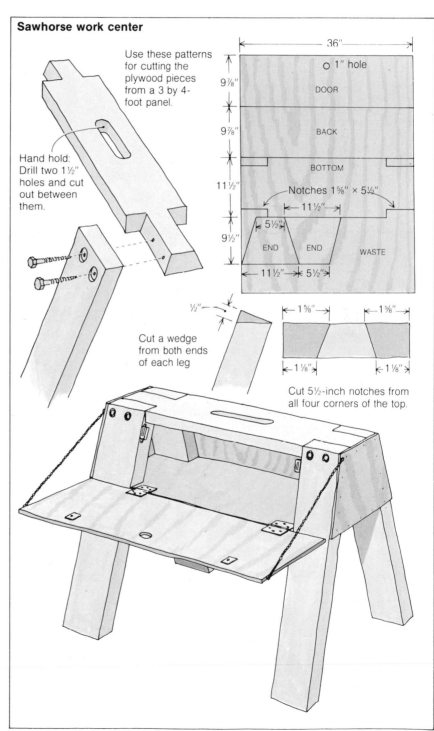

Sawhorse work center

Use these patterns for cutting the plywood pieces from a 3 by 4-foot panel.

Hand hold: Drill two 1½″ holes and cut out between them.

Cut a wedge from both ends of each leg

Cut 5½-inch notches from all four corners of the top.

On Gathering Tools

One mark of the careful craftsman, a person who loves his work, is fine tools. When you begin building your own tool center, always buy the best quality tools even if you think at the time that you can't quite afford them. A cheap tool often cannot do the job properly or will soon become dull or inoperative and have to be replaced.

If you're starting from scratch, probably the most basic tool you should have is a hammer. Now, you might think that if you need a hammer, you just go out and buy the first one you see. It's not quite that simple, however, because there is such a great variety: curved-claw, straight-claw, ball peen, tack and club, to name just the most common of hammers. In addition, they all come in several weights and in various styles and patterns for specialized uses.

For a person buying one hammer for all round use, the one to buy is a 16-ounce curved-claw hammer. It's light enough to swing comfortably but still heavy enough to drive large nails.

If you plan to do a lot of nailing with big nails, perhaps in building a deck or framing a room in the basement, buy yourself a straight-claw hammer. These range from 18 to 28 ounces. The heavier it is the faster the nails go in, but consider your own wrist strength. The average man should be able to handle a 20-ounce hammer.

When using a hammer, hold it at the very end of the handle. After one or two taps to start the nail, swing in increasingly longer strokes with the whole arm, concentrating on smoothness and accuracy.

When pulling nails that won't come easily, don't keep pulling or jerking on the hammer handle. You may break it. Instead, catch the nail in the claw and push the hammer first to one side and then the other to loosen the nail. This carpenter's trick works best with a straight-claw hammer.

The next basic tool to have in the house is a screwdriver. The two most common varieties are the standard for slotted screws and the Phillips for cross-slotted screws. Not only do you need both, but you really need two or three sizes of each so the tip will properly fit the screw. Trying to turn a screw with a tip too small can so badly damage the slot that you may never get the screw out. A driver that's too big may not fit into the slot or can mar the surface around the screw.

You will also need a stubby screwdriver for working in tight places, a long slender one for places difficult to reach, and a heavy-duty screwdriver for large or especially stubborn screws.

Driving screws straight and without marring the slots takes some practice. Always make a starter hole, either pre-drilling for large screws or punching a hole with an awl for smaller ones. Lubricating wood screws with wax or soap makes them much easier to drive, too.

Next, consider the tape ruler. Probably the most practical type is the self-retracting flexible steel tape. It comes in lengths from 6 to 25 feet. Buy one at least 8 feet long, since that is the standard length of such common items as wall paneling, Sheetrock, and 2 by 4 studs. Better yet, buy a 12 foot tape so you don't have to measure twice when working on something over 8 feet long.

Of course, you can't really get along without a fine hand saw, even though you plan on getting a power saw. Buy the best one there is and have the teeth set and sharpened periodically. If you take such care of it, it can last you a lifetime.

The most useful saw is the cross-cut saw, designed to cut across the grain of wood. Buy one with 8 to 10 teeth per inch. Fewer than 8 teeth per inch gives you a rough cut and more than 12 gives you a very fine but very slow cut.

There's an art to sawing, as you will soon learn. Start the cut with small pulls toward you, using your bent-in thumb as a guide. Once you start, move your hand well away so that, if the saw jumps out of the kerf, it won't bite your fingers. Saw with a smooth, straight stroke using your whole arm and keeping the saw at about a 45 degree angle. The cut is made as you push, but don't force the saw down; let it work by itself. It will work even more smoothly if you rub the sides with a candle or paraffin.

As you build your tool collection, you will need a backsaw with a rigid back for precisely angled cuts, a keyhole saw for starting cuts from holes drilled in the middle of boards, a coping saw for tight curves and a hacksaw to cut metal.

The rip saw has big teeth designed for rapid cutting with the grain of wood. It is being replaced in many homes by power saws that do the job much faster and easier.

Now, you can't cut a board accurately unless you can mark one accurately, and for that you need a square. This tool has a perfect 90 degree angle. One arm fits against the edge of a board while the other reaches across it to mark for a square cut.

For general work, the try square is fine. It's a small, one-piece square with a 6-inch tongue. A more useful tool is the combination square with an adjustable tongue. It can be turned to mark 45 degree angles and slid back

and forth so you can measure inside or outside a corner. It also has a built-in level.

For larger projects, the steel framing square is a must. Its body or blade is 24 inches long and its tongue is 16 inches, two common spacing distances between joists and studs. The tongue is 1½-inches wide, the same as all 2-by lumber. The body usually has incised tables for figuring stairs and rafters and for calculating board feet.

A good level is another must, even for the beginning tool set. One that will do almost any job is the 2-foot carpenter's level. Its bubbles will tell you when something is either level or plumb. Some levels are also made with vials to show 45 degree angles, but these are generally not worth any added expense.

There are also the small torpedo levels, the extra long masonry levels for use in building walls, and the very handy little line level that can be hung along a stretched string.

The number of different tools available can be overwhelming, especially when you first start buying. It can also overwhelm your pocketbook. So before you start, make a list of exactly what you need — **need**, not just want — and then buy those first, in the very best quality.

On the following pages are our ideas of primary, intermediate, and advanced tool sets. You'll probably modify these choices as you start working on particular projects.

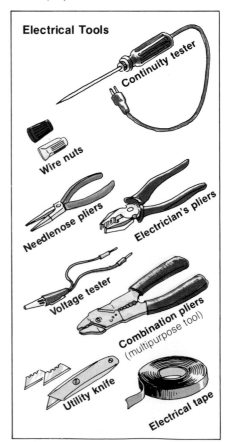

Electrical Tools

Continuity tester

Wire nuts

Needlenose pliers

Electrician's pliers

Voltage tester

Combination pliers (multipurpose tool)

Utility knife

Electrical tape

Primary Tool Set

This array of tools may seem large for a starting set. And it is for someone who plans to do only a few very minor household repairs. However, this list is designed to cover all the most basic needs, and includes tools for the most minor plumbing and electrical repairs as well as general repairs and basic carpentry.

Of course, you do not have to buy all of these tools in one bunch, but if you do, the money will be well spent. Having the right tool for the job when it needs doing may make it a pleasant task instead of frustrating drudgery.

You may also want to get a small tackle box or tool holder to keep your small tools organized and handy.

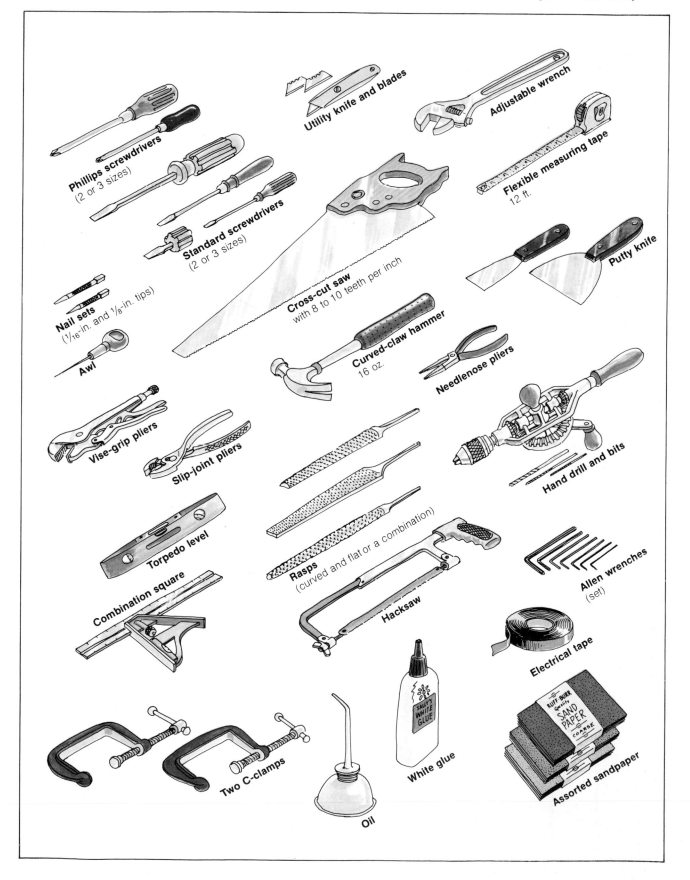

Phillips screwdrivers (2 or 3 sizes)

Utility knife and blades

Adjustable wrench

Flexible measuring tape 12 ft.

Standard screwdrivers (2 or 3 sizes)

Cross-cut saw with 8 to 10 teeth per inch

Putty knife

Nail sets (1/16-in. And 1/8-in. tips)

Awl

Curved-claw hammer 16 oz.

Needlenose pliers

Vise-grip pliers

Slip-joint pliers

Hand drill and bits

Torpedo level

Rasps (curved and flat or a combination)

Allen wrenches (set)

Combination square

Hacksaw

Electrical tape

Two C-clamps

Oil

SALLY'S WHITE GLUE

White glue

RUFF-BURR Quality SAND PAPER COARSE

Assorted sandpaper

Intermediate Tool Set

These tools are the ones we consider the most useful additions to your primary tool set. Here are tools for somewhat more elaborate electrical, plumbing, and carpentry repairs. With these you can even make some modifications or additions to your house and its most vital systems.

Since these tools are not all needed for repair of emergency problems, and some of them are fairly expensive, we don't recommend you buy them all at once. You may just want to pick up the appropriate ones when you are about to embark on a project or when you see them at a good price.

At this intermediate stage, you may also want to expand the range of your screwdrivers, hand saws and other basic hand tools to make every little job easier.

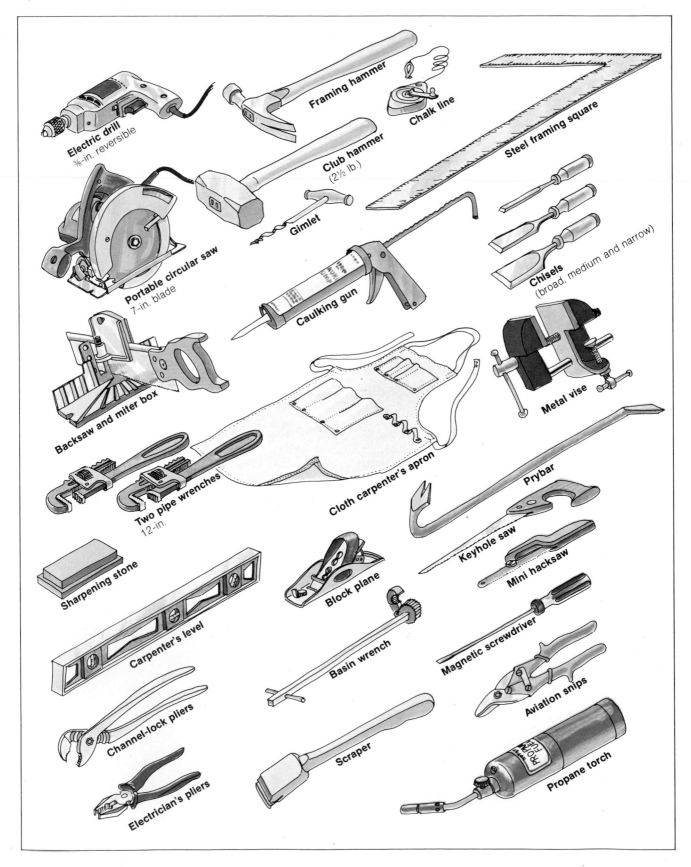

Electric drill
⅜-in. reversible

Portable circular saw
7-in. blade

Backsaw and miter box

Two pipe wrenches
12-in.

Sharpening stone

Carpenter's level

Channel-lock pliers

Electrician's pliers

Framing hammer

Club hammer
(2½ lb.)

Gimlet

Caulking gun

Cloth carpenter's apron

Block plane

Basin wrench

Scraper

Chalk line

Steel framing square

Chisels
(broad, medium and narrow)

Metal vise

Prybar

Keyhole saw

Mini hacksaw

Magnetic screwdriver

Aviation snips

Propane torch

Advanced Tool Set

As your budget permits, your confidence increases, and your projects become more complicated, you will want additional tools that make the big jobs easier and give a professional looking finish. The ones shown below are some suggestions gleaned from the multitude of power tools and specialized tools on the market. Power tools, for instance, usually come in several different horsepowers and with optional blades, bits and attachments. And almost all tools come in grades of quality from supreme (usually expensive) to practically useless (usually cheaper).

Before you decide to buy a particular tool, shop around a little and satisfy yourself that it's exactly what *you* need for the jobs you want it to do, both now and in the future.

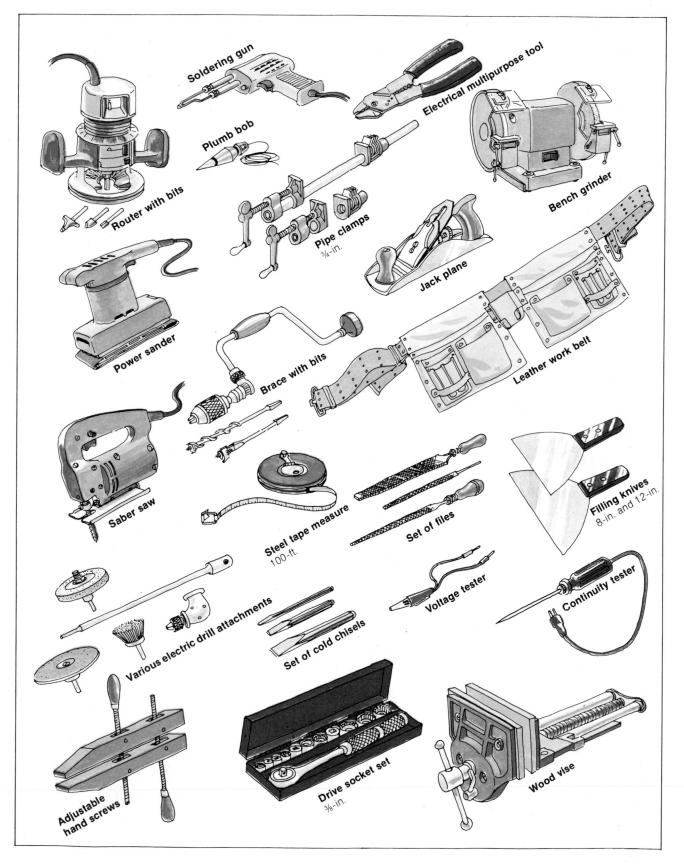

Soldering gun

Electrical multipurpose tool

Plumb bob

Bench grinder

Router with bits

Pipe clamps
3/4-in.

Jack plane

Power sander

Brace with bits

Leather work belt

Saber saw

Steel tape measure
100-ft.

Set of files

Filling knives
8-in. and 12-in.

Various electric drill attachments

Set of cold chisels

Voltage tester

Continuity tester

Adjustable hand screws

Drive socket set
3/8-in.

Wood vise

Nails

The oldest metal fastener invented by man is the nail, and nails are still the most efficient and commonly used. There are a great variety of nails, each with its own range of sizes and finishes. Here we show only a few that you may find useful around the house.

Sometimes nail sizes are designated in inches, but more commonly the antiquated term "penny" is used. It is abbreviated "d" after the denarius, a small silver coin of ancient Rome. It is referred to as a penny in the New Testament. The penny number was originally used to indicate how many pennys it would cost to buy one hundred nails.

When choosing nails, decide which size will provide the most holding power for your purpose without splitting the wood. Ideally, a nail should be three times as long as the thickness of the material it's holding. In real life, this long a nail would often go right through the second member, too.

Select the right style as well as size of nail for the job you are doing. For instance, the large heads of common and box nails spread the load over more wood surface and resist pulling through. Conversely, finishing nails and brads pull through quite easily — a welcome propensity for home repair purposes because they allow casings, trim and other finish carpentry to be pulled apart with virtually no damage to the exposed surfaces.

To get the best holding power, drive nails at an angle to each other or the direction of stress (toenailing). Sometimes, especially in rough work, you can drive the nail clear through and bend the point over. This is known as clinching and makes an extremely strong joint. You also get much more holding power with barbed, annular-ringed or screw-nails. They are made for special purposes, such as installing

Some of the most useful nails

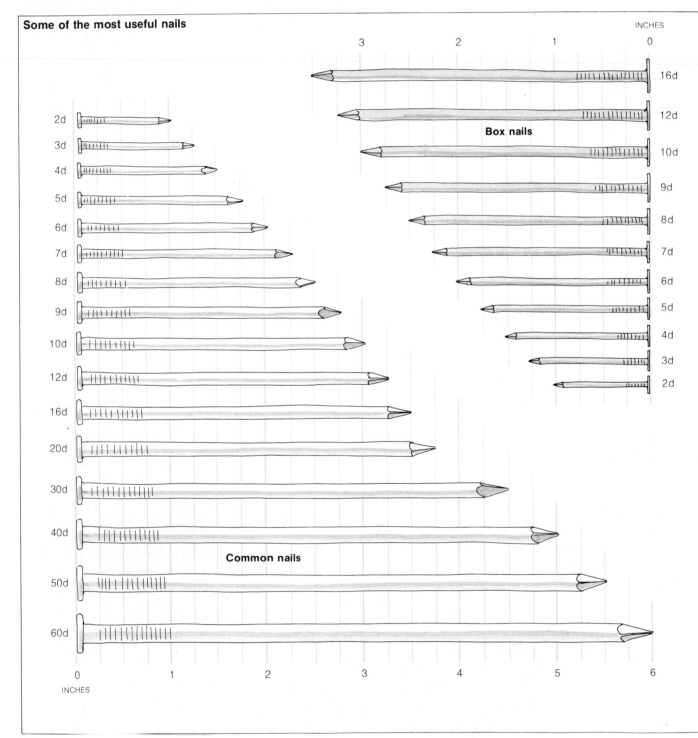

flooring, roofing and drywall panels.

Here is a brief description of the more familiar types of nails:

■ **Common nails.** Large head, thick shaft, good for the widest variety of general construction and framing purposes.

■ **Box nails.** Much like the common nail but thinner. Use where the common would cause splits.

■ **Finishing nails.** Where you don't want nails to show. The small head is designed to be countersunk (set) and the depression filled and painted over.

■ **Brads.** Similar to finishing nails but thinner and in a smaller range of sizes.

Specified by length in inches and wire gauge number from 11 to 20.

■ **Casing nails.** A little thicker than finishing nails with small, flat heads designed to be driven flush with the surface and painted rather than countersunk and filled. Used for casings and rough moldings, and for installing paneling.

■ **Panel nails.** Small casing nails, usually paint-dipped to match wood veneer paneling. Sometimes barbed or annular ringed.

■ **Roofing nails.** Extra large head and barbed shank to hold roofing materials securely.

■ **Drywall nails.** Similar to box nails but with slightly concave heads designed to dimple gypsum board. Some have annular rings.

■ **Screw-nails.** Usually used for flooring but also can be used for any rough carpentry. Spiral shank gives it a tenacious, screw-like grip.

■ **Masonry nails.** Made of case-hardened steel. Mostly used to attach studs to masonry walls or 2 by 4 plates to concrete floors.

■ **Duplex nails.** Designed for temporary bracing or forming, the double head of the nail makes it easy to remove.

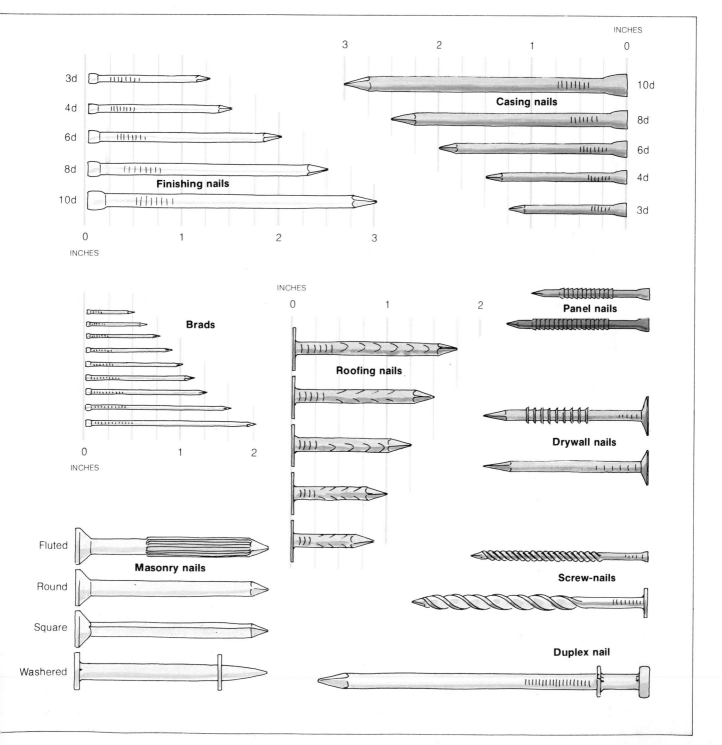

Screws

The vast majority of carpentry joining is done with nails, but screws are more desirable in some instances. Screws have much greater holding power than nails. They are easier to remove when parts must be taken apart later. They are usually used to hold hardware to wood, and they are often used on wood parts to harmonize with the hardware. The main disadvantages of screws are that they require more time and effort to install and they are much more expensive to buy than nails.

Screws probably come in as many sizes and styles as nails, but again, we show only the few that are generally useful in home repairs. When selecting screws you must decide on length, diameter (gauge), head, slot, and finish.

The length of a screw is designated in inches. Usually they are available from ¼ inch to 6 inches long, but when you need screws over about 3½ inches, consider using lag screws. They are much easier to drive. Screw diameters range from 0 to 24 gauge but the most commonly available are from 5 gauge (about 3/32 inch) up to 14 gauge (about 7/32 inch).

The most useful screw for wood construction is the flathead. It can be driven flush with the surface or countersunk and hidden with filler. Round heads are easier to turn down tightly and they can be used with flat washers for more holding power. Since round heads must be exposed, they are often used where appearance is of little matter.

Oval head screws are considered

A guide to screws

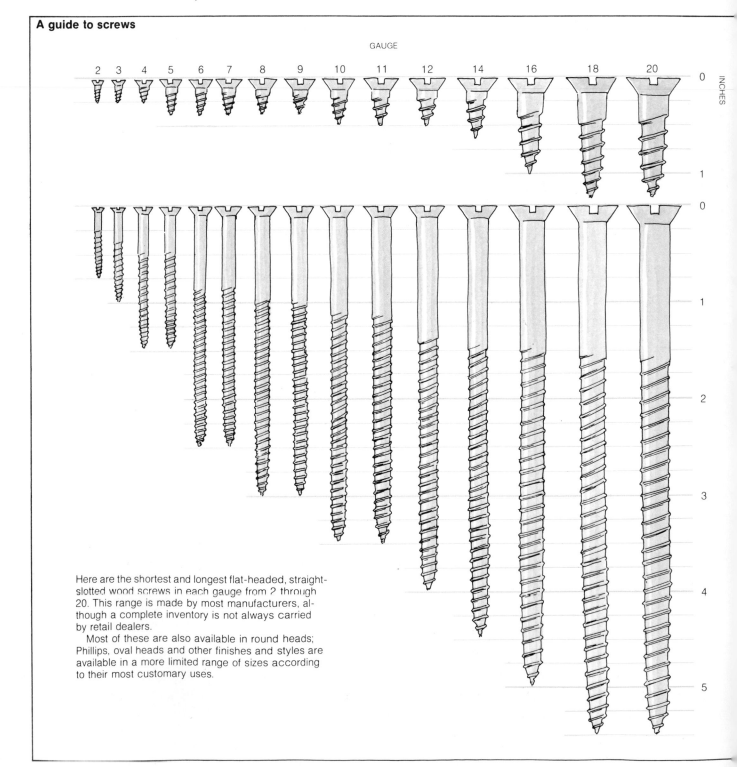

GAUGE

2 3 4 5 6 7 8 9 10 11 12 14 16 18 20

0 INCHES
1
0
1
2
3
4
5

Here are the shortest and longest flat-headed, straight-slotted wood screws in each gauge from 2 through 20. This range is made by most manufacturers, although a complete inventory is not always carried by retail dealers.

Most of these are also available in round heads; Phillips, oval heads and other finishes and styles are available in a more limited range of sizes according to their most customary uses.

decorative and usually come in brass or chrome finish. They are most often used to apply hinges, latches or other hardware or with washers to secure panels — such as the back of a speaker case — that need to be removed periodically.

The two universal slot designs are the straight slot and Phillips. Both are available in most kinds of screws. You should have at least two sizes of Phillips screwdrivers and three or four sizes of standard screwdrivers to fit all of the screws that you are likely to find around the house.

There are several other types of screw heads that you may run across on various objects — One-way, Reed and Prince, Posidriv, Robertson, Clutch head and Torx. These have probably been used by a factory to provide a more positive screw location during manufacture, or to discourage you from removing the screws.

Lag screws (or bolts) are used usually in sizes from 3½ to 6 inches, when real holding power is required. They have square or hexagonal heads that are turned with a wrench.

Sheet metal screws differ from wood screws mainly in that there is no smooth shank. The threads continue all the way up to the head. They are designed to tap their own threads in the sort of thin sheet metal you find in aluminum screen doors or storm windows.

Most screws come in a number of finishes. In ascending order of resistance to corrosion, these are: bright steel, blued, dipped, galvanized, brass or chrome plated, and solid brass. Stainless steel screws are also made, but they are not always easy to find in retail shops.

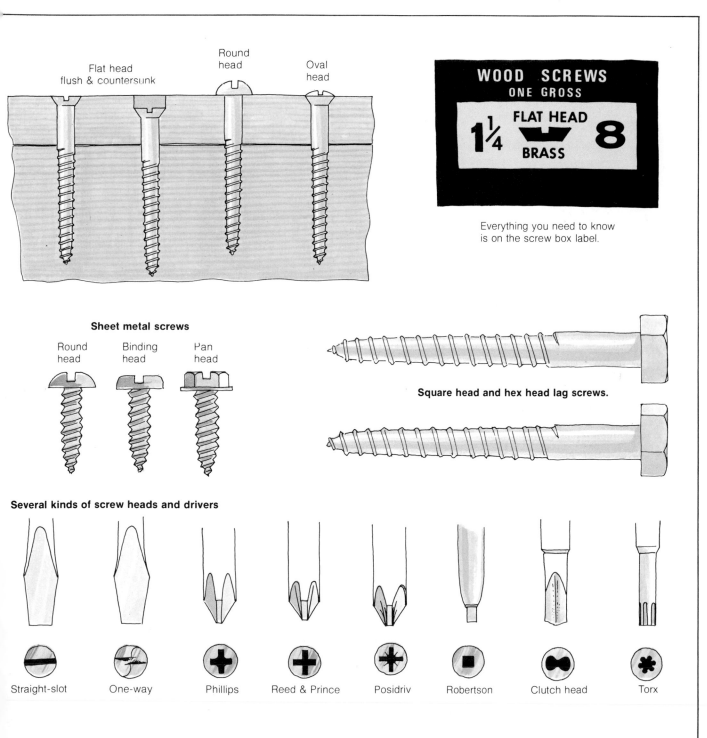

Flat head flush & countersunk

Round head

Oval head

WOOD SCREWS
ONE GROSS
1¼ FLAT HEAD 8
BRASS

Everything you need to know is on the screw box label.

Sheet metal screws

Round head

Binding head

Pan head

Square head and hex head lag screws.

Several kinds of screw heads and drivers

Straight-slot   One-way   Phillips   Reed & Prince   Posidriv   Robertson   Clutch head   Torx

Hardware

It's presumptuous for us to suggest that we can even begin to cover the subject of home repair hardware on these two pages. There are thick books on the subject that are woefully incomplete.

If you have become interested in doing a lot of your own home repairs, or maybe even attempting some modifications or additions to your home, you would benefit greatly by finding the one or two best and most completely stocked hardware stores in your area. Spend a few Saturday afternoons just browsing around in them. Especially check out the ones that are used most by local contractors. Don't hesitate to ask questions, either. Even experienced contractors often learn new ways of doing things from knowledgeable clerks.

Some people see a library as a building full of books — others see it as a place full of knowledge, adventure and delight. If you really become interested in the doing of projects, you'll discover that a hardware store can be a little like a library.

It is possible to discover two, three and sometimes a multitude of ways to

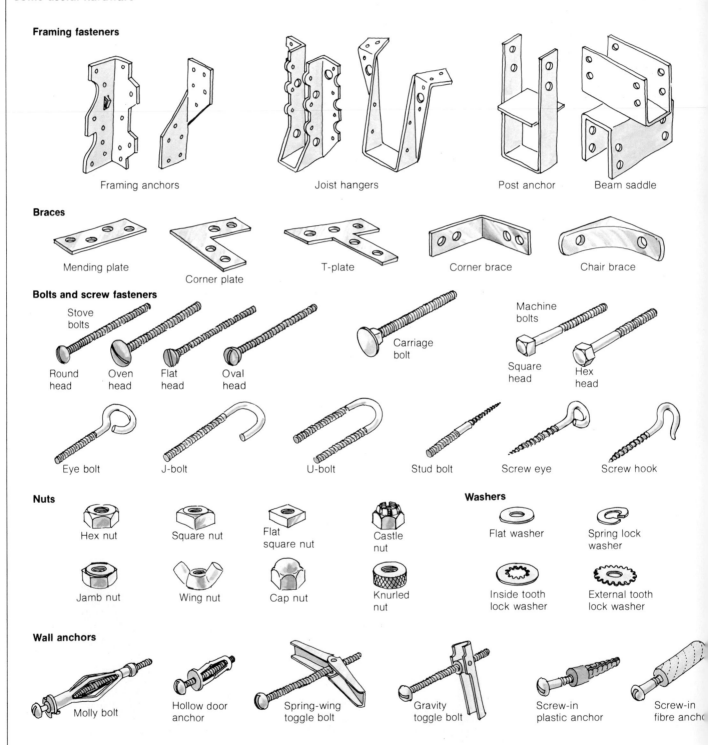

Some useful hardware

Framing fasteners

Framing anchors

Joist hangers

Post anchor

Beam saddle

Braces

Mending plate

Corner plate

T-plate

Corner brace

Chair brace

Bolts and screw fasteners

Stove bolts

Round head

Oven head

Flat head

Oval head

Carriage bolt

Machine bolts

Square head

Hex head

Eye bolt

J-bolt

U-bolt

Stud bolt

Screw eye

Screw hook

Nuts

Hex nut

Square nut

Flat square nut

Castle nut

Jamb nut

Wing nut

Cap nut

Knurled nut

Washers

Flat washer

Spring lock washer

Inside tooth lock washer

External tooth lock washer

Wall anchors

Molly bolt

Hollow door anchor

Spring-wing toggle bolt

Gravity toggle bolt

Screw-in plastic anchor

Screw-in fibre anchor

solve a problem you thought had only one solution — or maybe no solution at all. For instance, there's a drawer in your kitchen that's been driving you crazy because it keeps pulling out and spilling silverware all over the floor. A well stocked hardware store may have two or three different kinds of little metal or plastic wheels, slides or stops to fix the existing mechanism. You could also find another three or four complete wheel-and-track or slide devices that would be simple to install and make the drawer better than it was when new.

Just to give you a little idea of what is available, here are some of the more common hardware items that are useful in basic home repairs. Even a rather poorly stocked hardware store will have many variations within each of these categories.

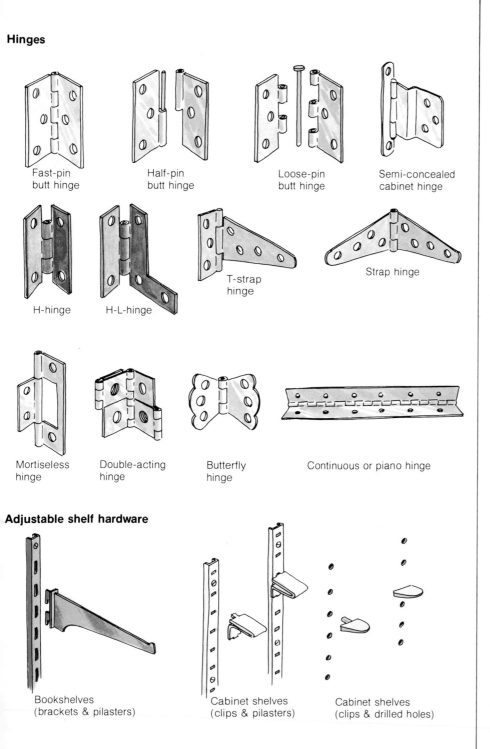

Hinges

Fast-pin butt hinge

Half-pin butt hinge

Loose-pin butt hinge

Semi-concealed cabinet hinge

H-hinge

H-L-hinge

T-strap hinge

Strap hinge

Mortiseless hinge

Double-acting hinge

Butterfly hinge

Continuous or piano hinge

Adjustable shelf hardware

Bookshelves (brackets & pilasters)

Cabinet shelves (clips & pilasters)

Cabinet shelves (clips & drilled holes)

When to Call a Professional

Although the philosophy of this book is that you can do it yourself, there may come a time when the advice and service of a professional are necessary. Sometimes a carpenter, plumber or electrician can do one part of a project that has you stumped, then you can go on and finish the rest of it.

Before you call in the pro, jot down a list of questions you would like to ask about things you don't quite understand. The good professional craftsman should be willing to sell advice as well as skilled labor.

Here are some factors that should go into your decision about calling a professional:

—If the job is a one-shot operation that requires expensive special tools, you might have a pro do it. The fee may not be too much more than the cost of the tools, which you may never use again.

—If you are physically unable to do the job or consider the risk to your health too great, as in roof repairs, let the pro do it. He will cost less than the hospital.

—If the project is going to be highly visible and requires expert craftsmanship, you might disrupt the decor of the whole room if the job is botched. Some things, such as fine woodwork, take years of practice.

—If you are really pressed for time and the job must be done now, immediate attention may be essential to prevent further damage or a dangerous situation for your family. Leaking or broken pipes or loose wiring are among these situations.

The project may be so big it would take many hours of your spare time during the coming weeks or months. Perhaps you'd really rather spend some of that time at your own profession earning the money to pay a carpenter, electrician or plumber.

Although there are times you should call in the professional, you can still save money by doing some preliminary work yourself, such as pulling out the old fixture or tearing off the old paneling. Have the pro do just the detailed work while you take care of all the common labor that he would otherwise do and charge you for.

To find a good professional ask around your neighborhood, the local stores or your bank. Seek several different opinions and if one craftsman's name keeps popping up, you can assume that person does good work. It also helps to choose a pro from your own area — better work seems to get done when a good reputation needs to be maintained.

Index